The Economy of Religion in American Literature

NEW DIRECTIONS IN RELIGION AND LITERATURE

This series aims to showcase new work at the forefront of religion and literature through short studies written by leading and rising scholars in the field. Books will pursue a variety of theoretical approaches as they engage with writing from different religious and literary traditions. Collectively, the series will offer a timely critical intervention to the interdisciplinary crossover between religion and literature, speaking to wider contemporary interests and mapping out new directions for the field in the early twenty-first century.

Series editors: Emma Mason and Mark Knight

ALSO AVAILABLE IN THE SERIES:
The New Atheist Novel, Arthur Bradley and Andrew Tate
Blake. Wordsworth. Religion, Jonathan Roberts
Do the Gods Wear Capes?, Ben Saunders
England's Secular Scripture, Jo Carruthers
Victorian Parables, Susan E. Colón
The Late Walter Benjamin, John Schad
Dante and the Sense of Transgression, William Franke
The Glyph and the Gramophone, Luke Ferretter
John Cage and Buddhist Ecopoetics, Peter Jaeger
Rewriting the Old Testament in Anglo-Saxon Verse, Samantha Zacher
Forgiveness in Victorian Literature, Richard Hughes Gibson
The Gospel According to the Novelist, Magdalena Mączyńska
Jewish Feeling, Richa Dwor
Beyond the Willing Suspension of Disbelief, Michael Tomko
The Gospel According to David Foster Wallace, Adam S. Miller
Pentecostal Modernism, Stephen Shapiro and Philip Barnard
The Bible in the American Short Story, Lesleigh Cushing Stahlberg and Peter S. Hawkins
Faith in Poetry, Michael D. Hurley
Jeanette Winterson and Religion, Emily McAvan
Religion and American Literature since the 1950s, Mark Eaton
Esoteric Islam in Modern French Thought, Ziad Elmarsafy
The Rhetoric of Conversion in English Puritan Writing, David Parry
Djuna Barnes and Theology, Zhao Ng
Food and Fasting in Victorian Religion and Literature, Lesa Scholl

FORTHCOMING:
Marilynne Robinson's Wordly Gospel, Ryan S. Kemp and Jordan M. Rodgers
Weird Faith in 19th Century Literature, Mark Knight and Emma Mason

The Economy of Religion in American Literature

Culture and the Politics of Redemption

Andrew Ball

BLOOMSBURY ACADEMIC
LONDON • NEW YORK • OXFORD • NEW DELHI • SYDNEY

BLOOMSBURY ACADEMIC
Bloomsbury Publishing Plc
50 Bedford Square, London, WC1B 3DP, UK
1385 Broadway, New York, NY 10018, USA
29 Earlsfort Terrace, Dublin 2, Ireland

BLOOMSBURY, BLOOMSBURY ACADEMIC and the Diana logo are trademarks
of Bloomsbury Publishing Plc

First published in Great Britain 2022
This paperback edition published 2024

Copyright © Andrew Ball, 2022

Andrew Ball has asserted his right under the Copyright, Designs and
Patents Act, 1988, to be identified as Author of this work.

For legal purposes the Acknowledgments on p. vi constitute an
extension of this copyright page.

Cover design: Rebecca Heselton
Cover image: Victor Dubreuil, *The Cross of Gold*, ca. 1896, oil on canvas,
14 x 12 in. Crystal Bridges Museum of American Art, Bentonville,
Arkansas, 2011.40. Photography by Edward C. Robison III.

All rights reserved. No part of this publication may be reproduced or transmitted
in any form or by any means, electronic or mechanical, including photocopying,
recording, or any information storage or retrieval system, without
prior permission in writing from the publishers.

Bloomsbury Publishing Plc does not have any control over, or responsibility for, any
third-party websites referred to or in this book. All internet addresses given in this book
were correct at the time of going to press. The author and publisher regret
any inconvenience caused if addresses have changed or sites have ceased
to exist, but can accept no responsibility for any such changes.

A catalogue record for this book is available from the British Library.

A catalog record for this book is available from the Library of Congress.

ISBN: HB: 978-1-3502-3167-2
PB: 978-1-3502-3170-2
ePDF: 978-1-3502-3399-7
eBook: 978-1-3502-3168-9

Series: New Directions in Religion and Literature

Typeset by Integra Software Services Pvt. Ltd.

To find out more about our authors and books visit www.bloomsbury.com
and sign up for our newsletters.

Contents

Acknowledgments		vi
Introduction: A New Theory of the Sacred		1
1	The Boiled-Over District: Effervescence and Adaptation during the Market Revolution	29
2	The Salvific Power of Affect: Sentimentalism in the Labor Fiction of Rebecca Harding Davis and Elizabeth Stuart Phelps	59
3	The American Fetish: Religious Economics in the Novels of William Dean Howells	89
4	Mistaking "Shadows for Gods": Class and the Christ Novel in the Progressive Era	111
5	"Christianity Incorporated": Sinclair Lewis and the Taylorization of American Protestantism	137
6	Gastonia Revisited: Religion, Literature, and the Loray Mill Strike of 1929	165
7	"The Blackness of God": Race and Religion in the Literature of the Harlem Renaissance	203
Works Cited		242
Index		255

Acknowledgments

This book has been many years in the making and would not have been possible without the support of my friends and colleagues. I owe special thanks to Lori Branch, Harold K. Bush, Susan Curtis, John N. Duvall, Wendy Flory, Sandor Goodhart, Daniel T. Kline, William McBride, Paul R. Petrie, Thomas Ryba, and Daniel W. Smith for their mentorship and advocacy on my behalf.

I am particularly grateful for my colleagues in the *American Religion and Literature Society*, J. Laurence Cohen, Kenyon Gradert, Ray Horton, Kathryn Ludwig, Jonathan McGregor, Catherine Rogers, Ryan Siemers, Tae Sung, and Hannah Wakefield. Thank you for the community you're building and the remarkable scholarship you're producing.

As a so-called alternative academic, I appreciate the professional and institutional support of my co-workers at Harvard University and Berghahn Books, Vivian Berghahn, Janine Latham, and Horng-Tzer Yau. Your patience, understanding, and the space you gave to this project were invaluable.

I have had the privilege of working with a superb group of editors over the course of this project. In particular, I would like to thank Ben Doyle, Mark Knight, Emma Mason, and the entire Bloomsbury Academic team. Thanks as well to Duncan Faherty at *Studies in American Fiction*, Romana Huk at *Religion & Literature*, Gary Scharnhorst at *American Literary Realism*, and to the referees of those journals, where earlier versions of Chapters 4 and 5 previously appeared.

Most importantly, I am endlessly grateful for my amazing support system of family and friends, Connie and Demetrious Turner, Terry Ball, Cory Ball, Michael Ball, Teresa and Joe Whitford, Chris and Laura Harris, Sue and Charles Harris, Audre Schoof, Brian Bergen-Aurand, Jennifer Backman, Jillian Canode, Tim Gaines, Jeff Heinle, and Monica Osborne.

Introduction: A New Theory of the Sacred

On May 19, 2018, new media artist Avery Singer and entrepreneur Matt Liston announced the creation of a new religion modeled on blockchain technology and the economics of cryptocurrency. The pair unveiled the new religion at the New Museum's annual Seven on Seven exhibition[1] along with its first sacred objects, a 3D-printed sculpture and an animated video representing the religion's totem, the Dogewhal.[2] The founding of the religion—0xΩ—was also accompanied by the release of its own cryptocurrency token, Omega, on the Ethereum platform. At the rollout, Singer and Liston explained that, in addition to introducing new religious doctrines and practices, 0xΩ incorporates traditional religious functions and promises by replacing them "with token-based consensus mechanisms"[3] (Avery and Singer). Using commerce on the blockchain, group members engage in prayer, evangelism, holy acts, pilgrimage, worship, and can even gain entry to a digital afterlife. To attain salvation in this religion, members must make an offering of their data. This data, combined with further information gleaned from the member's interaction with a chatbot, is used to generate a "mind model" that can be uploaded to the blockchain,

---

[1] "Seven on Seven" is an event organized by the new media art organization Rhizome and hosted at the New Museum in New York City. As Rhizome explains, "Seven on Seven pairs seven leading artists with seven visionary technologists, and challenges them to make something new—an artwork, a prototype, whatever they imagine. What's created is premiered at the annual flagship event." Singer and Liston took part in the tenth edition of "Seven on Seven," on May 19, 2018.

[2] A narwhal with the head of the Doge meme.

[3] Before Liston and Singer introduced the first new religion to be entirely modeled on cryptoeconomics, traditional world religions and blockchain start-ups had already begun to accommodate one another. Numerous companies offer digital commerce that incorporates religious law. For example, Blossom Finance promises that their blockchain "is designed with end-to-end shariah compliance in mind" (Blossom website). Similarly, the Lotos Network assures investors that their system is "compliant with the Noble Path" and conforms to the ethics of "Buddhist economics" (Winchester). Each of the world religions has their own cryptocurrency as well. For example, the "Karma Token" is a Buddhist digital currency, "BitCoen" is a kosher token, and the satirical but ultimately successful "Jesus Coin" was marketed as "the currency of God's Son" (Reiff). In addition to these religiously themed businesses, digital currencies and blockchain technology have significantly altered the way long-established religions function as institutions with respect to church finances, capital campaigns, and charitable giving.

enabling the member's virtual duplicate to exist and invest their wealth for eternity. Singer and Liston say that the members' combined mind models will ultimately form "a discrete... collective consciousness" (Avery and Singer). This collective representation of the group, they explain, constitutes "transcendence or meaning within the structure of this religion" (Avery and Singer).

Singer and Liston defend what appears to be an irreverent pairing of the sacred and the secular by arguing that religion and cryptoeconomics are eminently compatible. Liston, a lifelong atheist, says that once he began to look at religion through the "technical lens" of cryptoeconomics, he saw that religions are "coordination tools" that "allow humans to coordinate as society toward common utility" (Avery and Singer). Similarly, "cryptocurrencies are mechanisms to coordinate society without a central trust authority" (Avery and Singer). In this sense, he concludes, "cryptocurrencies as they exist in and of themselves are already religious structures" (Avery and Singer). They argue that religion and cryptoeconomics are both systemic means of actualizing the will of a group. However, by using blockchain technology—which advocates believe is a perfect consensus system—their cryptoreligion is better equipped to express group interests than any established religion. Singer explains that their "consensus-based religion could better reflect how quickly we feel things in culture change, how our needs change, how technology changes, how our lives are changing" (Avery and Singer). Liston adds, "Religion can evolve and adapt by using a system like this" (qtd. in McKinley). In their view, a blockchain religion is preferable to mainstream religions because it will more effectively mirror society and its political exigencies. For example, through the circulation of cryptocurrency, group members collectively determine the religion's defining ideas and practices, such as its deities, symbols, doctrines, rituals, sacred objects, and forms of social action.

In the case of 0xΩ, we observe a contemporary instance of a universal social phenomenon, and that phenomenon is the focus of this book. Singer and Liston's project exemplifies the way economic and technological change reshapes religion and gives rise to new forms of the sacred. These forms are expressed symbolically, in ideas, practices, and artistic representations collectively designed by the members of a group. Though novel, they are adaptive and incorporate aspects of established religion. Singer points to the specular structure of this phenomenon, that is, to its mirroring quality when she claims that cryptoreligion is a superior means of reflecting group interest. Like all forms of the sacred, 0xΩ is created in the likeness of an economic system and is determined by the traits and material relations of its members. Just as Singer and Liston look at religion through the lens of a new economic form during a period of significant material change, earlier Americans redesigned their conceptions of religion to accommodate new technologies and forms of economy during the Market and Industrial Revolutions. The religious innovations of the Information Age are the most recent iteration of a process that also marked the Machine Age.

In this book, I show that economics has a determining influence on religion that is necessarily mediated by the symbolic, most notably, by literature and print culture. I explain how the sacred is created and how it operates socially within an assemblage of groups that are in a perpetual state of mutual contestation. I forward a general theory that is applicable to any region, time, and religion, but my focus here is on Protestant Christianity during the Market and Industrial Revolutions in America. Contrary to the once dominant notion of a secular age, overwhelming evidence shows that modernity in America was far from disenchanted. Rather, the development of capitalism and the process of class formation intensely invigorated religious enthusiasm and transformed every facet of Protestantism, in particular its central doctrine: salvation.

Raised on Robbery: Max Weber and the American Mythos

Today, though academics have grown suspicious of grand narratives, the American public's conception of the nation remains in thrall to a foundational mythos. One of the unwitting authors of this mythology was the German sociologist Max Weber, who put forward theories of economy and religion that significantly influenced America's image of itself. In *The Protestant Ethic and the Spirit of Capitalism* (1904), Weber argued that Calvinism's ideas concerning work and its relation to salvation morally prepared the ground for the flourishing of capitalism, and in this way he established a line of consistency between Christianity and capitalism. Though Weber was just one of many machine age thinkers who were arguing for the compatibility of Christianity and capitalism, his account proved integral to the sacralization of capitalism in the American imagination. Now, its citizens largely view capitalism, religion, and authentic Americanness as inextricably linked[4] and Weber's *Protestant Ethic* is one of the central works responsible for popularizing that belief.

---

[4] For example, in a study of the religious makeup of the 116th Congress of the United States, the Pew Research Center found that just one member out of 535 identified themselves as "unaffiliated" (Sandstrom). Similarly, in 2021 the 117th Congress includes just four socialists, again out of 535, Jamaal Bowman, Cori Bush, Alexandria Ocasio-Cortez, and Rashida Tlaib. This is not to suggest that these statistics are reflective of American demographics but rather that the American citizenry does not regard atheists and anti-capitalists to be fit for positions of political authority.

Of course, Weber's contribution to the American mythos is ironic because he believed that capitalism would ultimately secularize society. Weber argued that history had been marked by the inexorable march of reason, and he predicted that this centuries-long development would culminate in modernity with the rationalization of all things and the thoroughgoing "disenchantment of the world" (FMW 351). Weber maintained that, like a tragic hero, religion would bring about its own downfall. He claimed that the world religions were engines of secularization because over time they developed ever more rational norms in their quest to achieve salvation.[5] Weber held that Calvinism's salvation ethic in particular made the advancement of rational, capitalist society possible. It is in this sense that, for Weber, Protestantism "produces... its own grave-diggers," carrying "within it the seeds of its own destruction," and would lead inevitably to a secular age and "a world robbed of gods" (Marx and Engels 483, 506; FMW 282).

Weber's teleological secularization narrative draws from a long-challenged[6] tradition[7] of cultural evolution theory that envisions humanity as necessarily progressing from primitive superstition to modern reason. However, as Talal Asad recently put it, "If anything is agreed upon" among scholars of religion and culture, "it is that a straightforward narrative of progress from the religious to the secular is no longer acceptable" (1). Weber predicted that, once capitalism fully developed, it would no longer require the religious legitimation afforded by the Protestant salvation ethic.[8] The expansion of industrial capitalism and its attendant social norms would rationalize the world and eliminate religious superstition for good. As I will show, contrary to Weber's theory of disenchantment, capitalism, like all forms of economy, derives its social authority and transcendent legitimacy from the sacred. Economic life is not purely rational. Our material relations are infused with feelings and ideas about the sacred and the profane—with, as Tillich put it, matters of ultimate concern.

As American society was increasingly conditioned by the development of capitalism in the nineteenth and early twentieth centuries, rather than becoming secular as Weber predicted, modern America was instead characterized by

---

[5] Weber writes, "And not only theoretical thought, disenchanting the world, led to this course, but also the very attempt of religious ethics practically and ethically to rationalize the world" (FMW 357).

[6] E.g., Latour, Bruno. *We Have Never Been Modern*. Cambridge: Harvard UP, 1993.

[7] Others have sought to root this tradition in the Enlightenment, but it is a classical notion that gained further currency during the Renaissance and colonial Age of Discovery.

[8] Weber writes, "victorious capitalism, since it rests on mechanical foundations, needs [religion's] support no longer" (*PESC* 181-2).

an intensified production of the sacred. The economic paradigm shifts that occurred during the Market and Industrial Revolutions, roughly 1820–1940, were the cause of nearly unmitigated religious proliferation. There is much more to be said about the nature of this causal relation, but what is clearly self-evident is that, from the Second Great Awakening and the Social Gospel to the rise of fundamentalism and the creation of countless new belief systems, modernity in America was hardly a period of disenchantment.

The general position Weber defends—that religious ideas shape the economy—represents a widely held philosophical orientation. Those who study religion and its role in society fall into two groups: idealists and materialists. The fundamental disagreement between the two camps comes down to a question of primacy and derivation. Idealists maintain that the material world is derived from the world of ideas, while materialists claim that ideas are derived from the material world. For example, figures like Weber,[9] Georg Simmel, and Clifford Geertz argue that religious ideas determine the material order of society whereas for those like Ludwig Feuerbach, Karl Marx,[10] and Émile Durkheim, the material conditions of society determine religious ideas. Put another way, idealists like Weber see the economy as a dependent variable; materialists, on the other hand, see religion as a dependent variable. In the context of contemporary America, this is more than a matter of esoteric academic debate because Weber's account remains a major feature of the nation's dominant origin story.

Durkheim's protégé Marcel Mauss wrote that "social life in all its forms—moral, religious, and legal—is dependent on its material substratum... at the very moment when the form of the group changes, one can observe the simultaneous transformation of religion, law and moral life" (Mauss and Beuchat 1979, 80). This exemplifies the Durkheimian stance, which comports with Marx's more polemical theory of base and superstructure. Mauss makes two claims here that are central to this book: first, that religion is dependent on material conditions, and second, that material change alters the form of social groups, which in turn causes a "simultaneous transformation of religion." In this book, I give a materialist account of American religious history and show how economic change reshaped religion in modern America. I examine how the new material conditions brought about by the Market and Industrial Revolutions—in particular, the process of class formation—led believers to redesign Protestant

---

[9] Weber writes, "It is not our thesis that the specific nature of a religion is a simple 'function' of the social situation... or that it represents the stratum's 'ideology,' or that it is a 'reflection' of a stratum's material or ideal interest-situation. On the contrary, a more basic misunderstanding of the standpoint of these discussions would hardly be possible" (FMW 269–70).

[10] "Consciousness does not determine life, but life determines consciousness" (Marx and Engels 93).

concepts, practices, and institutions. As we will see, the culturally formative relation of economy and religion is mediated by the symbolic, most importantly, by literature, and by collective symbolic activities like labor strikes and revivals. Therefore, to develop a model that explains the entanglement of economy and religion and rectifies the fundamental errors of the idealist theory of secularization, we must focus on these modes of expression.

Over the last twenty years or so, scholarly debate about secularization and the so-called post-secular has become an increasingly important matter in every discipline in the humanities and social sciences. Taken together, this debate now comprises a vast and diverse literature. In this book, I did not set out to rigorously engage with questions concerning the secular or secularism writ large, either in the context of current geopolitics or with respect to the more meta-critical directions of this scholarship, though I do hope this book can contribute to those conversations. However, I would also say that the position I lay out in this book does not align with concepts of the post-secular that presuppose theories of "resacralization,"[11] "desecularization,"[12] or notions of a return to religion[13] in modern and contemporary society. This book not only refutes Weber's theory of disenchantment but also challenges forms of the post-secular that forward a resurgence theory of religion.

Within the broader debate across these disciplines, this book participates in the ongoing conversation among a diverse group of scholars that is focused on the relation of economy, religion, and art. Of course, a comprehensive accounting of these works cannot be given here, but a number of noteworthy texts exemplify recent and current attempts to understand this relation. In the sociology of religion, a group of social scientists including Roger Finke and Rodney Stark have empirically proven that economic change determines the development of religion.[14] Similarly, like Finke and Stark, economists in the emerging field of the economics of religion, such as Rachel McCleary, Robert Ekelund, Robert Tollison, and Laurence Iannaccone, apply rational choice theory to explain the necessary

---

[11] E.g., Davie, Grace, "Resacralization," in *The New Blackwell Companion to the Sociology of Religion*, ed. Bryan S. Turner. Chichester: Blackwell, 2010, 160–77.

[12] E.g., Berger, Peter L., ed., *The Desecularization of the World: Resurgent Religion and World Politics*. Washington, DC: The Ethics and Public Policy Center, 1999.

[13] E.g., Partridge, Christopher, *The Re-enchantment of the West (vol. 1): Alternative Spiritualities, Sacralization, Popular Culture and Occulture*. London: Continuum, 2004.

[14] E.g., Finke, Roger, and Rodney Stark. *The Churching of America, 1776–2005: Winners and Losers in Our Religious Economy*. New Brunswick: Rutgers UP, 2005; Finke, Roger, and Rodney Stark. *Acts of Faith: Explaining the Human Side of Religion*. Berkeley: University of California Press, 2000.

connections between economics, religion, and culture.[15] While Ekelund and Tollison focus on capitalism and Catholicism in Europe, Finke and Stark use the same methods in their groundbreaking work on capitalism and American Protestantism. In this school of thought, scholars apply the tools of economics to interpret religion. However, though this group has done as much as anyone to disprove Weber's secularization thesis, they are contemporary proponents of his idealist position, in that they are methodologically committed to the notion that it is individuals' ideas—their beliefs, desires, choices, and preferences— that shape the material order of society. These multidisciplinary scholars have marshalled an enormous amount of data to show that there is an inextricable link between economy and religion but, as Weberians, their assumptions about that link are fundamentally at odds with a materialist approach.

Historians like Jama Lazerow, Teresa Anne Murphy, Paul Johnson, Mark Schantz, and William Sutton have written remarkable regional studies that examine the relationship between the Industrial Revolution and nineteenth-century American revivalism, and show how antebellum class conflict influenced the development of American Protestantism.[16] Some of the best works to recently appear in the areas of religious studies and Christian theology have also sought to better understand the link between economy and religion. In contrast to the cultural historians' in-depth analyses of narrow locales, Devin Singh and Eugene McCarraher's new works are broad in scope, the former covering Christianity in the West from antiquity to the present, and the latter, Christianity in America from the colonial period to the 1970s.[17] Singh

---

[15] McCleary, Rachel M. and Robert J. Barro. *The Wealth of Religions: The Political Economy of Believing and Belonging.* Princeton: Princeton UP, 2019; McCleary, Rachel M. ed. *The Oxford Handbook of the Economics of Religion.* New York: Oxford UP, 2011; Ekelund, Robert B., Robert F. Hébert, and Robert D. Tollison. *The Marketplace of Christianity.* Cambridge: MIT Press, 2008; Ekelund, Robert B. and Robert D. Tollison. *Economic Origins of Roman Christianity.* Chicago: University of Chicago Press, 2011; Ekelund, Robert B., Robert F. Hébert, Robert D. Tollison, Gary M. Anderson, and Audrey B. Davidson. *Sacred Trust: The Medieval Church as an Economic Firm.* New York: Oxford UP, 1996; Iannaccone, Laurence R. "Introduction to the Economics of Religion," *Journal of Economic Literature* 36.3 (1998): 1465–95. For a more polemical branch of scholarship that explicitly conflates economics and theology, see Nelson, Robert H. *Economics as Religion: From Samuelson to Chicago and beyond.* University Park: Pennsylvania State UP, 2001.

[16] Lazerow, Jama. *Religion and the Working Class in Antebellum America.* Washington: Smithsonian Institution Press, 1995; Murphy, Teresa Anne. *Ten Hours' Labor: Religion, Reform, and Gender in Early New England.* Ithaca: Cornell UP, 1992; Johnson, Paul E. *A Shopkeeper's Millennium: Society and Revivals in Rochester, New York 1815–1837.* New York: Hill and Wang, 1978; Schantz, Mark S. *Piety in Providence: Class Dimensions of Religious Experience in Antebellum Rhode Island.* Ithaca: Cornell UP, 2000; Sutton, William R. *Journeymen for Jesus: Evangelical Artisans Confront Capitalism in Jacksonian Baltimore.* University Park: Pennsylvania State UP, 1998. See also Davenport, Stewart. *Friends of the Unrighteous Mammon: Northern Christians and Market Capitalism, 1815–1860.* Chicago: University of Chicago Press, 2008.

[17] Singh, Devin. *Divine Currency: The Theological Power of Money in the West.* Stanford: Stanford UP, 2018; McCarraher, Eugene. *The Enchantments of Mammon: How Capitalism Became the Religion of Modernity.* Cambridge: Harvard UP, 2019.

adeptly shows how economics shaped early Christianity, while McCarraher demonstrates that the sacralization of capitalism was central to American modernity, and makes Weber the primary opponent of his sacramental theology. In her excellent new book, Kathryn Lofton takes a Durkheimian approach to examining the "persistent commiseration between religion and economy" in modern American culture.[18] In the field of literary studies, Lori Merish and Josef Sorett have written exemplary works that revisit two of the discipline's perennial concerns, namely, how labor[19] and religion[20] impact modes of representation in American literature.

While works like these have significantly advanced our understanding of American culture, scholars tend to focus on the comparative pairs, economy and religion,[21] religion and literature,[22] and economics and literature.[23] In this book, I draw from diverse resources in the humanities and social sciences to create a coherent theory that explains the interrelation of economics, religion, and literature in American culture.

In the following section, I put forward a synthetic social theory that explains the genesis of the sacred and its part in group dynamics. In the subsequent chapters of the book, I further elaborate this theory and apply it to the analysis of modern America. I believe that this approach can resolve numerous open problems and critical stalemates in multiple fields. This theory gives us new tools for understanding the relation of the sacred and the secular and offers an alternative to both Weber's "straightforward narrative" of disenchantment and post-secular concepts of religious resurgence.

---

[18] Lofton, Kathryn. *Consuming Religion*. Chicago: University of Chicago Press, 2017, pg. 8.

[19] Merish, Lori. *Archives of Labor: Working-Class Women and Literary Culture in the Antebellum United States*. Durham: Duke UP, 2017.

[20] Sorett, Josef. *Spirit in the Dark: A Religious History of Racial Aesthetics*. New York: Oxford UP, 2016.

[21] E.g., Cox, Harvey. *The Market as God*. Cambridge: Harvard UP, 2016. Hudnut-Beumler, James. *In Pursuit of the Almighty's Dollar: A History of Money and American Protestantism*. Chapel Hill: The University of North Carolina Press, 2007; Noll, Mark A., ed. *God and Mammon: Protestants, Money, and the Market 1790–1860*. New York: Oxford UP, 2002.

[22] E.g., Lundin, Roger, ed. *Invisible Conversations: Religion in the Literature of America*. Waco: Baylor UP, 2009. More broadly, on religion and art, see for example, Graham, Gordon. *The Re-enchantment of the World: Art versus Religion*. Oxford: Oxford UP, 2007.

[23] E.g., Seybold, Matt, and Michelle Chihara, eds. *The Routledge Companion to Literature and Economics*. London: Routledge, 2019; Woodmansee, Martha and Mark Osteen, eds. *The New Economic Criticism: Studies at the Intersection of Literature and Economics*. London: Routledge, 1999.

Specular Phenomena: From Anthropotheism to Apotheosis

The desire to demystify the genesis of religious ideas has been a motivating Western concern since antiquity. The moment we began to systematically reflect on ourselves, we asked, what is the origin of our concept of the divine? One of the earliest and most charming examples of this line of inquiry comes down to us from the fifth century BCE, in the fragments of Xenophanes, who writes, "If horses had hands, or oxen or lions, or if they could draw with their hands and produce works as men do, then horses would draw figures of gods like horses, and oxen like oxen, and each would render the bodies to be of the same frame that each of them have" (Curd 34). Here, Xenophanes acknowledges that an image of god is necessarily the outcome of a creative act of symbolization and satirizes what Ludwig Feuerbach would later call *anthropotheism*, that is, attributing human traits to the gods. Xenophanes writes, "Mortals suppose that gods are born, have human clothing, and voice, and bodily form" (Curd 34). He further explains that the features we assign to the gods are not simply general human characteristics—a voice and body—but are dependent on the differentiating traits of a given social group. Xenophanes writes, "Ethiopians say that their gods are snub-nosed and dark, Thracians, that theirs are grey-eyed and red-haired" (Curd 34). A few centuries later, the Church Father Clement of Alexandria would echo these pagan remarks, writing, "the Greeks assume their gods to be human in passions as they are humans in shape; and each nation paints their shape after its own likeness… For instance, the barbarians make them brutal and savage, the Greeks milder, but subject to passion" (36–37). Like Xenophanes, Clement explains that concepts of God are the product of self-portraiture and reflect the traits unique to "each nation."

Statements like these abound in the canon. For centuries, anthropotheism was generally accepted as a universal aspect of human culture but no one bothered to rigorously examine the phenomenon. That is, until Ludwig Feuerbach took up the subject in his book *The Essence of Christianity* (1841)—a work that would have a tremendous impact on modern European and American politics. Like Xenophanes, Clement, and so many others, Feuerbach claims that we create God in our own image. However, unlike his predecessors, who observed that social factors like race and nationality influence the creation of god images, Feuerbach is more of an essentialist. He argues that Christians imagine God by absolutizing essential human traits. For instance, it is in our nature to love but we love imperfectly. God, on the other hand, is thought to love infinitely and unconditionally, indeed for Christians, God *is* love. This is an example of our tendency to ontologically elevate features of human experience. Feuerbach posits that we fashion our idea of God by converting the mundane into the metaphysical, or the material into the ideal, by projecting essential human predicates into the heavens and investing them with unity and autonomous being. Humanity then forgets how its god images were originally produced and comes to misrecognize them. This misrecognition is characterized by an inversion of subject-object relations. That is, human subjects mistake objects they create for independent subjects, and mistake themselves for dependent, created objects. Put another way, anthropotheism entails both falsely investing objects with agency and divesting subjects of agency—personification and depersonification, the reversal of subject and object. Anthropotheism is a specular phenomenon in that it is structured like a mirror, only here, the real person mistakes herself for a reflection. Feuerbach's discovery of the specular form of religion led him to famously conclude that "theology is anthropology" (x).

This profoundly influenced Marx and Engels but ultimately Feuerbach's materialism did not go far enough for them. Like Xenophanes and Clement, Marx and Engels believed that we create transcendent norms not by deifying immaterial human essences but by sacralizing the attributes of a social group, as well as its material relationships and forms of work. Marx writes that "Feuerbach resolves the religious essence into the human essence. But the human essence... in its reality... is the ensemble of social relations" (183). From Feuerbach, Marx and Engels learned that "the religious world is but the reflex" or "duplication" of the material world (164, 183). However, they took Feuerbach's model of anthropotheism further to develop a more general theory of norm production which maintained that the dominant ideas that guide behavior in a given social group, including those pertaining to "politics, law, morality, religion, [and] metaphysics," are "the direct result of their material behavior" (Marx and Engels 99). Building on Feuerbach's theory that religious ideas are produced by sacralizing aspects of human life, Engels argued that

> all moral theories have been hitherto the product... of the economic conditions of society obtaining at the time. And as society has hitherto moved in class antagonisms, morality has always been class morality; it has either justified the domination and the interests of the ruling class, or, ever since the oppressed class became powerful enough, it has represented its indignation against this domination and the future interests of the oppressed.
>
> (726)

As is clearly apparent here, Marx and Engels use the specular structure of anthropotheism elaborated by Feuerbach as the model for their theory of base and superstructure. Ultimately, Marx secularized Feuerbach's theory of religion and made the specular structure of anthropotheism the foundation of many of his core concepts like alienation, commodity fetishism, and ideology.

However, Marx and Engels made a vital contribution to this area of inquiry by displacing the human individual as the original model for conceptions of God and reinstating the social group as the determining exemplar. They further recognized that the moral norms of each group are determined by class interest, that these economically oriented norms are legitimated through sacralization, and that the metaphysical elevation of class interest is a major factor in the continual struggles for power among these conflicting groups. Unlike Feuerbach, Marx and Engels recognized that the images of God humans produce and the religious norms they develop on the basis of those symbols are created by projecting the defining attributes of the class onto the group's conception of God and by sacralizing the interests of the group. These developments begin to give us some indication that anthropotheism is merely one aspect of a much larger social process. While Feuerbach was the first to map the specular structure of sacralization, leading him to conclude that "theology is anthropology," later figures, most notably Émile Durkheim, made the crucial discovery that in fact theology is sociology. With respect to the origin of god images, Durkheim writes that "the gods are no other than collective forces personified and hypostasized in material form. Ultimately, it is society that is worshiped by the believers; the superiority of the gods over men is that of the group over its members" (PECM 161).

Figures like Feuerbach, Marx, and Freud were preoccupied with a negative view of anthropotheism, seeing it only as a deceptive fantasy that justifies oppression and distorts reality to fulfill our desires.[24] Conversely, Durkheim and his adherents represent those who take a broadly positive view of the phenomenon. Durkheim writes, "Far from ignoring real society and turning it into an abstraction, religion is the very image of it. It reflects all its aspects, even the most ordinary and repulsive" (316). He contends that "reality can be clearly glimpsed through mythologies and theologies" where it appears "enlarged [and]

---

[24] Cioran, for example, writes that humans are possessed by a "mania for salvation" (4). "Man animates ideas, projects his flames and flaws into them... Idolaters by instinct, we convert the objects of our dreams and our interests into the Unconditional. History is nothing but a procession of false Absolutes, a series of temples raised to pretexts... Even when he turns from religion, man remains subject to it; depleting himself to create fake gods, he then feverishly adopts them: his need for fiction, for mythology triumphs over evidence and absurdity alike" (3).

transformed" (316). Here, Durkheim adopts specular language to argue that religion is a kind of mirror image of society and can therefore serve as a crucial means of understanding culture. Further, Durkheim maintains that religion is not merely a social sedative that promotes docility—though it can be used to that end. He writes that "A god is not only an authority to which we submit, however; it is also a force that supports our own. The man who has obeyed his god, and therefore believes he is on his side, approaches the world with confidence and the feeling of accumulated energy" (157). Crucially, Durkheim recognizes that religion is not primarily repressive—it is the source of tremendous power. However, anthropotheism, god-making, is only one aspect of the way that power is generated and regenerated.

Durkheim made a crucial breakthrough when he recognized that gods are not essential to religion. Of course, he was by no means the first to acknowledge this but it was Durkheim who discovered and elaborated the full significance of this fact; and in doing so, shifted the focus of religious study from gods—given the form of animals, plants, and humans—to the more abstract concept of the sacred. Durkheim observes, "there are rites without gods, and there are even rites from which gods derive. Not all religious qualities emanate from divine personalities, and there are cultic practices that have other goals than man's union with a divinity. Religion therefore transcends the idea of gods or spirits, and so cannot be defined exclusively as a function of that idea" (35). This insight led Durkheim to define religion as "a unified system of beliefs and practices relative to sacred things… that unite its adherents in a single moral community" (46). This brief definition supplies many of the key ideas that I will return to throughout this book. First, that in order to understand religion in modern America, we must focus on the sacred. Second, that religion extends well beyond formal institutions to include any concepts, practices, feelings, and events that pertain to the sacred. And third, that religion functions to integrate social groups through a shared moral code.

So, where does this leave Xenophanes's horses and oxen? Since antiquity, when westerners sought the origin of their concept of the divine, they looked to theogenesis, to the way gods are made. With his theory of anthropotheism, Feuerbach appeared to provide a final account of the process, while Marx and Engels demonstrated its role in macro-scale power dynamics and the establishment of social norms. But Durkheim's findings prove that the sacred is the essential element of religion, not God. Of course, this raises the question, then what is sacred? Durkheim found that "anything at all, can be sacred" (36). The sacredness of a thing "does not inhere in any of its intrinsic attributes" and so "the most trivial, the most ordinary object" such as "a rock, a tree, a spring, a stone, a piece of wood, a house," can be regarded as sacred (Durkheim 240–241). Sacredness, therefore, is not inherent in anything, but is something "*added...* The world of the religious is not a particular aspect of empirical nature: *it is superimposed*" (Durkheim 174). With these facts, Durkheim makes a seemingly slight but ever so important alteration to the perennial question with which we began. The question is not, how are gods made? but, how is the sacred produced? If the sacred is something superimposed, then what is the nature of that process?

Like Feuerbach's, Durkheim's model is specular, but it is not the predicates of human nature that are mirrored in our representations of divinity; instead, he observes that "god is merely the symbolic expression of society" (Durkheim 171). The sacred is "society hypostasized and transfigured" (Durkheim 257). Simply put, the sacred is social. However, "society" is not a unified, autonomous agent but instead consists of groups. Consequently, "the idea of religion is inseparable from the idea of a church" or moral collective (Durkheim 46). Religious ideas and actions are therefore created by social groups; they are "products of collective thought" and experience that "express collective realities" (Durkheim 11). While Durkheim would not go as far as Marx to claim that religion is determined by material conditions, he argued that religious ideas, actions, and feelings "depend on social conditions" and that all religions "respond, if in different ways, to the given conditions of human existence" (14, 4). Where Feuerbach saw God as a representation of immutable human nature, Durkheim saw the sacred as a dependent variable, contingent on the diversity and plasticity of human culture. Most importantly, what their models share is a recognition of the specular framework of sacralization. With Durkheim's results, we discover that anthropotheism is only one form of the process. All things sacred, including god images, are a projection of social groups and the conditions unique to them in a given time and place. The sacred is created when the defining traits, ideas, customs, and interests of a social group are transfigured and regarded as objects of veneration. The multifunctional social process of making-sacred and its corollary, god-making, I call *apotheosis*. Apotheosis determines how representations of gods are created as well as the sacralization of things, people, practices, events, and feelings. Apotheosis is elevation is this dual sense. It involves both consecrating aspects of the material world and conceiving of the metaphysical as an idealized reflection of that world, as it is experienced by a particular social group.

In every age and place, we find that concepts of the supernatural within a given group correspond to the defining characteristics of their social life.

Apotheosis is a universal phenomenon readily observable throughout history, from the fertility gods of agricultural communities to the warrior gods of imperial societies. But, as Heraclitus put it, πάντα ῥεῖ, everything flows, social life changes as a consequence of changing material conditions. New groups emerge and dissolve, new tools are adopted and with them, new ways of working. The sacred is a projection of the social so when material relations change, religion necessarily changes in kind. Wherever new forms of social organization emerge or differentiation increases, such as in the division of labor, those changes are reflected in theology. As Weber put it, "the forms of the gods vary, depending on natural and social conditions" (SR 20). Though we tend to think of God or religion as something solidified and more or less unchanging, "now as in the past, we observe society constantly creating new sacred things" (Durkheim 160).

Apotheosis is not a process limited to how people conceive of the formal, visible, or tangible aspects of the sacred. Apotheosis entails the sanctification of "social sentiments" as well (Mauss 149). Just as Feuerbach was alive to the deification of human sensibility, Durkheim and his protégés Marcel Mauss and Henri Hubert observed that religious concepts and practices are the product of the "collective desires" shared by a social group (155). Durkheim explains, "even the most impersonal and most anonymous forces are none other than objectified feelings. Only by viewing religions from this perspective is it possible to perceive their real significance" (314). "Religious force," he writes, "is the feeling the collectivity inspires in its members, but projected outside and objectified by the minds that feel it. It becomes objectified by being anchored in an object which then becomes sacred, but any object can play this role" (174). We will return to the question of how such an anchoring works but for the moment it is crucial to underscore that the sacred is not an inert mirror image; it does not just reflect already existing feelings, but inspires feeling and action. Apotheosis is generative and propulsive. It is the current of the Heraclitian flow of culture.

The Symbolic

I have established that the sacred is social. Further, we will find that the sacred is always already symbolic. Apotheosis is the process whereby the differentiating traits, interests, and feelings of a social group are "projected outside" and "anchored in an object which then becomes sacred" (Durkheim 174). We should recall here Geertz's inclusive definition of a symbol as "any object, act, event, quality, or relation which serves as a vehicle for a conception—the conception is the symbol's 'meaning' " (97). It is through the symbolic that groups collectively elaborate their representation of the divine, in texts, images, rituals, and sacred practices. To study religion, therefore, is to study collective representations. The sacred, and in particular the god image, is the social group's conception of itself rendered symbolically. Ernst Cassirer writes that the social group "finds and constitutes itself only by projecting itself outward" (*Symbolic* 223). The group creates its image of God by objectifying its defining characteristics, and this god image is "the sign by which each clan distinguishes itself from others, the visible mark of its personality, a mark that embodies everything that belongs to the clan in anyway" (Durkheim 154). The god image is a collective emblem that expresses the "personality" of the group and serves to strengthen or reinforce the bonds between its members. This is what Durkheim means when he writes that the god of the group is "the clan itself, but transfigured and transformed by the religious imagination" (160).

As Cassirer so elegantly put it, humanity "finds itself only through the detour of the divine" (*Symbolic* 205). His take on apotheosis draws our attention to the epistemological aspects of this phenomenon and the kind of hermeneutic approach it demands. He contends that "man can apprehend and know his own being only insofar as he can make it visible in the image of his gods" (*Symbolic* 218). Humanity "can contemplate itself only in this kind of projection" (*Symbolic* 217). Our knowledge of humanity in general, and modern America in particular, is necessarily mediated by our interpretation of sacred symbols.

Apotheosis structures a group's relation to itself and to other groups. Durkheim observed that religion is "a system of notions by which individuals imagine the society to which they belong and their... relations with that society. This is its primordial role" (170–171). Religion is the symbolic representation of the collective life of a social group, and the collective life of the group is determined by its material conditions. Therefore, to modify Althusser's formulation, religion is humanity's imaginary relation to its real social conditions. Apotheosis is the sacralization of an *imaginary* conception of one's group. Though we are considering for the moment the creation of god images, we must keep in mind that apotheosis entails both transcendent and immanent projections; its specular structure causes the heavens to mirror human society and causes elements of that society to be made sacred. Durkheim finds that "what defines the sacred is that it is superimposed on the real" (317). Apotheosis "can turn the most ordinary object into a sacred and very powerful being" (Durkheim 173). If Cassirer and Durkheim are right, and I think they are, then in order to understand humanity, in order to understand modern America, we must understand how we produce the sacred. Durkheim writes, "we cannot explain one without explaining the other" (317). To know the real world, we must explain the nature of apotheosis, "we must reach beneath the symbol to the reality it embodies and which gives it its true meaning" (Durkheim 4). To find modern America, then, we must detour through the divine and through the symbolic. However, we must recall that sacred symbols and collective representations are not passive things, "they determine man's conduct as imperatively as physical forces" (Durkheim 173). Now that we have established the basic structure of apotheosis, we can examine how sacralization conditions individual and large-scale social action.

Salvation Ethics

So far, we have laid the groundwork for how the sacred is made but that is only to bring us to the more important matter—what the sacred *does*. Apotheosis does not simply explain how people create religious symbols or why most Americans worship a white Jesus; apotheosis is the mechanism that produces social norms. The sacred-symbolic directs action, and not just practices that are overtly religious, like formal rituals, but the activity of everyday life. As Feuerbach recognized, apotheosis creates an idealized reflection. As an imaginary rendering of real conditions, it does not express what is, but rather what believers feel they ought to be. The sacred does not just reflect the actions and feelings of a particular social group, it models how believers should act and feel, and is in this sense normative. Apotheosis is the process that provides group members with a normative code of conduct that guides their behavior. However, it should also be noted that collective representations not only express a group's conception of itself, but, more broadly, provide "an authoritative conception of the overall shape of reality" and give them resources for acting in a manner consistent with that conception of reality (Geertz 112). Groups' sacred symbols provide them with a "cosmic framework" or conception of the general order of existence and they establish social norms that are intended to replicate or conform to that order (Geertz 105). Therefore, it is through apotheosis that a group establishes its ontology and ethics. As Geertz put it, "sacred symbols function to synthesize a people's ethos—the tone, character, and quality of their life, their cosmology and shared morality" (96).

The sacred directs action and the ultimate objective of that action, indeed the very substance of that action, is salvation. Weber argues that every religion is a "quest for salvation" (SR 149). Similarly, Durkheim writes that "the first article of all faith is the belief in salvation" (311). From their perspective, it seems that soteriology, the study of salvation, should be at the very heart of any examination of religion. To inquire into the nature of American Protestantism, where salvation is undoubtedly its foremost idea, further demands our focus on this concept. Weber explains that a group's religious system hinges on their concept of salvation. He writes, "the various ethical colorations of the doctrines of god and sin stand in the most intimate relationship to the striving for salvation, the content of which will be different depending upon what one wants to be saved from, and what one wants to be saved for" (SR 147). The content of redemption is variable and contingent on the material conditions of the group, which determine what they want to be saved "for and from." Salvation is a universal religious concept with seemingly endless permutations. For example, Weber reports,

> One could wish to be saved from political and social servitude and lifted into a messianic realm in the future of this world... One could wish to escape being incarcerated in an impure body and hope for a purely spiritual existence. One could wish to be saved from the eternal and senseless play of human passions and desires and hope for the quietude of the pure beholding of the divine... One could wish to be redeemed from the barriers to the finite, which express themselves in suffering, misery and death, and the threatening punishment of hell, and hope for an eternal bliss in an earthly or paridisical future existence. One could wish to be saved from the cycle of rebirths with their inexhaustible compensations for the deeds of the times past and hope for eternal rest.
> (FMW 280–81)

Though Durkheim acknowledged the universality of salvation in religion, he failed to fully recognize the power and centrality of this concept. In this respect Weber, who gives the study of salvation priority in his work, surpassed Durkheim. We can, however, reconcile their results to develop an upgraded theory of apotheosis.

While social scientists like Durkheim and Geertz recognized that religion consists of a system of practices related to a group's concepts of the sacred, that is, that it embodies a group's ethos, it was Weber who found that salvation is the *sine qua non* of religious action. Simply put, salvation is activity in conformity with the sacred. All groups develop a salvation ethic, a set of codified norms of thought, feeling, and conduct, fidelity to which members believe will confer or reinforce redemption. A salvation ethic is a moral code, shared by a community, that prescribes social actions conducive to salvation. Durkheim called this "collective conscience" and Weber, "the religious systematization of the conduct of life" (SR 149). Even in the worship of non-anthropotheistic religions that do not possess self-mirroring images of God, the believer still conditions their conduct according to a concept of the cosmos modeled on their social group. The content of redemption is variable but salvation ethics are ubiquitous in all social groups, whether they are self-consciously religious or not. Members "believe they are held to certain kinds of behaviour imposed by the nature of the sacred principle with which they are engaged" (Durkheim 154). It is crucial to emphasize once again that salvation ethics, and the concepts of the sacred they are based on, are derived from the symbolic stage of apotheosis. Cassirer explains that humanity "draws from his spiritual creations—language, myth, and art—the objective standards by which to measure himself and learn to understand himself" (*Symbolic* 218).

Durkheim explains that "collective ideas and sensations are possible only thanks to the external movements that symbolize them... Therefore action dominates religious life" (313). Salvation is the performance of that action. Salvation is a condition of continued purposive action in the world, it is not a destination or passive quality. We must therefore think about salvation sociologically, as an element of social activity rather than a metaphysical state or theological fantasy. A group's concept of salvation is an expression of its differentiating characteristics, and has inherent value from a cultural studies perspective for that reason alone. But what is most important about salvation is what it does, not only with respect to the conduct of single individuals, but to behavior within and among social groups. Salvation ethics require group members to behave in a manner that is meant to mimic or otherwise appease the sacred. Weber argues that salvation must be viewed as "active ethical behavior performed in the awareness that god directs this behavior, i.e., that the actor is an instrument of god" (SR 164). Salvation, he writes, is a "quality of conduct... an awareness of having executed the divine will" (SR 168). For Christians in particular, salvation is the belief that one possesses "an ethical justification before god, which ultimately [can] be accomplished and maintained only by some sort of active conduct within the world" (SR 178). Therefore, salvation religion affords a "transcendental anchorage for ethics" (SR 90). This is the sanctioning function of redemption, one element of the way that apotheosis serves as the source of authority and legitimation for all social groups.

Social Reproduction, Group Solidarity, and Class Formation

Now that I have delineated the specular, symbolic, and ethical aspects of apotheosis, we can look to the macroscale social function of apotheosis.

Apotheosis is the process by which social groups are created, maintained, and reproduced. First, let's consider how the symbolic serves as the medium of group integration. The bonds that unify a social group are formed and maintained through sacred symbols. To have its own identity as a genuine group, it must have a symbol of the divine that functions as an objectified "personification of tribal unity" (Durkheim 216). These symbols mediate how a group both relates to itself and to other groups. A group's concept of the sacred or image of God is not only an emblem of solidarity directed toward others; the group needs the sacred-symbolic "to explain to themselves the bonds that unite them to one another, to whatever clan they belong to" (Durkheim 215). A clear illustration of this universal phenomenon can be observed outside the context of modern America, in the case of occupational or vocational gods. Occupational gods, "functional deities," "gods of locality, tribe, and polity" who are "only concerned with the interests of their respective associations" have existed globally from antiquity to the present day (FMW 333). However, it was the Romans, Cassirer writes, who developed this practice "with the greatest precision" (*Symbolic* 202). Elsewhere one finds "a god of blacksmiths and brassfounders, a god of tinsmiths," and so on, but among the ancient Romans, "every action and particularly every activity necessary to the cultivation of the fields has its own god and its own organized priesthood" (*Symbolic* 202).[25] Likewise, Weber reports that "there is no communal activity… without its special god. Indeed, if an association is to be permanently guaranteed, it must have such a god. Whenever a grouping… appears as a genuine group, it has need of a special god of its own" (SR 14). Also turning to Italian religion, Weber gives some indication as to the way apotheosis conditions group dynamics and political relations. He writes that

> every permanent political association had a special god who guaranteed the success of the political action of the group. When fully developed, this god was altogether exclusive with respect to outsiders, and in principle he accepted offers and prayers only from the members of his group… The stranger was thus not only a political, but also a religious alien. Even when the god of another society had the same name and attributes as that of one's own polity, he was

---

[25] Usener explains in greater detail: "For all actions and conditions special gods are created and clearly named; and it is not merely the actions and conditions as a whole which are deified in this way but also any segments, acts, or moments of them that are in any way conspicuous… In the agricultural sacrifice the Flamines had to invoke twelve gods in addition to Tellus and Ceres, and these twelve corresponded to as many actions of the tiller of soil: Veruactor for the first breaking of the fallow field, Reparator for the second plowing, Inporcitor for the third and final plowing… Insitor for the sowing, Oberator for the ploughing over after the sowing, Occator for the harrowing, Saritor for the weeding… Subruncinator for the pulling out of the weeds, Messor for the reaping, Convector for the transportation of the grain from the fields, Conditor for the garnering, Promitor for the giving out of the grain from granary and barn" (Cassirer, *Symbolic* 202–3).

still considered to be different. Thus the Juno of the Vejienti is not that of the Romans, just as for the Neapolitan the Madonna of each chapel is different from the others.

(SR 17)

Later, we will examine the way this phenomenon appears in America, where the Jesus of one class is not that of another. But the point to reemphasize here is that apotheosis is a necessary condition of social integration. Sacred symbols strengthen group unity by conveying, with a narrative or image, its shared identity, purpose, and place in society.

Though apotheosis is the process by which social groups are reproduced, this is not to say simply replicated. Despite their reputation, gods and rituals are changing all the time. Indeed, everything flows. It would be more accurate to say that apotheosis is, in biological terms, a homeostatic regulatory mechanism. Like all things, social formations are subject to entropy; they are dynamic, unstable assemblages that require regulatory mechanisms to maintain equilibrium, preserve cohesion, and generate renewal. A people's religious symbols, what they make sacred, are therefore not simply expressions of belief but are integral to sustaining the group itself. Durkheim writes that "it is man who makes his gods, or at least makes them endure, but at the same time it is through them that he himself endures" (253). A social group, he explains, "can neither create itself nor recreate itself without at the same time creating the ideal. This creation is not a kind of optional step, a finishing touch that society adds once it has been formed; it is the act by which it fashions and refashions itself periodically" (317). As we further examine this phenomenon, we will come to see, as Durkheim indicates here, that apotheosis is the force that propels cultural motion. The possession of shared interests, mores, and goals that have been deemed sacred is necessary for the stability and reproduction of the group; therefore, salvation ethics are an essential feature of apotheosis. A group's salvation ethic serves as an integral means of normative integration by modeling the ideal behaviors, values, and affects that will maintain the endurance and continual recreation of the group. An example from an American Indian religion, that of the Standing Rock Sioux, perfectly illustrates how apotheosis generates social reproduction. Vine DeLoria writes that, among his people, "religion is not conceived as a personal relationship between the deity and each individual. It is rather a covenant between a particular god and a particular community. The people of the community are the primary residue of the religion's legends, practices, and beliefs. Ceremonies of community-wide scope are the chief characteristic feature of religious activity... There is no salvation in tribal religions apart from the continuance of the tribe itself" (194).

Up to this point, I have been referring a great deal to social groups and that is because I contend, with Durkheim, that "wherever we observe religious life, its foundation is a defined group" (42–43). If we wish to understand religious life in modern American society, then we must focus on the group. Thinking about "society" as a unified totality that possesses agency, as an entity that does things—which Durkheim was famously wont to do—is itself a form of apotheosis. The same can be said for the commonplace practice of earnestly regarding the mood of the market. Recently, thinkers like Levi Bryant, Bruno Latour, and Manuel DeLanda among others have demonstrated that society consists of a nested set of assemblages that operate at varying levels of scale. For example, each person is affiliated with numerous groups that are of different sizes and which direct their actions in manifold ways and degrees. Analogously, society consists of groups that are similarly bound up with others in a kind of ecosystem of assemblages. That is, we must acknowledge that modern Americans, like people of other periods and places, were associated with multiple social groups that impacted them in significant ways, but the fundamental group from which they derived their identity, purpose, aims, and code of conduct—the group that was the foundation of their religious life—was their class.

It is through religion, in particular through the process of apotheosis, that social groups are integrated and reproduced. The period of the Market and Industrial Revolutions in America was one of acute social reorganization. With the rise of a new economic order, the former social structure was breaking down and there was a general dissolution of social solidarity. Old groups were dissolving; new ones were forming and needed to be solidified. Amid this fragmentation, newly forming classes had a great need for unification and a sense of shared identity and purpose. Therefore, as in the case of occupational gods, where each labor group develops its own concepts of the sacred and profane that reflect it and attend to its unique needs, so too in modern America. With modern class formation came the proliferation of new gods, rites, taboos, and new salvation ethics. This was necessarily accomplished through the symbolic, in literature, print culture, and collective rituals like revivals and labor strikes. Durkheim wrote that a group "whose members are united because they share a common conception of the sacred world and its relation to the profane world, and who translate this common conception into identical practices, is what we call a church" (42–43). In modern America, whether self-consciously or otherwise, one's class was one's religion. I have touched on the way apotheosis conditions how groups relate to themselves by producing consensus and endurance, but what is as important is how the sacred shapes group dynamics, that is, the way groups relate to one another.

Conflict and Consensus

Sacralization bestows power, legitimacy, and authority. Through apotheotic symbolization, the worldview and traits of the group, both real and ideal, are endowed with transcendent legitimacy. Apotheosis is the process of transforming group interest into ontological law. It is that special sleight of hand that imbues a particular conception of reality with ultimate authority, consequently rendering the norms derived from that conception inviolable. However, this is not to reduce religion to a mere instrument used by one group to deceive another. As Weber put it, "The fortunate is seldom satisfied with the fact of being fortunate. Beyond this, he needs to know that he has a *right* to his good fortune. He wants to be convinced that he 'deserves' it, and above all, that he deserves it in comparison with others" (FMW 271). Though directed at the wealthy, this holds generally. People of every class want to believe that their way of life is right and good, particularly "in comparison with others." When their defining qualities and rules appear to mimic or conform to the sacred, they can rest assured that they are redeemed. Again, the specular nature of apotheosis causes the real thing to mistake itself for a reflection.

Apotheosis legitimates and thereby confers power on the members of the group. As Mircea Eliade put it, "the *sacred* is equivalent to *power*" (12). This underscores that, contrary to Marx's view, religion is not a political soporific, but is rather immensely vivifying. Durkheim reports that believers

> feel, in fact, that the true function of religion is... to make us act, to help us live. The worshiper who has communed with his god is not only a man who sees new truths that the unbeliever does not know; he is a man who is *capable* of more. He feels more strength in himself, either to cope with the difficulties of existence or to defeat them. He is raised above human miseries because he is raised above his condition as man; he believes he is saved from evil, in whatever form he conceived of evil.
>
> (311)

I have said that salvation is activity in conformity with the sacred. We recall that salvation is an affective "quality of conduct" characterized by the invigorating feeling "of having executed the divine will" (SR 168). Salvation, then, is a vital and ubiquitous form of collective action performed by those who feel they are authorized by God or by fidelity to the order of existence. When viewed from this perspective, the full political power of apotheosis becomes clear.

The power of religion is not in the god image itself but in the way that image impacts the social group and its relations with other groups. God is always "God for-us"; God is always the god of the group (Althusser 119). However, the concept of the sacred entails its "essential duality" with the profane—God for-them (Durkheim 38). Durkheim finds that the relationship of the sacred and the profane is one of "serious antagonism... The two worlds are not only conceived as separate, but as hostile and jealous rivals" (39). We must go a step further to see that the antagonism of the sacred and the profane is the apotheosis of class conflict. Each group regards itself and its ethic as sacred and its rivals as profane. Gods are the legitimating projections of adversarial social groups. Ultimately, politics is theomachy, a battle between gods. In the context of modern America, accelerating social differentiation caused by the Market and Industrial Revolutions led to a situation where groups with different value orientations were in a continual state of emergence, tension, and conflict. As is the nature of apotheosis, the drama of *fin de siècle* class antagonism was staged in the theater of religion.

Apotheosis is a universal phenomenon; however, the economic and accompanying social development of modern America provides us with a particularly clear illustration of how it functions within and among groups to shape culture. Prior to the Market and Industrial Revolutions, the social ecology of the new nation remained in flux; clearly defined and persisting classes did not yet exist. The sociality of the sacred is such that, as they developed, nascent classes necessarily differentiated themselves from other groups through religion—through religious concepts, practices, symbols, and institutions. Each class crafted its identity through religion by creating new god images and salvation ethics that served as sources of legitimation, unity, and power in their conflict with other groups. Drawing from Georg Simmel, Eric W. Rothenbuhler argues that, in situations of conflict, group interests override the individual interests of group members, producing integration. Struggling together against a common foe creates solidarity. Rothenbuhler calls this "the communitas of the fight" (74). Conflict at the macro level, among groups, generates consensus at the micro level, within groups. The economic conflict that defined American modernity accelerated class formation and reproduction in a time of general social disintegration. Further, the material antagonisms of the period were necessarily mediated by the symbolic. Such conflict is always a conflict of symbols, of narratives, of imagined relations.[26] Evidence shows us that apotheosis is central to both group formation and inter-group relations, that is, to internal consensus and external conflict. It is this dynamic interaction of groups that propels society, culture, and politics.

Apotheosis and Modern America

Now that we have established the basic premises of the theory of apotheosis, let's return to the example of Singer and Liston's cryptoreligion. Given the artistic context of the Seven on Seven exhibit and 0xΩ's Doge-headed totem, the audience was understandably incredulous about the new religion. Surely this was an ironic art project or a gimmick to sell Liston's newest venture. In discussion with the audience, Singer was jocular and noncommittal but Liston insisted on his sincerity, "I am cryptospiritual. This is legitimate" (Singer and Liston). But, by the end of the event, people were unconvinced. Why would an avowedly atheistic cryptocurrency entrepreneur appeal to religion and art? Were they really suggesting that capitalism should be worshipped? By turning religion into commerce didn't they mock and diminish it? Tellingly, Liston said that his interest in combining economy, religion, and art in this way "comes from a drive to use cryptocurrency technologies to take central trusted authorities and replace them with decentralized trust systems because... that will effectively lead to a smoother and more equitable state transition from one mode of capitalism to another" (Singer and Liston). Liston recognized that religion and art are the necessary means to successfully transition from one economic form to another, in this case, from centralized to decentralized finance capitalism. After the initial rollout, Liston doubled down on the incorporation of art into the religion and announced that he would be collaborating with authors to write speculative fiction about 0xΩ. He explained, "I want to paint a picture of how people could be thinking about this in several decades' time... It's an experiment in taking a fiction and using accelerated hype cycles to make the fiction more real over time"[27] (McKinley). By sanctifying cryptocapitalism, Liston sought to invest it with legitimacy, to strengthen the bonds between those who favor

---

[26] However, this is not to say that cultural or theological conflict is material conflict carried out at the abstract, ideal level of the symbolic. The symbolic is concrete and corporeal.
[27] "Hype cycle" is a marketing term that refers to the lifespan of a new technology, from breakthrough and mainstream adoption to obsolescence.

decentralization, and ultimately to bring about the widespread acceptance of a new economic order. This exemplifies how apotheosis necessarily entails the use of literature and visual art as media of conflict with the advocates of rival economic forms. Singer and Liston's blockchain religion is just one of the diverse ways apotheosis appears in contemporary American society. In the following chapters, I will examine how this phenomenon functioned in the United States from the mid-nineteenth to the early twentieth centuries. Along the way, we will meet numerous figures like Liston who use literature to campaign for the compatibility of established religion and a new kind of economy. And we will look to artists like Singer who give form to the collective representations of competing groups.

In the first chapter, I argue that the Second Great Awakening was a religious response to the Market Revolution. I show that the new religious norms established during this period of intense revivalism were part of an effort to accommodate the novel social relations and patterns of behavior created by the expansion of market capitalism. I analyze the new doctrines, practices, and polities observed by emerging sects and mainline denominations as well as works of political economy written by the nation's leading clerics to show that antebellum Protestantism was defined by an effort to reorient Christianity to make it compatible with market capitalism. I contend that this process of accommodation was integral to the further advancement of capitalism in the United States. Further, I show that Protestant denominationalism and the theological variations that proliferated during the Awakening were the by-products of early class formation.

In Chapter 2, I turn from the Jacksonian era to early years of industrialization. In particular, I reassess the labor fiction written by Rebecca Harding Davis and Elizabeth Stuart Phelps in the 1860s and 1870s. I argue that these works were not early examples of realism that advocate on behalf of the working-class, as they are generally regarded to be, but are rather conventional products of the sentimental culture industry that sought to integrate and secure the dominance of the middle-class by sanctifying its defining traits, values, and objectives. In keeping with sentimental theology, Davis and Phelps believe that economic inequality can be moralized by inculcating middle-class ideals of domesticity throughout the nation. In their labor fiction, they promote a form of maternalism that aims to reform rather than abolish industrial capitalism and class difference.

William Dean Howells rose to literary stardom over course of the 1870s and 1880s. By 1890, he had become America's foremost cultural gatekeeper and an exemplar of bourgeois Victorianism. However, after having a conversion experience, Howells began to endorse Christian socialism and to critique American capitalism on religious grounds. In Chapter 3, I turn to the series of "economic novels" he wrote over the next decade. In these books, Howells aligns himself with the antebellum tradition of "social Christianity" which has its roots in Transcendentalism, abolitionism, and early labor activism. The focus of this liberal theology is "social salvation" or the collective redemption of the nation, as opposed to saving individual souls. Howells advances his own take on apotheosis in these novels, arguing that the recent shift in dominant American values stems from the sacralization of capitalism. He argues that capitalism has become the new American religion, and that its attributes and ethos have been made sacred, leading Americans to confuse economic norms with the means to salvation.

Chapter 4 is devoted to examining anthropotheism in the modern American novel and the role of this phenomenon in early-twentieth-century politics. More specifically, I focus on the life of Christ novels that constituted the most popular genre of American fiction at the turn of the century. Giving particular attention to the work of Jack London, Upton Sinclair, and Bruce Barton, I analyze the Christologies expressed in literature by members of conflicting classes, and the way they appeal to apotheosis to legitimate their group's traits, values, practices, and political interests.

In Chapter 5, I show that Sinclair Lewis's popular novels from the 1920s are devoted to satirizing the conflation of economy and religion in modern America. In particular, Lewis takes aim at Frederick Winslow Taylor's principles of scientific management, the source of an efficiency craze that was sweeping across the nation. Lewis contends that Taylor's industrial reforms had been recast as divine truth, causing them to transcend the factory to become the dominant system of norms operative in American society. In his most famous novels, Lewis looks at the apotheosis of Taylorism from multiple perspectives. For example, in *Elmer Gantry* (1927) he caricatures the way Protestant institutions have adopted the priorities and procedures of modern industry, and in his classic *Babbitt* (1922), he examines the sanctification of business culture, consumerism, and the managerial middle-class.

In 1929, a textile mill in Gastonia, North Carolina called a strike to protest the implementation of the Taylor system in the factory. Though the Loray Mill strike was one of hundreds in the South that year, it inspired six novels and was the subject of Liston Pope's landmark sociological study *Millhands and Preachers* (1942). In Chapter 6, I show that the Gastonia novels convey the vital role of religion in Depression-era class conflict in the American South and, more broadly, provide insight into the relationship of religion and economy in modern America.

Chapter 7 is about the literature of the Black God created by Harlem Renaissance authors in the 1920s and 1930s. By examining how Black modernists developed new religious symbols to legitimate and mobilize Black liberation, and how reactionary white writers appropriated those symbols to reproduce existent relations of oppression and exploitation, this chapter further illustrates how apotheosis mediates both systems of domination and liberation. This analysis reveals the vital role of religion in modern American race struggle and the crucial function of literature in that conflict. More broadly, this chapter concerns how the sacred was used in the formation of race as a concept and mechanism of domination. Looking forward, it shows how the Harlem Renaissance literature of the Black God laid the groundwork for the liberation theologies produced by Black and Latin Americans in the decades to come, who employed apotheosis to formulate anti-colonial, anti-racist theologies.

1

The Boiled-Over District: Effervescence and Adaptation during the Market Revolution

During the first decades of the nineteenth century, the growth of free-market capitalism wholly transformed American society. Advancements in communication, transportation, and production technologies allowed for the rapid expansion of domestic markets, connecting distant members of society for the first time. At the end of the Revolutionary War, 3.9 million people populated America's thirteen coastal provinces, where citizens predominantly made their living in rural areas through subsistence farming, local trade, and by laboring in small workshops that were founded on the guild system. Within just a few decades, America's population swelled to nearly 32 million people; citizens flooded into burgeoning urban centers, labored in factories and mills mass-producing commercial goods, and converted their subsistence farms into those that produced specialized goods to be sold on the national market. American farmers and artisans who had formerly traded their goods in small communities were now required to conduct business with anonymous consumers in distant locales. Artisans adopted a new mode of production, replacing traditional handicrafts with a divided and deskilled form of work. Master craftsmen implemented the wage system for the first time, making journeymen's income subject to fluctuations in the market. While these changes enriched masters, allowing for the development of a more robust middle-class, the deskilling and commodification of journeymen's labor depressed their income and led to the formation of a proletarianized working-class. In the highly unstable boom and bust market economy, short spells of prosperity were punctuated by periods of financial panic and economic depression—first in 1819 and again in 1837 and 1857—that bankrupted thousands of families and businesses. This economic paradigm shift—what has come to be known as the Market Revolution—fundamentally changed how Americans worked and lived. Though the acceleration of domestic trade brought prosperity to a minority of antebellum

Americans, the masses experienced a loss of security, autonomy, and a general decline in their quality of life. This led to widespread social unrest and gave rise to the conflict between capital and labor that would shape American culture for the next 100 years.

The economic changes that reshaped American society between 1815 and 1860 dramatically altered existing norms and power relations, creating a world that antebellum Americans did not recognize or understand and therefore aroused intense feelings of fear and anxiety at all levels of the new order. Early Americans were a theocentric people so they inevitably turned to religion "to find some providential meaning and design in the trials they and the Republic were enduring" (Scott 152). Charles Sellers, the foremost historian of this period, contends that the extent to which religion organized the experience of early Americans is "almost incomprehensible" to us today (29). Market capitalism was a system of beliefs, behaviors, and values that were anathema to traditional Christian principles. For example, "the market's competitive ethic defied the Biblical injunction" against acquisitiveness and individualism (Sellers 137–8). This conflict of foundational value systems caused Jacksonian Americans to suffer an identity crisis marked by a profound sense of "cultural disorientation" and "a kind of vertigo" (Sellers 138; Larson 11).

Suffering and confused, the citizens of the city on a hill collectively "cried out for redemption," and the expression of that outcry has come to be known as the Second Great Awakening (Lazerow 31). The Second Great Awakening was a period of intense religious activity that transformed the doctrines, practices, and institutional framework of Protestantism in order to reconcile free-market capitalism and Christianity, and thus resolve the cultural crisis. The modes of apotheosis employed to accomplish this adaptation created the religious concepts, moral norms, and denominations that continue to define American Protestantism today.

William G. McLoughlin argues that religious awakenings are periods of ideological "reorientation" that occur in response to "a general crisis of beliefs and values" (*Revivals* xiii). When the routine "patterns of thought and behavior that guide individuals in their daily lives" no longer produce "expected results," people experience immense confusion and despair. When the members of a society experience a fundamental "disjunction between… old beliefs and new realities," between "dying patterns and emerging patterns of behavior," this necessitates a "profound reorganization" of the principles and conventions by which they define themselves, thereby altering "the whole world view of a people or culture" (*Revivals* 14, 10, xiii). An awakening, revival, or collective eruption of religious enthusiasm is the social process by which a group reorients and redefines its core beliefs and practices in response to critical disjunctions in its dominant forms of self-understanding. In fact, such awakenings are "necessary if a culture is to survive the traumas of... adapting to basic social... and economic change" (*Revivals* 8). McLoughlin explains that "a religious revival or awakening begins when accumulated pressures for change produce acute personal and social stress," and when "the whole culture" feels it "must break the crust of custom... and find new socially structured avenues along which members of the society may pursue their course" (*Revivals* 15).

The Second Great Awakening is a textbook example of what Émile Durkheim termed *effervescence*. The etymology of the word illuminates the kind of social phenomena Durkheim had in mind, as it means "to boil over." Durkheim writes, "when collective life reaches a certain degree of intensity it awakens religious thought, because it determines a state of effervescence that changes the conditions of psychic activity. Vital energies become overstimulated, passions more powerful, sensations stronger" (317). He continues,

> In certain historical periods, under the influence of some great collective upheaval, social interactions become more frequent and more active. Individuals seek each other out and assemble more often. The result is a general effervescence characteristic of revolutionary or creative epochs... People live differently and more intensely than in normal times... all these mental processes are so clearly those at the root of religion.
>
> (158)

As Tiryakian has observed, effervescent events are mechanisms of "societal renovation" (45). When formerly dominant norms break down and come into conflict with a new moral paradigm, the people become increasingly distressed until their emotions "boil over" into volatile mass demonstrations. In these emotionally charged assemblies, group members collectively reinforce old bonds, establish new ones, and alter prevailing conventions in light of new conditions. Effervescence is ultimately about social adaptation. During the Market Revolution, relationships and customs were in flux; many were passing away entirely and being replaced by new obligations and social classes. The Second Great Awakening was a series of effervescent social events triggered by the Market Revolution that gave rise to new sacred concepts, practices, and institutions; in combination, these innovations functioned to reconcile Christianity and capitalism.

Figure 1.1 In this picture, the artist conveys how an evangelist provokes collective emotions to produce conversion experiences. "Camp-Meeting" by Alexander Rider (ca. 1829), Library of Congress.

Awakening revivalism served three primary functions: to repair alienation by building solidarity among foundering and emerging groups, to vitalize the disempowered, and, most importantly, to adapt religious ideas to new material conditions. Durkheim explains, "No society can exist that does not feel the need at regular intervals to sustain and reaffirm the collective feelings and ideas that constitute its unity and its personality" (322). Therefore groups "hold periodic meetings in which their members may renew their common faith… by some collective demonstration" (Durkheim 157). "This moral remaking," he continues, "can be achieved only by means of meetings, assemblies, or congregations in which individuals, brought into close contact, reaffirm in common their common feelings" (Durkheim 322). It is in this way that effervescence plays an essential role in social reproduction. Tiryakian further explains that "the act of coming together, of uniting in collective assemblies, generates societal… exaltation and a feeling of force or energy which, on an aggregate basis, conveys a sense of power" (49). Awakening revivals vivified the disenfranchised and provided a means for new groups to develop their identity using forms of apotheosis.

Sellers was right to argue that only religion could "nerve" Americans for the cultural trauma of accommodating free-market capitalism, but the Second Great

Awakening was much more than a psychological coping mechanism (137). The Market Revolution caused a rift to grow between Americans and their absolutization. The sacred was no longer an accurate reflection of society, and this caused such anxiety among the people that it "boiled over," giving rise to the effervescence of the Second Great Awakening. To remedy this incongruity, the sacred—God, cosmology, ritual, salvation ethics—had to be transformed to restore the specular accuracy of humanity's divine reflection. The Awakening was a series of rites intended to re-establish followers' bond with God by eliminating the discrepancy between humanity and its symbol. This renewed bond with God—that is, the apotheosis of group solidarity—was experienced as a rebirth or revival. The Second Great Awakening successfully refashioned the sacred to more perfectly mimic the new socioeconomic order, inaugurating the Protestant system that still prevails today.

Evangelical revivalism was particularly important for the burgeoning working-class who were drafting their metaphysical likeness for the first time. Durkheim writes, for any social group

> to become conscious of itself and sustain its feeling of itself with the necessary degree of intensity, it must gather individuals together in sufficient concentration. Now, this concentration determines an exaltation of moral life that is expressed by a set of ideal conceptions in which the new life thus awakened is portrayed. These conceptions... are then superimposed onto those [psychological forces] at our disposal for the ordinary tasks of existence.
>
> (Durkheim 317)

To unpack this a bit, Durkheim is saying that periodic assemblies are necessary for established groups to reinforce their unity and shared identity, and for new groups to forge their self-image by apotheosizing the group's qualities and customs, and codifying them into a sacred ethic used to guide everyday behavior. To summarize, then, the Second Great Awakening was a religious reaction to the fundamental economic changes that were reshaping American society. Largely remembered as an eruption of intense religious feelings expressed collectively in gatherings where ecstatic forms of worship were the new norm, it is important to recognize that these outbursts of emotion were more than the sighs of the oppressed. What we call the Second Great Awakening was an adaptive phase in the development of American Protestantism when doctrines, institutions, and forms of religious practice were recalibrated to bring them into line with Americans' new social experience. Periodic religious awakenings are a universal feature of human societies. In the case of Jacksonian America, when the sacred no longer accurately reflected the people, new and long-established groups of Protestants were compelled to gather in assemblies where they exalted their respective forms of life and the traits that defined them, and formalized these into symbolic representations of the sacred, which served as models for group ethics. The Second Great Awakening is an exemplar of Durkheim's conception of effervescence, but one that must not be mistaken for a fleeting expression of emotion alone. Rather, it was a complex and prolonged social phenomenon where diverse groups adapted their sacred dogmas and organizations to accommodate new material conditions.

Doctrines and Denominations

The primary attributes of the Second Great Awakening concern (a) doctrine—namely, the transition from Predestination to Arminianism, (b) practice—the rise of enthusiastic forms of worship, and (c) institutions—a veritable explosion of religious innovation and denominationalism. I will touch on each of these in turn to show that the new religious concepts, practices, and organizations that were created during this time ultimately had little to do with theological disputes and more to do with a theocentric society's attempt to adapt its traditional religious norms to a new economic system. For many historians, the Second Great Awakening is primarily characterized by a departure from the Calvinist belief in the remoteness and inscrutability of God and by growing confidence in forms of intuitionism which held that the common individual has the ability to discern the laws of God's creation. The authority newly accorded to subjective insight empowered members of each social class to conflate their personal interests with their conception of the natural, ontological order of existence. Each class appealed to intuition to proclaim that their favored economic model was a reflection of God's design. Both the elite and the disenfranchised sought to prove that their economic commitments were not only compatible with Christianity but were mimetic earthly embodiments of God's will. This kind of exaltation serves the dual purpose of sanctifying an avowed economic philosophy while portraying an opponent's as a perversion of the natural order. The case of nineteenth-century anthropotheism amid the Second Great Awakening demonstrates that apotheosis is a cultural mechanism that allows one social formation to appear sacred and another profane.

However, it is crucial to recognize that the emergence of Arminianism in New England coincided with both the early period of the Market Revolution,

1815–30, and the "tide of disestablishment," during which the State renounced its financial and legal endorsement of Congregationalism (*Revivals* 110). Connecticut terminated its tax-supported church system in 1818 and the other New England states followed suit soon thereafter. The cessation of government funding and regulation initiated a shift from a State-sponsored church system to a voluntary or free church system. This inaugurated an era of intense religious pluralism where churches were forced to compete for congregants and financial support in a free religious market. Ernst Troeltsch explains that "the Free Church system... represented a subjective and relative form of religion... This meant that the question of Church membership now became a matter of individual choice" (657). By making the discernment of religious truth and the route to redemption an individual, subjective affair, Christianity was democratized. This was revolutionary, however, even if the Dutch theologian Arminius had not rejected predestination by asserting that salvation is attainable by all through the faculty of free will, Americans—in the liberal, free-market atmosphere of the early nineteenth century—would have invented Arminianism for themselves. William R. Sutton reminds us that " 'liberal' in the nineteenth-century vernacular referred to the removal of 'unnatural' restrictions to free individuals in all areas of human activity," including that of religion (9). The adoption of Arminian soteriology was the theological means by which Protestants adapted their doctrines to the free-market political economy of the Market Revolution. Disestablishment represented the deregulation of the religious sphere and the removal of the traditions and seats of authority that had previously restricted individuals' free religious activity and innovation. Arminian redemption was the theological expression of the free-market values of liberal individualism; it "represented a subjective and relative form of religion," a let-do approach to salvation that permitted Christians to innovate. It is no coincidence that free salvation, free labor, and the free market emerged at the same moment in American history, as the former were by-products of the latter. The opening of the soteriological market meant that anyone could devise for themselves the means to redemption, could bring their product—their doctrine of salvation—to the religious marketplace. Arminianism, like the free market, proclaimed that individuals could succeed—or be redeemed—by the power of their own self-reliant striving. However, by proclaiming that humanity could discern divine truths by its own subjective lights, Arminianism was preeminently vulnerable to apotheosis, that is, to turning man-made ideas and practices into divine laws, characteristics, and ontological structures. Because it was a subjective form of religion, the social conditions experienced by believers, especially those regarding class, fundamentally influenced the theology each incipient group developed. Therefore, the key to interpreting the cultural phenomenon of the Second Great Awakening is not to focus on the theological disagreements of the various denominations, but to examine the classed sources of those doctrinal differences. Ultimately, we find that Arminian soteriology was put to as many uses as there were social classes because class formation, not theology, was the basis of differing religious orientations.

H. Richard Niebuhr writes that "the sociological structure of religious groups" has invariably played a central role "in the determination of their doctrine" (17). Following Troeltsch, Niebuhr maintains that the formation of numerous denominations in countries where the church is not regulated and financially supported by the State "represents the accommodation of Christianity to the caste-system of human society" (6). Historical evidence clearly shows that "the division of the churches closely follows the division of" social classes (Niebuhr 6). The work of Troeltsch and Niebuhr represents a commonly held view among historians, sociologists, and theologians concerning the shared development of a society's economy and its religious systems, one that turns the once popular Weberian schema on its head. Scholars have found that the religious development of a society is critically influenced by material factors, most importantly by economy, class, and normative power relations. Their research conclusively shows that a society's religious rituals, doctrines, worship practices, church polity, and central theological tenants mirror the economic conventions, conflicts, and class structure of its people. As McLoughlin puts it, "insofar as a theological position... is an ideology, that is, gives meaning and order to the lives of a people, it is subject to reinterpretation... in the light of significant changes in the economic, demographic, political, or social affairs of the people who hold it" (*Revivals* xiii). Similarly, Niebuhr explains, "theological opinions have their roots in the relationship of religious life to the cultural and political conditions prevailing in any group of Christians... The religious life is so interwoven with social circumstances that the formulation of theology is necessarily conditioned by these" (14–15). Therefore, major changes in a society's economy, such as the adoption of free-market capitalism, will necessarily result in theological changes that will cause religious concepts, practices, and institutions to reflect those of the new dispensation. "Regarding theology from this point of view," writes Niebuhr, "one will discover how... the demands of national psychology... and the weight of economic interest play their role in the definition of religious truth. The importance of such elements is now generally recognized" (17).

Sociologists of religion have worked to dispel "the orthodox interpretation of denominationalism in Christianity" which "looks upon the official creeds of the churches" to explain the prevailing differences that divide them (Niebuhr 12–13). According to this formerly dominant view, denominationalism—the division of the church into diverse, mutually antagonist sub-groups—was caused by disagreements about points of doctrine. However, theologians and historians have proven that economic concepts and practices constitute a society's dominant "belief-value" system, fundamentally shaping its religious ideas. For instance, early Christian theology can only be fully understood by taking into account the social, political, and economic conditions of the Roman Empire. In order to fully understand the origins of American religious bodies and the doctrines, practices, and cosmological beliefs they profess, we must first understand the determining "relationship of ideas to underlying social conditions" (Niebuhr 14). For Niebuhr, the differences of creed and doctrine that are said to account for the division of the Christian denominations during the Second Great Awakening actually "had their roots in more profound social divergences," namely, those of social class. He writes that "denominations, churches, [and] sects, are sociological groups whose principle of differentiation is to be sought in their conformity to the order of social classes and castes" (25). While it would be false "to affirm that the denominations are not religious groups with religious purposes… it is true that they represent the accommodation of religion to the caste system" (Niebuhr 25). While Weber famously argued that the long-established mores of Protestant piety prepared the cultural ground for America's adoption of free-market capitalism, theologians and social scientists find the reverse to be true; that is, Protestant doctrine was refashioned by changes in the economic and social structure of the nation, by making free-market political economy America's new "belief-value" system. Niebuhr writes that religious "doctrines and practice change with the mutations of social structure, not visa versa"; therefore, the idea that denominational difference is a consequence of theological disagreements about salvation "quite misses the point" and runs counter to overwhelming evidence to the contrary (21).

Conflicting soteriologies are not the source of Protestant denominationalism. Rather, economic conditions, primarily those regarding class formation, shape concepts of salvation and the institutional norms of a given church. In antebellum America, "rich and poor [met] in their separate cathedrals and conventicles that each may achieve salvation in his own way and that their class loyalties may not be violated by the practice of the ethics they profess" (Niebuhr 11). Each economic group was positioned differently in the social milieu, and had, therefore, to create its own theological response to the market that would lend divine legitimation to its particular interests, whether they be in support or opposition to the new economy. The unique soteriologies, or theories of salvation, which each group developed were the doctrinal means through which each group adapted its theology to its social position. Each of the emerging social classes in antebellum America appealed to scripture to legitimize its response to the Market Revolution; each tailored its concept of redemption, its beliefs about the true nature of the church, its take on mediating religious authority, indeed every facet of religious life, to its particular social-political experience. Behind every divergence of doctrine "one must look for the conditions which make now the one, now the other interpretation appear more reasonable or, at least, more desirable" (Niebuhr 16–17). Which is to say, the class-based doctrines of antebellum Americans were not created in bad faith or in the knowledge that they were self-serving. Instead, a group's social conditions make a particular interpretation of scripture and the religious life appear more reasonable, appealing, or desirable. Niebuhr continues, by "advancing and defending their positions on the basis of proof-texts drawn from the Scriptures, it has been possible for various sects to take antithetical views," but "only the purest novice in history will seek the explanation of such opinions in the proof-texts from which they purport to derive" (14). The character of each group's exegesis, the foundation of its unique denominational perspective, betrays its social concerns. The most well-known characteristic of the Second Great Awakening is the proliferation of new doctrines, denominations, sects, communes, and cults. Each of these represented an alternative strategy for coping with economic change that was suitable to a particular social class.

Each of these newly formed Christian denominations, sects, and communes functioned as the religious body that gave expression to the classed perspective it represented and to its unique mode of accommodating—or rejecting as the case may be—free-market capitalism. Niebuhr writes that "each religious group gives expression to that code which forms the morale of the political and economic class it represents"; they function primarily "as political and class institutions" and only secondarily as Christian churches (24). Historians of the period roundly agree that the religious groups that emerged during the Second Great Awakening "showed themselves to be the mouthpieces of the economic and sectional groups they represented" (Niebuhr 24). In addition to reorienting doctrine, practice, and cosmology in light of new social and economic conditions, these emergent churches acted as "the religious spokesmen" of the classes with which they were allied (Niebuhr 25).

This religious spokesmanship, which expressed the "morale" of each class, was conducted in a number of interconnected venues: the pulpit, the revival, the religious press, the university, the lyceum circuit, and in the activism of "laborites" and utopian communitarians. These modes of expression were bound by their common function, to communicate the class-based soteriology and economized religious philosophy of a given social group. For example, antebellum evangelicals were self-conscious about the intimate connection of sermonic and literary discourse, stressing emphatically that "the PULPIT AND THE PRESS are inseparably connected" (qtd. in Hatch 143). In this period, print culture was believed to be as potent a means of conversion and ideological suasion as the camp meeting or Sunday sermon. This means that the culture industry as well as the revivalism and reform activity of the Second Great Awakening was equally utilized by emergent denominations, utopian communes, and evangelical labor radicals as a means to advocate the mode of redemption that developed out of their experience of the Market Revolution. By examining the cultural production of this period, from its literature to its sermonic discourse and modes of institutional and social reform, we can discern how antebellum Protestantism was fundamentally reshaped by the introduction of free-market capitalism, and by doing so we can begin to map how those alterations continue to govern Christianity in America.

Class and Soteriology

During the Second Great Awakening, religion was utilized by all classes as an instrument of divine legitimation and employed to advance opposing points of view. The middle-class used religion "to justify and applaud an emerging set of economic and social relationships... and thus their dominance over society" (Lazerow 9). The working-class, on the other hand, used religion to resist

> changes they perceived as threatening to their interests. In the hands of factory operatives, Scripture became the authoritative text for advancing labor's rights, and biblical figures the authoritative examples for questioning and criticizing social conditions on behalf of a growing, and increasingly aggrieved, population of wage workers.
>
> (Lazerow 9)

The salvation ethic developed by each of the social classes forming in the turbulent climate of the Market Revolution was constituted by "a class vision" (Lazerow 199). The religious perspective of each social group was fundamentally shaped by their experience of new social conditions and by the structures of America's new political economy. The exegeses, sects, and doctrines they developed, therefore, invariably lent divine sanction to their particular economic objectives and grievances.

The Social Control Debate

Social and labor historians who propound the "social control" thesis view "the awakening as a middle-class bourgeois phenomenon" (Bilhartz 135). These scholars argue that the revivalism and reform programs of the period were a religious vehicle for middle-class hegemony that served to impose industrial morality and disciplinarity onto the working-class. For example, Paul E. Johnson argues,

> the religion that [revivalists] preached was order-inducing, repressive, and quintessentially bourgeois. In no city is there evidence of independent working-class revivals before the economic collapse of 1837. We must conclude that many workmen... were adopting the religion of the middle class, thus internalizing beliefs and modes of comportment that suited the needs of their employers. [...] Evangelicalism was a middle-class solution to problems of class, legitimacy, and order generated in the early stages of manufacturing. Revivals provided entrepreneurs with a means of imposing new standards of work discipline and personal comportment upon themselves and the men who worked for them, and thus functioned as powerful social controls.
>
> (38)

For Johnson and the purveyors of the social control thesis,[1] the theology promulgated by Awakening revivalists, particularly ideas concerning the path to redemption, was calculated to "reinforce the dominance" of the middle-class (Johnson 137).

Johnson argues that "Charles Finney's revival [in Rochester, NY[2]] provided a solution to the social disorder and moral confusion that attended the creation of

---

[1] For examples of this perspective, see: Foster, Charles I. *An Errand of Mercy: The Evangelical United Front 1790–1837*. Chapel Hill: University of North Carolina Press, 1960; Griffin, Clifford S. "Religious Benevolence as Social Control, 1815–1860," *Mississippi Valley Historical Review* 44 (1957): 423–44; and Wallace, Anthony F. C. *Rockdale: The Growth of an American Village in the Early Industrial Revolution*. New York: Knopf, 1978. For critiques of the social control thesis see, for example: Banner, Lois W. "The Protestant Crusade: Religious Missions, Benevolence as Social Control: A Critique of an Interpretation," *Journal of American History* 60 (1973): 23–41; Howe, Daniel Walker. "Religion and Politics in the Antebellum North," in *Religion and American Politics: From the Colonial Period to the Present*, ed. Mark A. Noll. Oxford: Oxford UP, 2007, 121–45; Muraskin, William A. "The Social-Control Theory in American History: A Critique," *Journal of Social History* 9 (1976): 559–69.

[2] For a detailed account of the myriad forms of religious expression that proliferated in this area during the Market Revolution, see Whitney R. Cross's landmark regional history, *The Burned-over District: The Social and Intellectual History of Enthusiastic Religion in Western New York, 1800–1850*. New York: Octagon Books, 1981. See also Barkun, Michael. *Crucible of the Millennium: The Burned-Over District of New York in the 1840s*. New York: Syracuse UP, 1986.

a free-labor economy" (141). Antebellum revivalism, with its emphasis on self-discipline as a necessary means to salvation, convinced workers that humility, industry, and temperance—among other values calculated to maximize productivity and docility—were the mores required to achieve redemption. For the social controllers, the Second Great Awakening accommodated the newly forming market economy by lending divine legitimation to the social relations of wage labor. By asserting that salvation required workers to internalize "beliefs and modes of comportment that suited the needs of their employers," revivalists effectively sanctified middle-class hegemony.

In addition to sanctifying the exploitative relations of the free-labor economy, Arminian soteriology freed the middle-class from established relations that had previously held between employer and employee. The Arminian principle of free moral agency, which replaced the Calvinist belief in humanity's moral impotence, "stressed that each individual was responsible for achieving his or her own salvation" (Murphy 82). This doctrine was appropriated by the middle-class and adapted to the sink or swim, laissez-faire ideology of every man for himself that allowed them to renounce responsibility for workers and the impoverished masses. Teresa Anne Murphy writes, "in what was essentially a blow against the old patriarchal artisanal order in which masters assumed moral as well as economic responsibility for their journeymen, evangelical employers could feel justified in expecting moral behavior from their employees, without taking responsibility for them" (82). Johnson concurs, explaining that "the belief that every man was spiritually free and self-governing enabled masters to present a relationship that denied human interdependence as the realization of Christian ideals," thereby legitimizing the renunciation of social responsibility by proclaiming the egoistic individualism of laissez-faire political economy to be the God-ordained path to salvation (138). The bourgeois mode of redemption theologically codified competitive individualism, forming a kind of laissez-faire soteriology. By locating "the meaning of evangelism and antebellum reform in the matrix of a rising class's struggle to establish dominance over American society," social control theorists not only reveal how the bourgeois interpretation of Arminian salvation functioned to establish an exploited working-class for the first time but also show that "the 'Christian self-control' at the heart of evangelical Protestantism was the 'moral imperative around which the northern middle-class became a class' " (Lazerow 5). Therefore, by sanctifying an inequitable social economy, laissez-faire redemption acted as a cultural catalyst that helped to accelerate antebellum class formation.

The Clerical Economists

During the Second Great Awakening, a coterie of elite ministers served as a vanguard of apologists who leveraged new methods of inquiry and their social position to argue that unfettered capitalism was the hallowed manifestation of God's will. These powerful ministers, who Stewart Davenport has aptly dubbed "the clerical economists," were early practitioners of the new science of political economy; the group consisted of Francis Bowen, John McVickar, Alonzo Potter, Henry Vethake, and Francis Wayland. After 1820, the popularity of political economy as an academic discipline exploded and became an intellectual fad that was "regularly spoken of as 'the fashion' or 'the rage' " (Davenport 25). The clerical economists sought to use the tools of theology and economics to prove that market capitalism was the social mechanism through which Americans could fully realize their religious duties and secure salvation. Davenport writes that "from 1815 to 1860 the clerical economists argued forcefully that… [capitalist] political economy… [was] entirely compatible with their faith and intrinsically supportive of its central theology and morality" (35). These religious leaders "gave voice to the concerns of bourgeois Protestants on a national level" by working "to reconcile the spirit of capitalism with the ethics of Christianity" (Davenport 122). The work of the clerical economists represents yet another effort, one so characteristic of the Second Great Awakening, to overcome the incompatibility of a religious and economic system of value through the syncretization of Christianity and capitalism. This is the objective that led Rev. John McVickar to call Smithian political economy "the redeeming science of modern times" (qtd. in Davenport 9).

The cultural impact of the clerical economists must not be underestimated. With the exception of McVickar, each taught natural theology and moral philosophy at the nation's most prestigious universities before being appointed as a lead administrator of their respective schools. Moral philosophy was regarded as the most distinguished subject taught at university and was typically the final course taken by graduating seniors as the culmination of their learning prior to entering the professional world. Francis Wayland taught moral philosophy at Brown University, where he was named president and was best known for his *Elements of Political Economy* (1837); Henry Vethake served as Professor of Natural Philosophy at Columbia, Queen's College in New Jersey (now Rutgers), and the College of New Jersey (Princeton), until being named Provost and Professor of Moral Philosophy at the University of Pennsylvania. He was best known for his work *The Principles of Political Economy* (1838), in which he vehemently opposed labor unions and laws that limited the number of hours one could be made to work per day. Francis Bowen was Professor of Natural Religion, Moral Philosophy and Civil Polity at Harvard University and was well known for his *Lectures on Political Economy* (1850). Finally, Alonzo Potter, Episcopal bishop and author of *Political Economy* (1840), taught moral philosophy and political economy at Union College, where he was later named vice president.

From its publication in 1837, and into the 1840s and 1850s, Wayland's *Elements of Political Economy* "was the standard text in political economy at Yale, Amherst, Williams, Mount Holyoke, Wesleyan… New York University," and Brown where he taught (Davenport 36). It sold "ten thousand copies by 1843 and forty thousand by 1868," making it by far the most popular work of political economy in America prior to the Civil War. As Mark S. Schantz put it, Wayland "may well have been the most influential Protestant clergymen in the antebellum North," whose textbooks on political economy and morality "provided guidance to college students for decades" (154). Together, these ministers and educators economized Christian discourse. What Henry May called their "clerical laissez faire" constituted a "singular voice on the economic issues" of their day, determined the economic teaching of the nation's top universities for "at least a generation and in many institutions for longer," and thereby composed the received wisdom regarding the compatibility of free-market capitalism and Christianity (Davenport 36). Even "Abraham Lincoln counted himself among Francis Wayland's disciples" (*Piety* 154). While early labor activists argued that free-market capitalism inevitably impedes redemption, the clerical economists endeavored to convince the American populace that, by the lights of natural theology, capitalism is the realization of Christianity's moral principles. For the clerical economists, theology and economic theorizing were inseparable because, as they saw it, political economy was the science of discerning the natural laws that governed creation; in that sense, it was nothing short of a means to revelation.

As noted previously, during the Second Great Awakening, Arminian soteriology was adopted by all the primary denominations and emergent religious groups in one way or another. Among the Methodists, it appeared as evangelical anti-intellectualism, a religion of the heart, rather than the head, founded on the ability of the common person to determine religious truths for themselves, free from the mediating authority of a clerical elite. The deism of the Universalists accomplished the same thing but by the light of reason, while the Unitarians and Transcendentalists believed that humanity's "likeness to God" makes it possible for us to perceive religious truths through romantic intuition. Each of these denominations shares a common theological foundation: the belief that religious truths, particularly the right path to redemption, can be brought to light through free human agency; the clerical economists were no different. All of them "were staunch and unflagging disciples of Scottish common sense philosophy and natural theology" (Davenport 37). According to Scottish common sense philosophy, "the natural senses could be trusted to discover truths, or laws, about the external physical world" (Davenport 37). Similarly, natural theology was founded on the Enlightenment belief that the universe operates according to natural laws that can be discerned by human reason. That is, "the natural moral sense... that all humans possessed could be used to discover the... moral laws of the universe"; this was the first principle of the moral philosophy that clerical economists taught their students (Davenport 37). Moreover, they argued that human economy is also governed by natural laws and that political economy is the science by which we discern those laws; in this sense, political economy was, for them, a theological practice. Accordingly, Francis Lieber writes, "the Bible does not dispense with political economy. The Bible gives principles; political economy seeks to the means and methods of carrying them out... for, its subjects are closely connected with... the most sacred interests of man" (qtd. in Davenport 58).

As professors of moral philosophy—of the kind predicated on natural theology—they argued that God's moral laws are in harmony with His economic laws, that is, the laws of market capitalism. Alonzo Potter writes, "behold that perfect harmony which the Creator has established between his moral, intellectual, and economic laws" (qtd. in Davenport 35). Therefore, they claimed that Christian morality is exercised in the market through the individual pursuit of wealth and material accumulation. The clerical economists incorporated Adam Smith's economics into their religious cosmology to form a laissez-faire notion of redemption. Based on Smith's concept of the invisible hand, they taught a generation of Americans that it was through the pursuit of individual self-interest that Christians could best work to benefit the social whole. They asserted that God's natural moral laws were structured in such a way that the social amelioration the country so desperately needed could be achieved only through competitive individualism rather than through cooperative socialism, as advocated by many artisans and Transcendentalist intellectuals. Wayland "told his Brown students, in unmistakable terms, to get rich"; he writes, "it is a benefit to a whole neighborhood for a single member of it to become rich" (*Piety* 158). The message was clear: if you want to remedy the deteriorating conditions of your neighbor, get rich, accumulate, compete, assume the market mentality. These men believed that the emergence of market capitalism was a decisive event in the redemption history of humanity, that it was evidence of humanity's recognition of God's divine order. In contrast to the Puritan prohibition against excessive accumulation and contrary to John Wesley's advice, "having first gained all you can... give all you can," the clerical economists argued that the progress of a society, its level of civilization, and its place in redemption history are measured by its accumulation of wealth. They contended, moreover, that the structures and principles of market capitalism were earthly manifestations of the natural laws wrought by God. To obey those laws was therefore a sacred practice that brought one nearer to Him and would bring one favor, and ultimately salvation.

What we find in the textbooks and lectures of these men is the thoroughgoing sanctification of capitalism. John McVickar writes, "I cannot but reverence the claims of free commerce as something holy." Francis Wayland describes Smithian political economy as "the systematic arrangement of the laws which God has established." Potter argued that the laws of political economy are the "inviolable and resistless laws of nature, which are nothing less than the laws of God." Francis Bowen argues that political economists "discovered an economic order in the world that made 'manifest the contrivance, wisdom, and beneficence of the Deity.'" The clerical economists claimed that global free-trade was an integral part of God's natural order, the denial of which is sin. McVickar writes, "to forbid trade among nations is, therefore... a very wicked thing, for it is contrary to the will of GOD" (qtd. in Davenport 35, 42, 79). As Davenport put it, this represents "the ultimate sacralization of Adam Smith's economic order" by the clerical heads of the nation's leading universities and the figures that determined the conventional economic and moral wisdom of the antebellum era (79). Yet, these members of the elite class were not alone in elevating a mode of economy to the level of the sacred.

Religion and Radicalism

The religious innovations of the Second Great Awakening were not the sole province of the upper- and middle-classes. R. Laurence Moore explains that labor leaders "adapted Biblical ethics and the Christian vocabulary of hell, sin, and perfectionism to indict laissez-faire capitalism. The religious feelings in their statements were not peripheral to their mentality but central" (234). The antebellum labor movement utilized religion to craft an anti-capitalist message in the idiom of biblical literature. While the social control theorists argue that the revivals and reforms of the Second Great Awakening were "perpetrated by an unholy alliance of ministers and wealthy businessmen who exploited the power of religion to keep the masses in order and to preserve their personal status and wealth," subsequent scholars have proven that the gospel was also interpreted by disenfranchised artisans to form a theology of working-class liberation (Bilhartz

98). Murphy has shown that revivals and camp meetings were "arenas of... struggle" where traditional and emerging power relations were undermined (5). The perspective of artisans and unskilled workers "arose out of the popular evangelicalism of factory towns which challenged... authority [by] inverting traditional hierarchies and critiquing the pretensions of middle-class piety" (Murphy 5). Similarly, Nathan Hatch argues that the Second Great Awakening was a populist evangelical movement characterized by a "crisis of authority" in which the American everyman cast a vote of no confidence in all mediating religious and political bodies that condescended to determine truth for the common person. Artisanal evangelicalism was the religious milieu in which this delegitimation of the middle-class took shape. While "the entrepreneurial elite may have appropriated both religion and reform during this period to justify their position... that does not mean they controlled these arenas completely. Religion and reform," explains Murphy, "provided working people with a language of autonomy that was fundamentally at odds with" middle-class ideology, thus providing the working-class with "a critical site of conflict" (8). "Evangelical workers incorporated criticism of working conditions into their religious perspectives" by articulating their critique of the new modes and relations of production through the rhetoric and imagery of the Bible; being able to share this common "language of protest" helped to solidify labor activists' message and positively contributed to the young movement's cohesion (Murphy 3). Rather than hindering working-class self-consciousness, "religion and reform provided not only a way for working people to confront their employers, but also the means for working people from different backgrounds to communicate and engage in collective struggle" (Murphy 6). The theological perspective adopted by evangelical artisans, therefore, was a potent medium of class conflict that fostered organizing efforts and the development of working-class consciousness.

Examinations of "the relationship between religion and radicalism" in antebellum America reveal that "Protestantism [was] the handmaiden... of labor protest" (xiii). Jama Lazerow insists that "we cannot understand the emergence of an American working class before the Civil War—indeed, class relations generally in antebellum America—without first coming to grips with the powerful influence of religion," because, "in a fundamental sense... the early American labor movement was something of a Christian movement"; therefore, "it is a mistake to try to entirely separate the two" (Lazerow xvi, 31). Antebellum labor activists considered their movement a "religious enterprise" or a "religious crusade" (Lazerow 28). Sutton argues that artisans' "distinctive perspective on the socioeconomic and cultural transformation generated by the market revolution in America" critically determined the nature of evangelism practiced by the working-class (viii). Labor activists appealed to scripture to formulate their critique of market economy and its transformation of the crafts. By locating a working-class ethic in the New Testament and interpreting Jesus and his disciples as archetypical artisans, evangelical workers sanctified their class and put themselves on moral high ground in their conflict with "the rising hegemony of laissez-faire economics and industrial capitalism" (Sutton 8). For these workers, "the militant and righteous counter-hegemonic energy of... populist evangelicalism" was inseparable from "the moral imperative of producerism and the journeymen's movement" (Sutton 257). Questions concerning social justice and the distribution of power in society were central to artisan culture and, as a result, set the theological agenda of populist evangelicalism. Their notion of redemption, then, was wholly constituted by their experience of oppression and poverty in the era of the Market Revolution. Their conception of salvation had far more to do with their present material conditions than with esoteric theological speculations.

The examples recounted here, though emblematic, are part of such a wealth of corroborating evidence that it could fill volumes. Such comprehensiveness is unnecessary however as the matter, as we can see, is quite clear. The proliferation of new religious groups and forms of redemption that defined the Second Great Awakening was not the consequence of theological disagreements but was rather the product of class formation, born of "passionate social struggle" and the "deep-seated class antagonism" that Hatch describes as the "fundamental problem" of antebellum American society (14). Religion was the prevailing cultural site of class struggle; therefore, "blending the study of religious culture and social class" is necessary "to make sense of the conflicting social ethics" that were forwarded by diverse, emergent Protestant denominations (*Piety* 7). Members of the upper, middle, and working classes projected the economic theory and mode of social relation that best served their interests onto their theological ideas. Such forms of apotheosis served to legitimate each group's ideal set of values, practices, objectives, and power relations and to discourage opposition to these norms by turning them into immutable, divinely wrought structures of existence. Doing so enabled each group to construe contrary positions as blasphemous and to portray their own aims as the means to salvation.

The Free Religious Market

The birth of the American voluntary church system was fundamentally shaped by the social and economic conditions of the Market Revolution. Following disestablishment, free-market capitalism served as the practical and institutional model for American Protestantism. With the opening of the religious market, churches were indirectly mandated to assume capitalistic structures and practices if they were to continue to survive. In the laissez-faire environment of the Market Revolution, denominations were increasingly required to adopt new measures of evangelism to remain competitive and to increase market share through aggressive growth strategies. Consequently, revivalism and evangelicalism were transformed into marketing tactics calculated to convert new followers. Thus, salvation became a commodity that was produced and consumed on a mass scale in the conversions of awakening revivals, marketed in antebellum print culture and advertising, and sold in the "benevolent empire" of institutionalized charity. Each religious organization, new and old, produced a specialized soteriology—their "brand of Christianity"—that targeted a specific segment of the market (Bilhartz 11). Church polity and the role of the clergy were also redefined. As Donald Scott reveals, the structure of the major Protestant institutions became entirely corporatized by the mid-nineteenth century. Finally, the denominations, and the soteriological product they offered, became self-consciously representative of distinct social classes and therefore church affiliation and religious taste were a means of class distinction and conspicuous consumption. To say that salvation was produced, marketed, sold, and consumed in antebellum America is in no sense merely analogical or metaphorical. The process of apotheosis was such that every aspect of Protestantism was remade in the likeness of market capitalism; the church became a corporation, the clergy became salesmen, doctrines became products, and evangelicalism became a marketing strategy. The Second Great Awakening was the cultural expression of that transformation.

After disestablishment, the Calvinist church lost its state sponsorship, instantiating a voluntary church system that required every religious organization to depend on its members for financial support. By putting "all Christian denominations on equal footing before the law" states could "no longer… dictate religious uniformity or provide church financial assistance" (Bilhartz 11). In keeping with the liberal political economy of the era, all limitations to innovation were removed, allowing any individual or organization to sell their product on the religious market. While this deregulation increased religious freedom—inaugurating an era of religious innovation unmatched before or since—it also caused the newly opened market to be flooded with new denominations, sects, and communes. In order to remain solvent, each of these religious bodies was forced to compete for members and their financial contributions, and, as denominations multiplied, competition grew ever more fierce. Terry D. Bilhartz explains:

> in a pluralistic society the decision to associate with a given church is an act of free choice. But in any economy of exchange, individual choice is influenced by the supply of goods or services being offered and the marketing skills of the competing vendors. In the decades following disestablishment, when the virgin denominational market was unusually fluid, voluntary churches fiercely competed with each other for contributing members. The nature of this struggle encouraged churches to implement new strategies to enlarge their share of the population.
>
> (139)

As evinced by the rapid post-disestablishment decline of the Congregational church and the exponential growth of Methodism, the churches who were willing to embrace new, "more aggressive measures of recruitment" to increase their market share "prospered, while those reluctant to compete on such terms declined" (Bilhartz 139). Contrary to the demand-side interpretation of McLoughlin and Sellers, who claim that the Awakening was a response to the psychological demands of a nation in a time of economic crisis, Hatch and Bilhartz argue that understanding the nature of the Second Great Awakening requires a "supply-side interpretation" (Bilhartz 139). Bilhartz writes that Americans "bought into evangelical religion largely because the price was right and the streets were filled with venders" (139). For these scholars, the "fierce religious competition" of "religious entrepreneurs" produced the desire for redemption that impelled the "dynamics of revivalism" that we call the Second Great Awakening (Hatch 15).

Awakening evangelicals' top priority was the growth of their respective churches. They achieved that growth primarily through the conversions that occurred during revivals and protracted camp meetings. To this end, evangelists developed new methods of preaching and of staging revivals that were calculated to produce conversion experiences among spectators. Bilhartz writes that "revivalists were those evangelicals who insisted upon a special kind of conversion—an instantaneous experience of faith, preceded by a strong sense of personal guilt, and followed by a joyful assurance of forgiveness" (84). The popular endorsement of let-do Arminian soteriology meant that salvation was no longer a lifelong endeavor or a preordained gift but could now be had immediately, simply as a matter of choice. The job of the antebellum revivalist was to induce that choice, thereby producing a cathartic redemption experience. Preachers like Charles Grandison Finney, the primary designer of the "new measures" of revivalism, used "innovative measures calculated to provoke this type of religious experience" (Bilhartz 84). With this aim in mind, Finney created an efficient, dependable mechanism to mass-produce conversion. For Finney, redemption "is not a miracle or dependent on a miracle in any sense... It is purely a philosophical result of the right use of constituted means" (qtd. in *Revivals* 125). Such a result is as necessary and predictable as "the right use of means to raise grain and a crop of wheat" (qtd. in *Revivals* 125). Salvation was, therefore, perceived as a product that could be mechanically generated. In this way, Finney attempted to develop a rationalized, proto-industrial means for the mass-production of redemption.

Awakening revivalists were single-mindedly concerned with the soteriological bottom line, that is, increasing market share by winning over new customers. McLoughlin writes that measuring "success in terms of statistical results was central to Finney's revisionist view of what a revival was"[3] (*Revivals* 123). The New England establishment vehemently objected to the commodification of salvation, claiming that revivals had become superficial contrivances calculated to produce conversion. One clergyman writes, "they measure the progress of religion by the numbers who flock to their standards, not by the prevalence of faith and piety, justice and charity and public virtues in society in general" (qtd. in Hatch 13). The free religious market, on the other hand, rewarded this endeavor, regardless of the methods used to accomplish it. Finney put it bluntly: "the results justify my methods... Show me the fruits of your ministry, and if they so far exceed mine as to give me evidence that you have found a more excellent way, I will adapt my views" (qtd. in *Revivals* 126). He was the first to admit that his new evangelical measures were not intrinsically valuable but were designed to produce the greatest amount of conversions in the most efficient way. If a better mode of producing redemption could be devised, proclaimed Finney, he would adopt it. The new measures were simply a rhetorical and performative technology for the mass-production of salvation.

Mass conversions were commonplace in antebellum revivals and camp meetings. For example, one "Henry Smith described an October 1806 meeting that produced 579 conversions"; a Methodist itinerant, French Evans, recalled that a similar event occurred at the Rattlesnake Springs meeting in 1826, reporting that "250 persons" were converted; in the Methodists' General Convention of 1800, "some two hundred Baltimoreans were converted"; and in 1827 the First and Second Presbyterian churches of Baltimore gained "upward of one hundred new converts" (Bilhartz 89, 90, 96). Finney and his peers exhibited

---

[3] On revivalists' use of bookkeeping to record conversion statistics, see McLoughlin, *Modern Revivalism*, 262–5.

a let-do theological orientation that was open to any means that would further streamline the production of redemption, gain new consumers, and maintain the aggressive growth of the church. The theological novelties that we commonly associate with the Second Great Awakening—its sermonic rhetoric, soteriology, and aggressive evangelical tactics—were, therefore, expressions of the churches' assimilation of free-market values and modes of production.

In addition to employing new measures to attract and retain consumers, denominations had to set themselves apart from their competitors by offering ever more specialized doctrines that appealed to the needs of particular segments of the population. In order to "survive in the free religious marketplace, churches found it necessary to accentuate their distinctive attributes, and to persuade prospective converts why they should associate with a particular brand of Christianity" (Bilhartz 11). In their groundbreaking study, Roger Finke and Rodney Stark find that religious growth in America—what they call "the churching of America"—occurred precisely because of increased doctrinal specialization and denominational branding (20–21). Because no one religious organization could cater to the "divergent tastes," needs, and interests of every social class, each had to develop a distinctive product that appealed directly to the class concerns of its target market (Finke and Stark 18). The development of a free religious market, therefore, led to soteriological specialization, causing redemption to become a consumable product crafted and marketed to specific classes.

Daniel Walker Howe succinctly explains that "in antebellum America, religion was on its way to becoming what it would become more obviously in our own day, a consumer good that members of the public are free to purchase or not in any of a wide variety of brands. Revivalism in such a society can be interpreted as an effective form of the mass marketing of religion to the public" (269–70). According to McLoughlin's theory, religious awakenings occur in times of crisis when a society is forced to redefine its modes of self-understanding. During the Market Revolution, antebellum Americans who had traditionally looked to religion for self-understanding were now encouraged to self-identify on the basis of the goods they chose to consume. Religious consumption was, therefore, a transitional activity that advanced and even accelerated this cultural transition. The free religious market afforded antebellum Americans with a preponderance of consumer choice, giving them a "wide range of religious options" that "had never been equaled in any previous human society" (Howe 269). Hatch explains that such an excess of choice made it possible for an American to find an amenable group no matter what his or her preference in belief, practice, or institutional structure. Churches ranged from egalitarian to autocratic and included all degrees of organizational complexity. One could be a Presbyterian who favored or opposed the freedom of the will, a Methodist who promoted or denounced democracy in the church, a Baptist who advocated or condemned foreign missions, and a member of virtually every denomination that upheld or opposed slavery... One could opt for traditional piety or join a perfectionist sect. Religious options in the early republic seemed unlimited: one could worship on Saturday, practice foot washing, ordain women, advance pacifism, prohibit alcohol, or toy with spiritualism, phrenology, or health reform.

(65)

This abundance of options allowed consumers of religion to form their identity through consumer choice for the first time. Further, T. J. Jackson Lears writes that "the desire for a magical transformation of the self was... an essential part of consumer goods' appeal in nineteenth-century America" (43). Arminian salvation—in all of its myriad forms—taught Americans that this kind of immediate, magical self-transformation, or conversion, was simply a matter of choice. Through the specular process of apotheosis, salvation became a consumable good which was available in "a wide variety of brands," each tailored to the desires of the nation's newly forming classes, and at the same time, all acts of consumption were imbued with salvific potential, that is, with the transformative power of conversion.

As we see from Hatch's description of antebellum religious pluralism, doctrinal differences often turned, not on theological questions, but on social and political issues, such as regarding the distribution of power, the rights of women in church and society, sexual mores, slavery, and war. This exemplifies Niebuhr's contention that "theological opinions" are "necessarily conditioned" by prevailing "cultural and political conditions" (14). In the free religious market, each church was pressured by the abundance of competition to produce a specialized soteriological commodity that expressed "the morale" of a given "political and economic class." In the context of these politicized choices, antebellum Americans could use religious consumption and brand loyalty as a way of expressing solidarity with their own class, with a class with which they sympathized, or with one they aspired to join. Howe explains that one form of religious commitment "might represent the deliberate choice of a counterculture," while affiliation with a different denomination could be "a vehicle for upward social mobility" (269). In addition to being a means of self-identification, religious consumption was also a sociopolitical signifier that reflected one's class position or aspirations, and the political ideology one advocated.

Particularly in urban settings where there was more consumer choice, church was the dominant site where class relations were put on display and publicly reinforced. In his labor history of antebellum New York, Sean Wilentz found that, despite the aggressive expansion of the evangelicals, "the smaller churches continued to give New York high society much of its prestige" (77). In this era, one had to rent or purchase pews in order to attend church services. Therefore membership in the smaller churches was often cost prohibitive to all but the most wealthy. Religious consumption became a form of conspicuous consumption where congregants exchanged monetary capital for the social capital acquired through membership in the elite churches. In his study of antebellum Baltimore, Bilhartz found that church attendance was "significantly related to one's occupational status," that is, one's profession and social class (21). His research shows that each denomination was patronized by a particular "status group" which constituted the church's "status profile" (Bilhartz 22). He writes that "churches recruited most rigorously for those most able to... contribute toward the financial needs of the congregation. Laborers, in short, were not the best catch for voluntary churches struggling for survival" (Bilhartz 21). Therefore, competition in the free religious market put the working-class at a disadvantage, thus accelerating what Sellers called the "cultural imperialism" of the bourgeois churches, whose theology, politics, and mores were the most capitalistic. As a result of this, by 1830 Baltimoreans who worked in white-collar occupations, like lawyers, physicians, proprietors, and city officials, "overwhelmingly dominated local congregations" (Bilhartz 21). While some wanted to enlarge their congregation, they were ultimately unwilling to disrupt its status profile. Evidence clearly reveals that the competition and specialization required in a free religious market caused denominations to become "socially homogeneous" (Bilhartz 25).

The economic prosperity brought on by the Market Revolution "exacerbated the tendency toward congregational homogeneity" until "each reflected the ascendency of a particular occupational class" (Bilhartz 24, 25). Bilhartz writes, "the data indicate that for both the wealthier inner city and poorer peripheral congregations, the same denomination attracted the same status type in all parts of the city" (25). By 1830, it was clear that the "Roman Catholics embraced the poor... the Presbyterian and Episcopal denominations increasingly served social elites, [and] the Methodist Episcopal Church remained the church of the middle-class" (Bilhartz 25). "In any given neighborhood the white-collar workers were more likely to be Presbyterian or Episcopalian; the skilled artisans, Methodists or United Brethren, and the unskilled workers, Roman Catholic" (Bilhartz 25). Further, the "social complexion" of the German Reformed Church and the Baptist congregations was markedly working-class (Bilhartz 23, 24). The Old Otterbein Church had an "artisan-class orientation," the Swedenborgian New Jerusalem Church was attended by "low propertied artisans," and the Friends (Quakers) "were dominantly middle-class artisans"; and finally, the First Independent Unitarian Church "consisted overwhelmingly of merchants, physicians, and lawyers" (Bilhartz 24). The evidence gathered by Bilhartz and numerous other historians proves that church membership and doctrine developed along class lines and in response to market pressures. In the free religious market, dogma became a specialized commodity crafted to meet the social and political needs of differing "occupation classes." But this kind of specialization served to further entrench and codify those class divisions by naturalizing them, by transforming them into aspects of the natural order. Moreover, in this context of intensifying competition, the practice of selling and renting pews became a vehicle for conspicuous religious consumption, where antebellum Americans used denominational affiliation and religious taste to reinforce social exclusivity and class distinction.

In their respective studies of antebellum New York City, Baltimore, and Providence, historians Wilentz, Bilhartz, and Schantz find that pew renting was a way to establish economic criteria for church membership and to enforce exclusivity. Once commodified, church membership served as a mode of conspicuous consumption which "enhanced the prestige" of the cities' leading families (*Piety* 129, Wilentz 77). By setting high prices and through the practice of multiple pew ownership, members of the elite denominations were able to exclude the working-classes "from the ranks of respectable churchgoers" (*Piety* 132). Schantz reports an incident in which a Providence church eliminated an upper balcony that contained seats reserved for African Americans in order to construct "a more comfortable site for devotion... planned for a more fashionable, wealthy, and white congregation" (*Piety* 127). Such renovations were a common way to inflate pew costs to attract more wealthy, elite clientele, while excluding the less "respectable" classes and races, thereby elevating a church's status profile. Bilhartz and Schantz find that the average cost of pews coordinates with the class status of its members. For instance, in Baltimore, Methodists charged an average of $15 per seat, with the Presbyterian, Baptist, and Lutheran churches charging between $20 and $35; the Episcopal church charged between $35 and $50, and the Unitarian Church, over $65 per seat (Bilhartz 91). Schantz's research shows the same price distribution among the denominations, but with competition in Providence inflating costs to as high as "$350 per seat" in one Unitarian church (*Piety* 128).

The practice of multiple pew ownership enabled the wealthiest members of society "to exert extensive personal control within the denominations they funded" (*Piety* 129). This practice functioned much like owning stock in a church. Pewholders were like shareholders whose ability to exert denominational control was measured, in part, by the percent of pews—or shares—they owned. Purchased pews, therefore, were a kind of religious private property that imparted religious authority and social prestige to their lay owners. In order to maintain elite investment, churches had to pander to the social and political interests of its controlling shareholders. Wealthy investors were able to dictate everything from doctrine to the hiring and firing of clerics. Schantz writes that "these men and their extended families could not possibly have filled all of the seats in the pews they purchased," so they often gave them away as a conspicuous form of benevolence. This was, like much of the bourgeoisie's charitable activity in the voluntary associations of the "benevolent empire," one more mode of purchasing public esteem and respect, that is, of acquiring social capital through religious consumption. The leading historians of antebellum America agree that practices of pew taxation and multiple pew ownership "testif[y] to the profound linkages between the culture of the marketplace and that of the meetinghouse" (*Piety* 122).

In his seminal work *From Office to Profession: The New England Ministry 1750–1850*, Donald M. Scott examines how "the clergy's position in society and its character as a social institution... changed in ways that reflected the changes in society and the new definition of that society" (152). Scott's research reveals how the Market Revolution restructured the ministry and altered the way clerics understood their work. He writes that, by the 1850s, "a new kind of ministerial structure and consciousness had emerged, which... has endured to this day" (xiii). In the eighteenth century, the clergy, like artisans and farmers, exclusively served their local community and typically did so for the entirety of their career. Because of this, and the fact that the meetinghouse served as the central public space where an assortment of religious and non-religious activities took place, the local pastor played a central role in the social life of the community and in the lives of its inhabitants. During the Market Revolution, that all changed. Ecclesiastical modes and relations of production began to assume the shape taken in the national economy. Ministers no longer produced religious knowledge exclusively for provincial markets, but now addressed a dispersed, anonymous, national religious market "through such translocal agencies as the lecture and lyceum circuit, the religious press, and the American Tract Society" (Scott 154). By 1850, a cleric "was not in any necessary way integrated into the social structure of the town, rarely thought of himself as belonging to it, and rarely remained in a single town for much of his professional career" (Scott 154). The clergy was no longer a local institution, but was now "shaped by a new kind of translocal structure and professional consciousness," that is, by the structure and consciousness consonant with free-market capitalism (Scott 154).

By the mid-nineteenth century, the ministry was no longer seen as a calling, or a vocation, but had instead "become a 'profession' in a modern sense. Just like a lawyer or a doctor, the pastor now offered a specialized service to a particular self-selected clientele" (Scott xi). Scott writes,

> the young men entering the clergy in the teens and twenties... began to envision a career in the modern, technical sense—an occupational course composed of a sequence of steps upward to positions of greater prestige and influence... Their letters and diaries... betray a wholly new kind of self-consciousness about the relative merits and career potential of particular posts. They ranked pastorates or nonpastoral opportunities according to the kind of career they wanted and the chances for advance and influence the posts offered.
>
> (72)

In the wake of the Market Revolution, Protestantism became entirely corporatized. Ministers no longer felt obliged to remain in a single pastorate for their entire careers;[4] instead, a "prestige ladder" was introduced into the ministry where success was measured by one's ability to attain ever more esteemed, influential, and lucrative appointments (Scott 71). This introduced the ideal of free competition into the newly formed ministerial market, fostering intense competition among minsters for the most sought-after positions. This also changed relations between the ministry and the congregation. As voluntary religious consumers, "congregations became less hesitant to dismiss unwanted preachers," or those whose politics or style of worship was not in keeping with congregational demand (Bilhartz 46–47). This caused a reversal of ministerial priorities. Clerics were now expected to pander to the self-serving perspective of their employers. Bilhartz writes that "pastoral security depended largely on continued popularity... among the economic elites who controlled

---

[4] On the erosion of "the ideal of pastoral permanence," see Scott, 71–5; Bilhartz, 38.

local congregational decision-making" (39). In order to continue ascending the prestige ladder, clerics—the official exponents of Christian dogma—were obliged to conform the ethos they professed from the pulpit to the interests of their lay financiers.

The Market Revolution was experienced as a crisis that touched every facet of American life. The truths and mores that had formerly guided everyday life no longer held. Dominant social groups and seats of authority found themselves imperiled by newly emerging groups and ways of thinking. Overwhelming feelings of instability, insecurity, and moral confusion boiled over across New England, giving rise to the series of effervescent events that we now refer to as the Second Great Awakening. It is in the environment of such gatherings that human societies periodically create and recreate the sacred. However, we must keep in mind that effervescence is a form of extreme experience. Durkheim explains that, in the throes of terrified ecstasy,

> Man does not recognize himself; he feels he is transformed, and so he transforms his surroundings. To account for the very specific impressions he feels, he endows the things with which he is most directly in contact with properties that they do not have, exceptional powers, virtues that the objects of ordinary experience do not possess. On the real world in which his profane life unfolds he superimposes another one that, in a sense, exists only in his thought, but to which he ascribes a kind of higher dignity in relation to the first. It is an ideal world, then, in this double sense.
>
> (Durkheim 317)

Feuerbach famously argued that Christians' concept of God is the product of a specular projection—a vertical absolutization that models divinity and the metaphysical order on humanity. What Durkheim explains in this passage is that apotheosis—the creation of the sacred—also entails a horizontal introjection that invests "the real world," that is, the everyday material world, with the sacred. The sacred is indeed generated in a specular fashion, but rather than reflecting the fixed attributes of humanity writ large, the sacred is an ever-changing reflection of the material qualities and conditions of a given social group. When material conditions change, the sacred is recalibrated in kind. As the first decades of the nineteenth century drew on, established Christianity ceased to be an accurate reflection of American society. This caused horrifying feelings of moral vertigo to spread across New England like a contagion. The Second Great Awakening was the collective process of adapting Christian concepts, practices, and institutions to accommodate the material conditions of the Market Revolution, fundamentally transforming American Protestantism.

2

The Salvific Power of Affect: Sentimentalism in the Labor Fiction of Rebecca Harding Davis and Elizabeth Stuart Phelps

To us downright commonsensible Western people the gods are intelligible just in proportion as their bones ache or their clothes are cut like our own.
—Rebecca Harding Davis to Ralph Waldo Emerson, January 13, 1870

Rebecca Harding Davis and Elizabeth Stuart Phelps authored America's first labor novels: *Life in the Iron-Mills* (1861), *Margret Howth* (1862), and *The Silent Partner* (1871). On the basis of these works, modern critics[1] have refashioned Davis and Phelps into radicals and early realists. However, as enticing as this reading may be, it is aspirational. While these works depict aspects of society that had never before appeared in American literature,[2] and while the authors are critical of industrial relations, Davis and Phelps were firmly entrenched in the tradition of sentimental literature and the canon of domesticity. The novels' industrial settings, reformist sensibility, and focus on class relations may give, at first glance, an impression of nascent social realism but a closer look reveals the highly conventional tropes, plots, and objectives that were readily recognizable by mid-century readers of domestic fiction. Unfortunately, Davis and Phelps's reputations as would-be liberators of the working-class have been grossly overstated. Neither takes an anti-capitalist position in their sentimental labor fiction. Instead, they promote a form of middle-class maternalism as a means to redeem capitalism by accommodating rather than overcoming it.

Sentimental theology and print culture did the cultural work of middle-class formation in the nineteenth century by reconciling the mores of Christianity

---

[1] For example, Jean Pfaelzer describes Davis as "a pioneer of American realism [who] endowed social advocacy for workers with a feminist perspective" ("Rebecca" 39). See also Harde, Kelly, Lasseter, Olsen, and Privett. For an opposing view, see Mazurek, Watson.

[2] Perhaps with the exception of *The Lowell Offering* (1840–1845) and Herman Melville's "The Paradise of Bachelors and the Tartarus of Maids" (1855).

and capitalism.[3] Through literary types like the household saint, the angel in the home, and Christ-like mothers and female mentors, sentimental fiction sacralized the market-friendly morality and form of life that defined the emerging middle-class. The didactic canon of domesticity replaced Congregational fatalism with a theology of Christian nurture that taught Americans how to cultivate pious behavior and thus transformed capitalist norms into a salvation ethic. The sentimental and domestic culture industries were the means by which the middle-class conflated its defining traits, values, and objectives with those of Christianity. It was this apotheotic process that enabled capitalism to thrive and the middle-class to achieve cultural dominance.[4]

Rather than attempting to stoke class antagonism or advocate for the full inclusion of the working-class, Davis and Phelps's labor literature helped to perform the cultural work that secured the hegemony of the middle-class. Though critical of industrialism in their labor novels, Davis and Phelps sought to moralize capitalism, not to eliminate it. In keeping with the sentimental tradition and its ideology of instructive feminine nurture, they argued that middle-class domestic values could temper the immoral aspects of capitalism such as self-interest, lack of sympathy, individualism, and acquisitiveness. Sentimentalism and its function as a catalyst of middle-class formation were predicated on establishing and maintaining boundaries between the classes, not on dismantling them. Therefore, like other sentimentalists, Davis and Phelps moralized about the inhumane conditions of capitalism, but they had no interest in abolishing class difference or socioeconomic inequality. Instead, they forwarded a theory of social harmony modeled on middle-class domesticity that allowed for the kind of virtuous inequality that existed within the family. This, they argued, could be achieved by inculcating the kinds of sympathies and feelings favored by God. The figure called upon to lead that work of cultural-economic nurture was the spiritual mother, a projection of the middle-class domestic figurehead into the public sphere.

Domesticity, Sentimentalism, and the Middle-Class

The concept of domesticity was central to middle-class formation in the mid-nineteenth century. The middle-class in this period was nascent, immensely diverse, and unstable. It was composed of people from disparate occupations

---

[3] See Nelson, 6–11.
[4] "The 'spirit' of modern capitalism," writes Weber, "its specific *ethos*," is "the ethos of the modern *bourgeois middle classes*" (FMW 321).

and social backgrounds whose economic fortunes were as uncertain and fluid as the antebellum market. However, the middle-class established its unity and cultural authority by developing shared social and religious norms. As Mary Ryan has shown, "the American middle class molded its distinctive identity around domestic values and family practices" (*Cradle* 15). Richard Brodhead writes that "the antebellum decades were the time when the newly defined middle class began its push to establish its model as a social norm" (26). "At a time when it was in no sense socially normal, the new middle-class world undertook to propagate itself as American 'normality' " (Brodhead 27). This campaign of social reproduction and cultural hegemony was primarily accomplished through the medium of print, in "the canon of domesticity" that flooded the literary market with "essays, sermons, novels, poems and manuals offering advice and philosophy on family life, child rearing, and women's role" in American society (Cott 66, 63). Nancy Cott writes that "the canon of domesticity expressed the dominance of what may be designated a middle-class ideal" (92). Similarly, Stuart Blumin has found that "virtually every historian of the... canon of domesticity... has recognized its middle-class character" (187). "The emergence of a distinct middle class," he writes, "was closely connected with, and largely dependent upon, the development of the domestic ideal" promoted in this print culture (Blumin 187). Sentimental fiction was the literary expression of domestic ideology. Alongside works of theology and instructional books and magazines, sentimental fiction was central to the formation of middle-class subjectivity and the inculcation of norms concerning behavior, emotion, character, gender roles, and the family.

Affect was a primary feature of middle-class formation. Middle-class identity was contingent on a particular "structure of feeling" founded on sympathy and sentiment. The objective of sentimental fiction and the broader canon of domesticity was to inculcate normative affects that would unify the class and enable its reproduction. As Lori Merish put it, "domestic texts... construct class as a sentiment" (93). Because the middle-class was so diverse in the early stage of its formation, "middle-class consciousness was shaped less by structural circumstances than by ideological and emotional incentives. It required an act of imagination for such diverse individuals to conceive themselves as a community united by shared aspirations and cultural practices" (Applegate 111). Writers of sentimental fiction believed that literature could cultivate the kind of moral feeling inclusion in the middle-class required. As Harriet Beecher Stowe put it in *Uncle Tom's Cabin*, literature had the ability to make readers "*feel right*"

(404). When the cultural theorist Raymond Williams introduced the concept of "structures of feeling" as an affective supplement to ideology, he explained,

> The term is difficult, but "feeling" is chosen to emphasize a distinction from the more formal concepts of "world-view" or "ideology." It is not only that we must go beyond formally held and systematic beliefs... It is that we are concerned with meanings and values as they are actively lived and felt... We are talking about characteristic elements of impulse, restraint, and tone; specifically affective elements of consciousness and relationships: not feeling against thought, but thought as felt and feeling as thought: practical consciousness... in a living and interrelating continuity.
>
> (Williams 132)

Williams keenly observed that "specific kinds of sociality" are linked to "specific feelings" (133). He recognized that novel "forms and conventions... in art and literature, are often among the very first indications that such a new structure [of feeling] is forming" and, further, that "the emergence of a new structure of feeling is best related to the rise of a class" (133, 134). Sentimental fiction was integral to the affective formation of the middle-class and the inculcation of sympathy as its attendant structure of feeling. However, the function of this process was not limited to establishing social cohesion among a particular group of Americans but was necessary for the advancement of the burgeoning economic system. Merish astutely writes that sentimental "literary fictions construct market capitalism and middle-class personal life as mutually determining spheres, each dependent on the other, and they inscribe sympathy as the spontaneous emotional faculty that enables the flourishing of both" (4).

All ideology is inherently salvific in that it entails promises of reward for conformity to a particular set of norms. From the outset, the ideology of domesticity took the form of a religion. All class-specific forms of life are endowed with religious import for the purpose of legitimization and to assure the reproduction of the social assemblage. Middle-class formation in the nineteenth century required the creation of a salvation ethic that would endow the class's defining traits and values with transcendent authority and encourage their continued propagation. Print culture was vital to this process as the "canon of domesticity" gave rise to the "cult of domesticity" (*Cradle* 1). The cultural work performed by sentimental literature was to promulgate "the new domestic religion" as a mode of attaining salvation (Blumin 182). "Domesticity was a religion" in that authentic Christianity and the promise of redemption were now said to be contingent on conformity to middle-class ideals (Blumin 182). In this literature, "ministers and pious women made every effort to conflate domestic values with religious values" (Cott 136). Similarly, sentimental "writers' religious faith coincided with their conviction that God's values were domestic" (Baym 44). The transformation of middle-class norms into a salvation ethic required the creation of a sentimental theology, that is, a new image of God that would serve as the divine model and transcendent ground of these imperatives. Therefore, the attributes of God became those of the domestic mother; God was "spoken of as a parent" or a friend but "never the lover or bridegroom" as in eras past (Baym 44). In this sense, establishing the religion of domesticity required "the domestication of religion"[5] (*Cradle* 98). Sentimental literature expressed the apotheosis of domesticity and the defining attributes of the middle-class. By sacralizing domesticity and endowing it with soteriological power, sentimental print culture served as the principal catalyst of middle-class formation.

Sentimentalism was the literary product of the Second Great Awakening and shared its evangelical imperative. Writers of sentimental literature assumed the role of the evangelist and sought to incite religious conversion in readers. Nina Baym writes that domestic novelists "envisioned themselves lay ministers, their books as evangelical sermons that might spur conversion" (44). Just as revivalists utilized the dexterous manipulation of emotion to produce conversion experiences, sentimentalists used the rhetorical power of emotion to the same end. As Claudia Stokes has recently shown, literary sentimentalism significantly contributed to "the institutionalization of numerous new religious beliefs" during the Second Great Awakening, in particular "new ideas about salvation" (19, 22). One of the hallmarks of the Second Great Awakening was the prevalence of religious enthusiasm and a newfound belief in the salvific power of affect. Stokes summarizes the new doctrine of redemption, writing, "revivalists maintained… that conversion could be triggered solely through emotion," and that "one need only feel genuine religious emotion in order to convert and become Christian" (Stokes 41). Sentimental novelists took up this doctrine of salvation as a foundational principle. In the idiom of the revival, they believed that, if they appealed to the shared emotions of their readers through "narrative sympathy" and evoked deep moral feeling or sentiment, then readers would be "converted and redeemed" (Stokes 47). As Harriet Beecher Stowe put it in *Uncle*

---

[5] In his *Sociology of Religion*, Weber argues that the "middle-class transformation of religion in the direction of domesticity" is not limited to Christianity (SR 103). He continues, "the religious need of the middle and lower bourgeoisie expresses itself less in the form of heroic myths than in rather more sentimental legend, which has a tendency toward inwardness and edification. This corresponds to… the greater emphasis upon domestic and family life of the middle classes, in contrast to the ruling strata" (SR 103).

Tom's Cabin, literature had the ability to bring readers' sympathies "in harmony with the sympathies of Christ," it would enable them to *"feel right"* (404–405). Stowe's well-known formulation is indicative of the way the structure of feeling that supplemented middle-class ideology was sanctified. The apotheosis of the middle-class structure of feeling produced religious and social norms. Redemption was contingent on bringing one's feelings "in harmony with the sympathies of Christ," and as such, with the affective norms of the middle-class. To *be* right was to *"feel right."* Raymond Williams recognized that "the social content" of literature is often of an "affective kind, which cannot… be reduced to belief-systems, institutions, or explicit general relationships" (133). Christian sentiment was the affective element of middle-class consciousness and the new social relations engendered by the Market Revolution. This structure of feeling was not distinct from ideology but was rather a compendium to it. It was the way that the new "meanings and values" of the middle-class were "actively lived and felt." Sentimentalism was the means of inculcating the "practical consciousness" of the middle-class, of instilling middle-class ideology "as felt and feeling as thought" (Williams 132). The Second Great Awakening's emphasis on emotion and the salvific power of affect is a particularly stark example of the importance of feeling in the broad acceptance and reproduction of new ideas, values, and social structures.

In addition to appealing to readers' affects, writers modeled conversion in the narratives themselves in order to produce the experience of salvation in readers. As Jane Tompkins put it, sentimental novels are "spiritual training narratives" in which "the vocation to be mastered is Christian salvation" (184, 176–7). In these works, both the paragons of Christian piety and the characters who undergo a process of conversion are invariably women. In accord with the social and theological innovations of the Second Great Awakening, sentimental fiction invested women with religious authority. Amy Schrager Lang has argued that the new religious authority granted to women in sentimental fiction was predicated on the "reorganization of culture from the point of view… of the white middle-class woman" (141). Stokes goes a step further, arguing that sentimental texts sought to assign religious authority "specifically, to white, middle-class North Atlantic Protestant women"[6] (Stokes 24). Consensus holds that "middle-class formation was woman's work," and it was the apotheosis of motherhood and domesticity that gave the labor of cultural reorganization its power and effectiveness (Blumin 191). As Mary Ryan has observed, "a closer look at the

---

[6] See also Tompkins, *Sensational Designs*, 141.

Figure 2.1 "The Sphere of Woman," *Godey's Lady's Book*, March 1850. Courtesy of Rare Books, Special Collections, and Preservation, River Campus Libraries, University of Rochester.

Second Great Awakening indicates that the history of class and religion was hopelessly entangled with questions of family and gender" (*Cradle* 12).

During this period, the formerly dominant, paternal, stern, Calvinist soteriology was displaced by a maternal, nurturing form of salvation that made mothers the primary agents of redemption, affect its medium, and the home its site.[7] Middle-class womanhood and motherhood in particular were consecrated by "America's religion of domesticity" (Tompkins 125). Stuart Blumin writes,

---

[7] Mary Ryan argues that though the initiation of this transition to a nurturing, affectionate, maternal form of salvation is usually attributed to Horace Bushnell's *On Christian Nurture*, this theology can be traced back earlier to Reverend Beriah Green's 1836 tract, "The Savior's Arms Open to Little Children: A Discourse" (*Cradle* 100).

"the home, the traditional domestic tasks of women, and the particular task of childrearing... were increasingly sanctified during the early years of the nineteenth century" (184). Sentimental print culture played the foremost role in this shift, as it depicted women as "God in human form" and endowed mothers with the "power to dictate salvation" (Tompkins 142, *Womanhood* 99). Motherhood came to be regarded "as a project in salvation," as mothers, through nurturing character formation, sowed "salvation through motherly love" (Cott 88, Tompkins 125). Her domain, the domestic sphere of the home, was characterized "as a redemptive counterpart to the world" (Cott 98).

Nancy Cott has shown that "the central convention of domesticity was the contrast between the home and the world" (Cott 64). The canon of domesticity linked this division of home and world to the gendered doctrine of the spheres. The period's changing economic relations and division of labor—in which the family no longer worked as a unit and men ceased to work alongside women in the home—were conflated with Christianity's dualistic metaphysics. Home came to be analogous to heaven and the sacred, while the world of commerce and industry were associated with hell, the fallen, and the profane. Men's sphere was the immoral and sinful world of business and women's sphere was the redemptive sanctuary of the home, where their piety, affection, and sympathy could offer men respite and refuge from a world without feeling. Sentimental literature protested the "exploitation and pecuniary values" that defined American capitalism and argued that the domestic sphere provided the spiritual "antidote" to its "poisonous" effects[8] (Cott 68). Cott explains,

> In accentuating the split between "work" and "home" and proposing the latter as a place of salvation, the canon of domesticity tacitly acknowledged the capacity of modern work to desecrate the human spirit. Authors of domestic literature, especially the female authors, denigrated business and politics as arenas of selfishness... and degradation of the soul.
>
> (67)

Therefore, sentimental fiction was predicated on a religious critique of capitalism. However, sentimentalism performed the work of middle-class formation by investing domesticity with salvific power.

The middle-class's domestic doctrine of salvation was a consequence of economic change. As fathers' work took them out of the household and into the

---

[8] On the anti-pecuniary critique of marketplace values in domestic rhetoric, see Baym, 45, Cott, 68, Ryan, *Womanhood*, 77.

commercial and industrial world, childrearing responsibilities were transferred from authoritative patriarchs to affectionate mothers. As a result, at the direction of sentimental print culture "motherhood was invested with a new glory," giving rise to "the cult of the mother" (*Womanhood* 99). The Market Revolution had fostered Arminian theology, the soteriological counterpart to laissez-faire capitalism. This reformation of the dominant doctrine of salvation posited that individuals have the power to secure their own salvation. Just as pious Christians were obliged to strive for spiritual perfection, mothers were now responsible for their children's conversion and salvation. In this sense, women took the place of evangelists and the middle-class home took the place of the church or revival. Changing beliefs regarding the moral agency of children caused them to be seen as particularly susceptible to moral and spiritual formation. Led by Horace Bushnell's *On Christian Nurture* (1847), the canon of domesticity maintained that conversion and ultimately salvation was the outcome of long-term character formation, not an immediate ecstatic episode. This labor of subjectification was said to be conducted affectively, through the mother's loving nurture. Sentimental literature conflated salvation with a mode of socialization that entailed the adoption of the values, behaviors, and character traits that defined the middle-class. To be pious and authentically Christian was to conform to middle-class norms. Therefore, domestic soteriology was a means of reproducing and further consolidating the middle-class. According to sentimental literature, it was women's duty to instill this middle-class salvation ethic in the family home through affective means of character formation. However, domestic literature not only represented characters who achieved salvation through "spiritual training," the sentimental novel itself functioned as an "agent of discipline through love" (Brodhead 47). In the case of sentimental fiction, the author took on the role of the mother and the reader that of the child in "the domestic-tutelary complex" (Brodhead 43). The function of the sentimental author was that of the nurturing and instructive mother who cultivates the sympathy and feeling of the reader. "Like the mother's, the novel's intimacy is a tool for informing" the reader's mind and works to shape the structure of feeling proper to the middle-class (Brodhead 46). As mother-evangelists, the authors of sentimental fiction sought to produce the same conversionary, redemptive process in readers as that modeled in their narratives.

    Jane Tompkins incisively argued that the sentimental novel is "a political enterprise, halfway between sermon and social theory, that both codifies and attempts to mold the values of its time" (126). However, the precise nature of this political enterprise, the values it codified, and the manner of its molding require further clarification. It is clear that sentimental fiction was critical of capitalism and the pecuniary values it promoted. Davis and Phelps in particular have been applauded for writing some of the earliest works of American labor fiction that are generally regarded as being staunchly anti-capitalist. However, the reform strategies and proposed solutions to the problems of industrialization offered in sentimental fiction, and in the labor fiction of Davis and Phelps in particular, are supplied by the norms of sacralized middle-class domesticity. These authors did not advocate for fundamental systemic change but instead focused their attention on the moral and spiritual formation of individuals. When it came to economic matters, their interest was not in structural reform. Rather, their response to the problems of industrialization was drawn from the ethos of domesticity, which held that individuals must undergo a conversion of the heart before widespread cultural change can be achieved. They believed in the salvific power of affect and maintained that individuals must adopt the proper structure of feeling—the normative affects that they conflated with the "sympathies of Christ"—to remedy the ills of modern capitalism. Sentimental novelists and social reformers like Davis and Phelps contended that just feeling would give rise to a just society and in this way presented maternal affection and its focus on character formation as the means to the salvation of society. As Kenneth Warren has observed, a basic difference between literary realism and sentimentalism is that in realism, "the redemption of the individual lay within the social world," but in sentimental fiction, "the redemption of the social world lay with the individual" (75–76). Similarly, Nancy Cott explains that the domestic salvation ethic of the middle-class was founded on the view

> that individual moral qualities determined social gain or failure. Consequently, the only reliable means of initiating social progress appeared to be by strengthening individual character… In response to conditions of rapid change, people looked to individual initiative and to the resurrection of strength of character for their rescue.
>
> (96)

The cult of domesticity represented the separate sphere of the home as a moralizing influence that fostered sentiments that would leaven the exploitative degeneracy of the marketplace. Women were thought to be "naturally religious" and could therefore exert a corrective force on men and the fallen commercial world (Welter 153). By doing this, women worked "in cooperation with the Redeemer, bringing the world back 'from its revolt and sin' " (Welter 152). The mother in particular was regarded as a salvific agent of God whose influence could redeem the industrializing world through the affective formation of individuals. This was a role that was thought to be "hers by nature and divine decree" (Welter 174). However, the crucial distinction to be emphasized is that "the canon of domesticity did not directly challenge the modern organization of work and pursuit of wealth. Rather it accommodated and promised to temper them" (Cott 69). Davis and Phelps do not take an anti-capitalist position in their sentimental labor novels. Instead, they forward a form of middle-class maternalism or spiritual motherhood by projecting the ethos of maternal nurture outside of the home as a method of redeeming capitalism by accommodating rather than overcoming it.

Angels with Dirty Faces: The Religious Politics of Type

Davis and Phelps's stories about early industrialization are widely regarded to be among the first works of American literary realism. However, though they possess some of the nascent traits of realism, they are conventional works of sentimental fiction that do not exhibit the kind of radicalism that wishful contemporary critics have attempted to graft onto them.[9] It must be conceded that Davis writes the earliest American manifesto on realism in *Margret Howth*. Here, she promises to tell a "very crude and homely" story about the "plebeian" "dregs" of society whose "commonplace," "every-day drudgery" makes up "this vulgar American life," and criticizes the unrealistic, one-dimensional characters found in romantic literature (MH 6). But Davis fails to make good on these promises. *Margret Howth* is composed of long-established sentimental character types and plot conventions. Far from being a tale of the "crowded, tobacco-stained" working-class in "warehouses or back-streets," it is instead the story of a down on her luck but "high-bred" woman who "learned conservatism in her cradle" and her relationship with a soon-to-be mill owner (MH 6, 71). The only depiction of actual labor in the novel is a few hours of bookkeeping in Margret's quiet, personal office. There are undoubtedly aspects of burgeoning realism in Davis and Phelps's industrial fiction, but, more importantly, these texts contain all the defining attributes of sentimentalism. Like other contributors to the

---

[9] A rigorous examination of the complex and nuanced relation of realism and sentimentalism in the entirety of Davis's and Phelps's respective corpuses is beyond the scope of this chapter, which is limited to their labor fiction alone. For works that focus on this topic, see Harris (1991) on Davis's "metarealism," 19, Moody on her "sentimental realism," 43–106, and Pfaelzer.

canon of domesticity, Davis and Phelps are doing cultural work on behalf of the middle-class. They are not champions of working-class liberation, class struggle, or the creation of a classless society. The kind of reform they endorse assists in the formation and dominance of the middle-class.

All of the defining traits of sentimental literature are readily observable in Davis's *Life in the Iron-Mills*, *Margret Howth*, and Phelps's *The Silent Partner*, such as: the death or disability of a parent that propels the plot, the figure of the child angel, focus on the limitations placed on women and obstacles to their autonomy, the development of virtue through a series of trials, mentorship, emphasis on piety and self-sacrifice, maudlin scenes meant to evoke feeling from the reader, marginalized people as objects of sympathy, and domestic bliss as the ultimate goal. Like the heroines in such quintessential examples of the genre as Susan Warner's *The Wide, Wide World* (1850) and Maria Susanna Cummins's *The Lamplighter* (1854), the protagonists of Davis and Phelps's sentimental labor novels are literally or figuratively orphaned. The loss of parental support thrusts them into the world and initiates a process of moral tutelage. In Davis's *Life in the Iron-Mills*, Deb is adopted by a surrogate mother, the Quaker, who guides her domestic and religious cultivation. In *Margret Howth*, her father's blindness forces Margret to enter the fallen world of industry to support her family. Similarly, Phelps's *The Silent Partner* features three main characters, Perley, Sip, and Catty, all of whom are orphans. Each novel also features two sentimental character-types: the benefactress and the benefited. In sentimental fiction, the mentor or benefactress functions as a savior figure, "feminized God," or "God-deputy" who provides the heroine with nurturing "moral guardianship"[10] (Kessler 29, 27). Benefactresses are marginalized and disabled members of the working-class who teach the protagonists how to "*feel right*." In *Margret Howth*, Lois Yare mentors the titular character, and in *The Silent Partner*, it is Sip and Catty Garth who guide the moral *bildung* of Perley Kelso. Davis and Phelps's emphasis on character development and the inculcation of affective norms rather than on systemic change[11] reveal their allegiance to middle-class domestic ideology.[12] Despite Davis's pledge to write a gritty realist novel on the working-

---

[10] See also Kelly, 32, Kessler, 46.
[11] In her prefatory "Note" to *The Silent Partner*, Phelps makes clear that the novel is intended to critique the lack of Christian feeling in the "conduct of manufacturing corporations." It is not an indictment of industrial capitalism writ large. Phelps is careful to acknowledge those "intelligent" manufacturers who have "expended much Christian ingenuity, with much remarkable success, in ameliorating the condition of factory operatives" (7).
[12] See also Harde, 144; Lang, "The Syntax of Class in Elizabeth Stuart Phelps's *The Silent Partner*."

class, *Margret Howth* is a conventional work of sentimentalism that predictably ends with Margret engaged and in a state of domestic bliss. Perley and Sip's refusal of marriage proposals in *The Silent Partner* seems to subvert the norms of domesticity; however, these acts of self-sacrifice are performed so the women can transcend the home and become spiritual mothers who nurture the moral development of the working- and upper-classes. Rather than undermining domesticity, Phelps envisions the projection of middle-class maternalism into the public sphere as a means to reform and accommodate industrial capitalism.

One of the most typical features of sentimental fiction is the figure of the angel in the home. Claudia Stokes describes the angel in the home as "a devout female believer whose unwavering piety and altruism render her faultless and even incapable of sin... these women constitute the apotheosis of female piety in sentimental literature, whose example serves as a source of inspiration for the novels' heroines and presumably for the reader is well" (52). Their innocence and perfect religious devotion allows them to "commune so fully with the divine that he or she becomes a kind of mystic filled with boundless love who intuitively knows the divine will and automatically performs the work of the deity" (Stokes 53). Her intuitive connection to God's will makes her a kind of "divine presence on Earth" and her selfless devotion to the care of others cause her to be a "source of religious influence" on other characters (Stokes 173, 54).

Margret Howth's Lois Yare is a character straight out of sentimentalist central casting. She is mentally and physically disabled as a consequence of conditions in the mill where she worked as a child. She is comparable in many respects to little Eva in *Uncle Tom's Cabin*, a child-like angel in the home who possesses a saintly innocence, purity, and altruistic piety, who intuitively communes with the divine, and whose influence brings about the redemption of other characters in the novel. Lois is described as being, at once, a child and a motherly figure who is beloved by all.

Lois is inherently in tune with God and can therefore directly commune with His presence. We read that "her soul, being lower, it might be, than ours, lay closer to Nature" (65). To Lois, God was not simply an idea or object of faith but a self-evident truth that she could readily experience first-hand. Davis writes, "the owner of the mill was not a more real verity to this girl than the Master" (67). Despite "her marred senses," Lois is endowed with a special insight that enables her to see the "other light," "God's light," which reveals the divinity of all things, the immanent unity of heaven and earth, where the holy and the worldly are collapsed into a harmonic totality (100, 91). She saw divine truths that "her eyes were quicker to see than ours," particularly "in the homeliest things" (92).

We read that she "caught faint glimpses" of the sacred in "the fetid dens" and "the deepest mires of body where a soul could wallow" (91). Lois sees God "in everything that lived" and intuitively feels that all things, down to "the very worm in the gutter" are a part of God (95). "She saw the world [as] divine" (94). Lois's prophetic intuition makes her knowledgeable of God's will and thus a source of divine truth, as she is able to perceive "the message of God to man" that goes "unheeded by others" (100). Her holy insight into the sanctity of the wretched poor and her feelings' accord with the "sympathies of Christ" are evinced by an affective, sentimental response from Lois. We read, "she cried sometimes, looking at them" (92).

Lois precisely matches Stokes's description of the angel in the home as a "saintly domestic savior" whose tireless care for others makes her "a potent Christian missionary" (173). As an exemplar of domestic virtue and through a process of affective suasion, Lois brings about the redemption of the novel's main characters. In keeping with sentimentalism's *bildung* trope, *Margret Howth* features a highborn titular heroine who is forced by her father's disability and the family's resultant financial collapse out of her preindustrial, Edenic home and into the fallen world of industrial labor. In the course of overcoming a series of trials that often recall—sometimes overtly—Bunyan's *The Pilgrim's Progress*, Margret cultivates her morality and ultimately obtains salvation by adhering to a set of affective and behavioral norms. When the reader is first introduced to Margret, she is in the depths of despair over her family's decline and the bleak future of toil and poverty that lie ahead. After reading from scripture, Margret begins to experience a crisis of faith. We read, "she remembered a time when… she believed more in a God than she did now. When… He of whom she read to-night stood close… Now… the world was gray and silent… Christ was a dim ideal power, heaven far-off" (51–52). It is at this moment, which Davis suggests is an act of providence, that Lois Yare enters the scene. What follows is the first stage in the process of Margret's conversion, which is guided by Lois's maternal, religious mentorship. Immediately, if inexplicably, Margret is emotionally drawn to Lois. We read, "some strange sympathy drew her to this poor wretch, dwarfed, alone in the world,—some tie of equality, which the odd childish face… did not lessen" (63). On her long walk to work, Margret accompanies Lois, who trades with working people from her cart along the way. Margret initially resists the transformative affects that this series of interactions stir in her and renounces any responsibility for the conditions of the working-class. Davis writes, "What did she have to do with this gulf of pain and wrong?… was she to blame?… Her Virginian blood was cool, high-bred… So she put aside whatever social mystery or wrong faced her in this girl, just as you or I would've done... Was she her brother's keeper?" (71–72). In the course of their journey, Margret witnesses Lois's power to bestow grace on others and to lift their spirits with love and affection. "Some subtle power lay in the course, distorted body, in the pleading child's face, to rouse, wherever they went, the same curious, kindly smile" (76–77). The workers' reactions are not born of pity but rather from Lois's "faith in God, faith in her fellow-man, faith in herself. No human soul refused to answer its summons. Down in the dark alleys, in the very vilest of the... wretches that crowded... about her cart... Something in them struggled up to meet the trust in the pitiful eyes... some Christ-like power in their souls, smothered, dying, under the filth of their life" (77). Yet, Lois's motherly aura transcended class. Regardless of one's station, "nobody could help being kind to Lois" (54). Just as Lois's maternal, domestic love arouses that which is "Christ-like" in the working-class but has been repressed, "smothered" by the conditions of their work and lives, Margret too leaves Lois with "a different heart" (78). We read, "Margret... waked reluctantly to the sense of a different pain in the world from her own,— lower deeps from which women like herself draw delicately back, lifting their gauzy dresses" (70–71). Through this experience and the relationship that grows between them, Lois awakens Margret to the suffering of the working-class, to "a different pain... from her own." Subsequently, with an urgency born of her newly acquired sympathy, Margret becomes keen to help others. We read, "there was not a pain nor a want... that did not touch her sharply... with a keen pity, a wild wish to help to do something to save others" (88–89). She then acts on this desire by serving the poor at a benevolent institution called the House of Refuge. As a result of the affective conversion caused by Lois. Margret is redeemed, reconciled with God, and poised to further Lois's evangelical work. Davis writes, "Something of Lois's live, universal sympathy has come into her narrow, intenser nature; through its one love... the Helper yet waits near her" (266).

The death of the child angel is a vital part of their purpose as an evangelical device and was a defining feature of this popular character type in nineteenth-century fiction and devotional literature. Jane Tompkins explains that, "when the spiritual power of death is combined with the natural sanctity of childhood, the child becomes an angel endowed with salvific force" (129). In *Margret Howth*, written just ten years after *Uncle Tom's Cabin*, Lois Yare is cut from the same typological cloth as Stowe's little Eva. Lois's act of self-sacrifice and subsequent death, like that of Eva's, "enacts... the idea, central to Christian soteriology, that the highest human calling is to give one's life for another. It presents one version of the ethic of sacrifice on which the entire novel is based" (Tompkins

128). Stowe adapted this trope from one used in an evangelical sermon, "The Child Angel," by Dwight Lyman Moody. The dying child is an instrument of salvation for others: "in death she acquires a spiritual power... to redeem the unregenerate" (Tompkins 128). This highly conventional and popular trope was part of "a pervasive cultural myth which invests the suffering and death of an innocent victim with... the power to" initiate "a process of redemption whose power, transmitted from heart to heart, can change the entire world" (Tompkins 130, 131). Lois, and the angel in the home generally, is a Christ figure of perfect virtue, love, and innocence who serves as a moral exemplar for others and whose victimization and death brings about the salvation of others. In the canon of sentimentalism and the cult of domesticity, however, the Christ figure is a model of feminine, motherly love whose self-sacrifice takes place in the home. Moreover, Davis depicts Lois's ascent to heaven as a homecoming, where she is greeted by "the great mother" who "was glad to receive the form that want and crime of men had thwarted,—took her uncouth child home again, that had been so cruelly wronged,—folded it in her warm bosom with tender, palpitating love" (263). Here God, heaven, and salvation are figured in the idiom of domesticity. Those who employed this device believed that the child's self-sacrifice would not only lead to the salvation of other characters but could trigger an affective chain reaction that would cause mass conversion among their readership.

Sharon Harris has acknowledged that "Lois's death echoes little Eva's, acting as what Jane Tomkins has termed the epitome of Christian soteriology," but argues for "a significant distinction: Eva's self-sacrifice is redemptive for others, but there is no redemptive aspect to Lois's death" (*American* 67). However, the text does not support this claim. As she does with Margret, Lois brings about the redemption of Stephen Holmes.[13] We recall that the authors of domestic literature did not oppose capitalism outright; instead, they argued that domestic values could nurture sentiments that would mitigate the immoral behaviors learned in the marketplace, such as selfishness. Holmes's relationship with Lois exemplifies their belief that salvation is achieved through character formation or "spiritual training." Initially, Holmes embodies the masculine, romantic, self-oriented salvation ethic of industrial capitalism. For Holmes, "his work in the world was only the development of himself" (120). His chief aim was "to lift this self up into a higher range of being... Self-salvation, self-elevation,—the ideas," the narrator interjects, "that... destroy half of our Christianity!" (121). Whereas Lois sees "the world [as] divine" and God "in everything that lived," Holmes

[13] See also Yellin, 282–3, 286, Rose, 26, 30.

only sees "divinity within" the self (94, 95, 113). We read that "he was deaf... to any word of kindness or pity" and asserts, "There is no such thing as love in real life" (138, 143). However, after Lois commits an act of self-sacrifice by rescuing Holmes from a burning mill, which ultimately leads to her death, he undergoes a conversion experience and begins to regard his recent past as a "false life" (194). As she selflessly oversees his convalescence, Holmes's love for Lois warms his cold heart and leads him to renounce his individualism in favor of the love of Christ. He is drawn "out of his self-reliance by the hand of the child that loved him to the Love beyond, that was man and died for him, as well as she" (212). Though figured as a child, the angel in the home simultaneously assumes the role of a surrogate mother who nurtures the moral development of others. Stokes explains that a defining feature of sentimental literature was "the veneration of motherhood, which perceived angelic virtues in motherly sacrifice... Within this figuration, the devout, selfless mother functions as the paragon of sentimental femininity, whose example and moral tutelage enable the sentimental formation and consequent salvation of her loved ones" (173). Following Lois's example, Holmes relinquishes his former individualism and is redeemed by the kind of selfless love and recognition of mutual interdependence with others that is found in the family home. The pitiless man who had previously denied its existence was now filled with "love and warmth" (201). We read that Holmes went to see Lois with "his heart, full of a yearning pity for the poor cripple, who... had given her own life for his" (206). Through her nurturing friendship, motherly love, and selflessness, Lois guides the "sentimental formation and consequent salvation" of Margret and Holmes, who are shaken from their egoism and overriding self-concern and converted to the domestic ethos of self-sacrifice.[14]

Phelps's Catty Garth is also an example of the child angel character-type. Like Lois, Catty is an innocent, disabled orphan child whose influence causes the moral and affective development of others. Jaime Osterman Alves has shown that it is Catty who prompts Sip's religious awakening and her decision to become a preacher. Catty possesses the kind of intuitive religious feeling and communion with God that is typical of the angel in the home. Alves observes that "Catty displays a unique understanding and intelligence that Phelps clearly values for its ability to catalyze in Sip a personal relationship to, and emulation of, Christ" (139). Sip's captivation by the image of the crucifixion after her conversation with Catty and the image of the cross over the bridge after Catty's death invite the

---

[14] On the canon of domesticity's prescription of self-sacrifice as the means for women to remedy men's market-driven self-interest, see Cott 71.

reader to connect Catty to Jesus. In the novel, we read, "On the empty ruin of the sliced bridge, two logs had caught and hung, black against the color of the water and the color of the sky. They had caught transversely, and hung like a cross" (SP 278). Further, Alves has shown that Catty is the vehicle of Phelps's middle-class maternalism and her contention that cultivating "true Christian feeling toward one's fellow man will nurture moral change from the inside, obviating the need for" systemic social change (Alves 147). Though she is mute, Catty convinces Sip to relinquish her "righteous anger about workers' exploitation" and to accept "the inevitability of the factory system" (Alves 147). By identifying Catty with Christ and investing her with knowledge of God's will, Phelps sacralizes the middle-class desire to conserve capitalism and class hierarchy. Alves astutely argues, "Phelps does not ask readers to envision a world without capitalism or to abolish the factory system entirely. Instead, she imagines a way around the abuses of that system, in which Christian love between the owning and working classes softens the conditions and difficulties of poverty" (147). By adopting the proper structure of feeling and by accepting industrial capitalism and class inequality, Phelps suggests, one conforms to the will and likeness of God. In this way, Phelps uses the well-established sentimental figure of the child angel to conflate the path to salvation with the economic interests of the middle-class.

Conserving Distinction: Apotheosis and Class Formation

Davis and Phelps's sentimentalism is predicated on establishing and maintaining boundaries between the classes, not on dismantling them. Like other sentimentalists, they forwarded a moralistic protest against the conditions of industrial capitalism but they had no interest in eliminating class difference or economic and social inequality. As a function of its formation, the middle-class had to differentiate itself from the upper and lower classes and to demonstrate its superiority to them. It accomplished this through affective and religious means. In terms of affect, this was achieved by presenting new economic structures and class relations as structures of feeling.[15] Through apotheosis and the sacralization of domesticity, the middle-class further legitimated itself and its new position as cultural hegemon. The seemingly anti-capitalist maternalism that Davis and Phelps forward as an antidote to the ills of industrialism, and more broadly, the sentimental literature and theology that it issues from, is a product of middle-

---

[15] See also Alves, Brodhead, and Merish.

class formation. In keeping with the conventions of domesticity, their aim is not to defeat capitalism or eliminate class difference but to accommodate them.

Durkheim argued that "society is possible only if the individuals and things that compose it are distributed into different groups, that is, classes, and if these groups themselves are classified in relation to each other" (339). From this perspective, social life, and in particular religious life is largely a matter of continual boundary maintenance. Antonio Gramsci recognized that a class achieves "self-conscious awareness of itself as a class [by] distinguishing that class from competing social groups—as well as by representing its specific interests as 'natural' and necessary" (Merish 14). Put another way, apotheosis—the conversion of culture into nature—is an integral feature of class formation, as is establishing boundaries between completing classes. By sacralizing domesticity, sentimental literature codified the superiority of the middle-class over the working- and upper-classes, which were depicted as lacking moral and spiritual development. The apotheosis of domesticity through the sentimental culture industry was instrumental in establishing the authority and legitimacy of middle-class mores. Stuart Blumin has found that "middling families... perceived their homes and their domestic strategies to be distinct from those of manual workers, as well as from those of the fashionables who did not even aspire to the domestic ideal" (190–191). The middle-class regarded their domestic values and practices as that which set them "apart from both the rough world of the mechanics and the artificial world of fashion" (Blumin 188). Merish explains that sentimental fiction was a primary mechanism by which "the middle class family established boundaries between itself and other classes" (13). This work of sacralization and differentiation "suggests the cultural import of domestic fictions in mobilizing forms of class identification" (Merish 331–332n16).

Though they authored some of the earliest depictions of working-class life, Rebecca Harding Davis and Elizabeth Stuart Phelps were exemplars of the nation's new middle-class. In her youth, Davis's family gained entrance to Wheeling's middle-class; later, she lived the vast majority of her life "among the most elite circles of Philadelphia society where she developed friendships with US presidents and international figures" (*Life* 1). Davis's harrowing and initially anonymous descriptions of poverty and industrial labor make it easy to mistake her for a member of the working-class. In her diary, Louisa May Alcott remarks on the incongruity of Davis's fiction and personal experience, writing that Davis "says she never had any troubles, though she writes of woes. I told her I had lots of troubles; so I write jolly tales" (131). Despite her early focus on economic privation, Davis enjoyed a life of "comfort and security" (Rose 5). However, even as her family ascended to the highest echelons of society, Davis continued to privilege middle-class domestic values and considered homemaking and child-rearing to be her first priority. Tellingly, her son Charles Belmont Davis recalled that the family thought of their longtime home in Philadelphia as the "Centre of the Universe" (1). As a result of putting such emphasis on nurturing and cultivating her children, the Davises would come to be regarded as one of the nation's most distinguished families. Similarly, Phelps was securely middle-class and brought up in a highly respected New England family that traced its lineage to early colonists. The consensus among the foremost scholars of her work is that Phelps remained so "deeply entrenched in her middle-class mindset" that she was incapable of seeing beyond it[16] (Privett 64).

In their labor fiction, Davis and Phelps express their decidedly middle-class perspective by differentiating their values from those of both the upper- and working-classes in numerous ways. For example, both the narrator and reader of Davis's *Life in the Iron-Mills* are assumed to be middle-class. While the narrator is critical of the pitilessness and cold detachment of the upper-class characters who tour the mill and look upon its workers as scarcely human, her description of the degraded homes and inner lives of the working-class characters indicate that she too regards them as subhuman. Davis contends that the other classes are fundamentally deficient; whereas the upper-class lacks sympathy and pity, the working-class lacks respectable manners and behavior. *Life in the Iron-Mills* is a masterfully executed critique of industrial exploitation that interrogates the concept of criminality under capitalism, asking in effect, who is the true thief, one who steals a dollar or one who steals a million? However, despite the lamentable conditions outside of his control, and the unjust sentence he is given, Davis regards Hugh as fallen, as having sinned. Davis insists that though Hugh's plight is pitiable, direct action taken against the upper-class to reappropriate capital by force is not the solution. Hugh is no hero, no martyr for a cause. Hugh is a tragic figure in part because he is a good person that has done something the reader is to regard as foolish. In Davis's labor fiction, the working-class are noble, but they are still savages. Davis signals to her reader that authentic Christian morals and sympathies are solely possessed by the middle-class, those between the callous and dissipated rich and the wretched poor.

In *The Silent Partner*, Phelps's effort to emphasize and strengthen the boundaries between the classes is most evident when Perley Kelso organizes a party to bring the upper- and working-class together. The ostensible purpose

---

[16] See also Bennett, 58, Harde, 141, Kessler, 28.

of the party is to work toward reconciling capital and labor, but both the reader and the attendees leave the event with a revived certainty that class difference is insurmountable. The gathering is a narrative conceit that gives Phelps an occasion to show that both the haughty, overly refined, and insensitive upper-class and the uncultivated laboring-class lack the moral and spiritual development of the middle-class. Through Perley and the narrator, Phelps criticizes the deficiencies of the other classes and upholds the defining attributes of the middle-class as the remedy for the ills of industrial capitalism.[17] Throughout the novel, Perley remains estranged from the other classes. Her newly acquired class-consciousness alienates Perley from her former peers in high society. We read that her benevolent social work on behalf of the poor has caused Perley to be "dead and buried... as far as Society is concerned" (236). They are scandalized by her violation of the norm prohibiting social miscegenation. One of her wealthy guests remarks, "I am told that this superb house has been more like a hospital or a set of public soup-rooms for six months past, than it has like the retiring and secluded home of a young lady. Those people over run it. They are made welcome to it at all hours and under all circumstances. She invites them to tea, my dear! They sit down at her very table with her" (236). Perley's model of pious domesticity demonstrates that the middle-class's fidelity to Christian feeling distinguishes it from the other classes. However, though she welcomes them at her table, worships alongside them in the millhands' church, and takes action on their behalf, Perley remains decidedly separate from the working-class, draped in a mantle of saintly regality. The workers revere Perley as a maternal, Christ-like savior figure or domestic saint. Sip bears witness to Perley's work of redemptive nurture, insisting that

> There's those of us here, young girls of us... that she has saved from being what you would n't see in here to-night. There's little children here that would be little devils, unless it was for her. There's men of us with rum to fight, and boys in prison, and debts to pay, and hearts like hell, and never a friend in this world or the other but her... God bless her, and the ground she treads on, and the air she breathes, and the sky that is over her, and the friends that love her, and the walls of her grand house, and every dollar of her money.
>
> (238–9)

Perley functions as an idealized embodiment of the traits that distinguish the middle-class from competing social ranks. Just as a mother remains inherently

---

[17] See also Schrager, 279.

distinct from her children by virtue of her moral authority, and yet wholly invested in guiding the development of their character, Perley—that is, the middle-class—can nurture the other classes and help them to cultivate the feelings they lack, even as she remains morally and spiritually superior to them. By developing the proper structure of feeling, Phelps suggests, Perley's "grand house, and every dollar of her money" have been sanctified.

The way Perley handles the near-strike at her mill provides further evidence of Phelps's desire to conserve existent power relations between the classes. Amid financial trouble, the owners of the Hayle and Kelso mill decide to reduce the hands' wages. Learning this, the workers begin to plan a strike that could destroy the company. Perley urges Garrick to explain to the workers why the reduction is necessary, a step that the other mill owners had never taken in the past and thought absurd now. Garrick speaks to the crowd that has formed outside the gates of the mill but to no avail; they want to hear from Perley. Phelps describes the figure Perley cuts in language reminiscent of the biblical Transfiguration. She exudes a saintly or messianic aura. We read that, as "she stood in the mud and the rain... there seem to be a shining to her" (251). But rather than express her solidarity with the workers, she admonishes them for their lack of trust in the management. Sip recounts, "Then she blazed out at us!" (252). Perley scolds the millhands like so many petulant and naïve children. Sincerely ashamed, they accept the reduction in wages and slink back home, averting the strike. Perley echoes Maverick's contention that the workers are ignorant and untrustworthy children, that there is no "gratitude... among them. There's neither trust nor honor" (247). However, Phelps trades androcentric paternalism for domestic maternalism. Here, members of the working-class are depicted as children needing the guidance and nurture of a Christian mother. This important scene evinces the political tepidity of what has been falsely regarded as an anti-capitalist novel. Bennett has astutely argued that Phelps's representation of the owners is too generous. By representing the owners' problems "with as much understanding as those of their employees," Phelps diminishes her critique (63). "A successful propaganda novel is uncompromising, right being opposed to wrong" (Bennett 63). In *The Silent Partner*, on the other hand, Phelps tries to show "the right on each side" of the struggle, and in doing so reveals her disinterest in authentic economic justice (Bennett 63). Schrager maintains that this scene "is not, in the last analysis, about the strike at all but rather about the spiritual power to restore harmony invested in the true woman" (282). That is, Phelps endows the figure of the middle-class mother with the sanctified power and duty to reproduce harmony among unequal classes, thus conserving hierarchy.

Similarly, in Sip's sermon, Phelps ends the novel by presenting a middle-class salvation ethic in the guise of a proletarian doctrine of redemption that discourages class struggle and direct action.[18] Privett writes, "In a move bound to please the middle-class, peace-loving audience, Sip preaches *against* revolutionary responses to the social inequities" (100). Sip acknowledges that class interest shapes theology and assures her audience of workers that "It ain't a rich folks' religion that I've brought to talk to you. Rich religion ain't for you and ain't for me. We're poor folks, and we want a poor folks' religion or not at all... Now listen to me!... The religion of Jesus Christ the Son of God Almighty is the only poor folks' religion in all the world" (296). As is typical of proletarian Christology, Sip claims that Jesus was working-class: "this is what he says, '*I* was up, and down, and drove, and slaved, and hurried, myself,' he says, 'I was too hot, and too cold, and worried, and anxious, and *I* saw rich folks take their ease, and *I* was poor like you" (297–8). She also promotes a theodical response to economic injustice, as is often found in theologies of disprivilege. "You shake your head and you say, 'Capital has all the ease, Lord, and labor has all the rubs; and things ain't as they should be' " (297). However, Sip insists that despite this, workers must leave the judgment and punishment of the wicked to God in the hereafter, as He "knows where the fault is... and who's to blame, and who's to suffer" (298). Instead, members of the working-class should focus on themselves, on refining their own character, rather than trying to alter the structure of society. The solution to the problems of industrialization is not collective action but individual, affective self-transformation. Sip claims, "there 'll never be any way but his way to unsnarl us all... there's no way under heaven for us to get out of our twist, but Christ's way... That way is in the heart" (299). The way to reform capitalism and indeed the very pathway to salvation, Phelps argues, "is in the heart." While she purports to be preaching "poor folks' religion," Sip promotes the central doctrines of middle-class sentimental theology. She encourages her audience to have faith in the salvific power of affect, and assures them that, if they undertake a conversion of the heart and adopt the proper structure of feeling, then they can reform or "unsnarl" industrial capitalism from within. Phelps's principal figures of maternal nurture, Perley and Sip, both discourage efforts to directly combat inequality and instead espouse the cultivation of sentiments among members of the upper- and working-class as the way "to get out of our twist."

The middle-class primarily differentiated itself through the ethos of domesticity. The middle-class model of womanhood promulgated in sentimental print culture, in novels and such publications as *Godey's Lady's*

---

[18] See also Schrager, 283.

Book "eschewed the aristocratic lady of the federal period and celebrated instead the wholesome American woman who dedicated herself to the prosaic service of her family" (Ryan, *Womanhood* 76). The upper-class thrived on exclusivity and renounced the duties of housework and the care for children, which they delegated to servants. Lydia Maria Child writes in her *Letters from New York*, "of those duties which are feminine by universal consent, few are considered genteel by the upper classes. It is not genteel for mothers to wash and dress their own children, or make their clothing, or teach them, or romp with them in the open air" (280–1). Just as the middle-class distinguished themselves from the elite on the basis of the latter's refusal of homemaking and childrearing duties, Davis and Phelps express their distinction through working-class characters' failure to comply with domestic norms. This is evinced in the representation of the parenting practices and squalid homes of Welsh workers in *Life in the Iron-Mills* and by the emblematic Mell family in *The Silent Partner*.

Despite Phelps's desire to improve their lives, she represented working-class characters in an unflattering, if realistic, manner while idealizing heroines who "assumed an inherently superior attitude for the middle class toward the laboring class" (Privett 64). Like other sentimentalists, Phelps "did not question the social and economic structures that encouraged inequality" (Kessler 50–51). Instead, she depoliticized class relations by translating economic difference into affective difference (Poovey 9). While lamenting the impoverishment of industrial workers, Davis and Phelps define middle-class distinction on the basis of feeling, not money. Davis's Stephen Holmes and Margret Howth, and Phelps's Perley Kelso initially lack the proper sentiments. Their progressive salvation over the course of the narrative is achieved through the acquisition of right feeling. They achieve class-consciousness, but their redemption[19] and moral superiority over the other classes is a consequence of how they feel and relate to others, not of their commitment to altering the economic structures of society. Ultimately, Perley is transformed from someone who was "not used … to feeling at all" into a saintly savior figure whose conversion is a function of sympathy (39). Phelps writes,

> Wherever people were cold, hungry, friendless, desolate, in danger, in despair, she struck across his path. Wherever there was a soul for which no man cared, he found her footprints. Wherever there was a life to be lifted from miasmas to heights, he saw the waving of her confident white hand. If ever there were earnest

---

[19] Lang writes that Perley's redemption, in keeping with middle-class, sentimental soteriology, is "the raison d'être of the novel" (284). The same can be said about Davis's Margret and Holmes.

work, solemn work, solitary work, mistrusted work, work misunderstood, neglected, discouraging, hopeless, thankless,—Christ's work, to be done, he faced her... The woman's life had become a service in a temple.

(255-6)

Perley's work—Christ's work—is a matter of providing benevolent care and compassion to the working-class, not higher wages. Though Phelps wants her middle-class readers to experience a conversion of the heart, she reassuringly shows them that the new structure of feeling conserves and further strengthens class hierarchy.

Similarly, Davis's strategic use of the katabasis mytheme allowed her both to provoke sympathy from her readers and to endorse a social ontology that essentialized class difference, thereby advancing middle-class formation. In both of her labor texts, Davis employs the device of direct address, in which the narrator invites the reader to accompany her on a descent that mimics the journeys of epic, pagan heroes into the underworld, and later, in the Christianized versions of Dante and Milton, into hell. In each work, the narrator identifies herself and her assumed reader as middle-class. For example, when Margret Howth is confronted with the reality of extreme class inequality we read that she initially "put aside [this] social mystery *just as you or I would've done*" (71-72, emphasis added). When the narrator says to the reader, "you and I," she assumes a shared middling rank that looks down on the working-class and eschews interest in the cause of economic injustice.[20] Davis and her narrator take for granted that the reader's first reaction to the truth of working-class life will be one of revulsion, and that their impulse will be to "draw delicately back, lifting their gauzy dresses" (MH 71). Davis's labor novels call upon the reader to bear witness to the conditions of the working-class. However, the very exercise and necessity of this presupposes the readers' at least middling station and ignorance of working-class experience. This is clearly indicated in *Life in the Iron Mills* where we read, "This is what I want you to do. I want you to hide your disgust, take no heed of your clean clothes, and come right down with me,—here, into the thickest of the fog and mud and foul effluvia. [...] I want you to come down and look" (13, 25). Similarly, the narrator of *Margret Howth* entreats the reader, "I want you to go down

---

[20] Phelps uses the same tactic in *The Silent Partner*, where she also identifies clothing as a cultural signifier of class difference. Phelps speaks directly to the middle-class reader and writes that Sip's words, like Lois's, are calculated to awaken Christian feeling in them: "Here on the parlor sofa, in clean cuffs and your slippers, she harangues you" (SP 295).

into this common, every-day drudgery" (6–7). The narrator and reader must descend to be among the working-class. This emphasizes the essential nature of class difference—as the working-class dwell in a different world—and the moral superiority of the middle-class, as they must lower themselves to enter the realm of the damned.

Knowles plays the part of Virgil when he guides Margret Howth into the den of the underclass. He tells her, "I want to show you a bit of hell [...] only a glimpse of the under-life of America" (149, 152). He describes her religious duty to nurture the poor in the same katabatic language: "There is a cry going up... for help,—and no man listens... [God] calls you. He waits for your answer. Swear to me that you will help His people... go down as Christ did. Help me to give... Jesus' love to these wretches on the brink of hell. Live with them, raise them with you... It is your work" (155). When middle-class Americans "go down" among the poor for the purpose of reshaping their character, Davis indicates, they are mimicking the behavior of Jesus Christ. This is the apotheosis of middle-class benevolence—Davis invests middle-class mores with divinity and suggests that conformity to them will guarantee salvation.

Davis's hellish imagery is not simply meant to signify the suffering of the working-class, but their damnation and inherent depravity. In *Life in the Iron Mills* one of the wealthy visitors remarks to the mill owner's son, "your works look like Dante's Inferno... Judging from some of the faces of your men... they bid fair to try the reality of Dante's vision, some day" (27). In the original, serialized version of *Margret Howth*, Lois also uses katabatic language to describe the mill and the middle-class's view of workers: "Openin's to hell, they're like. People as come down to preach in them think that, 'pears to me,—"n" think we've but a little way to go, bein' born so near. It's easy to tell they thinks it,—shows in their looks" (Renfroe). In the novel version, it is the "alleys 'n' dark holes" where the poor are depicted as residing that are "like th' openin's to hell" (70). For Davis, the poor live in "Gehenna," a term used in rabbinic literature to describe the place where the wicked are punished and, in the Christian gospels, the place where the damned are sent to suffer in "unquenchable fire" (MH 70, Mark 9:43). When Davis figures the middle-class home as heaven—as she does in *Margret Howth*—and the factory and dwelling places of the poor as hell, and when she depicts the middle-class as virtuous and redeemed and workers as wicked and damned, she reinforces class difference and proclaims the salvific power of the middle-class structure of feeling.

As Merish has noted, "the conventional objects of sympathy in sentimental texts are socially marginalized and disempowered figures" such as the disabled, the poor, slaves, and criminals (23). In keeping with this tradition, Davis's objects of sympathy are abnormal figures who are excluded from the middle- and upper-class. Her working-class characters are grotesques; they are invariably deformed, disabled, and animalistic. Their humanity, she suggests, is deficient or incomplete. Not only do they exist on the margins of society, without power, they elicit disgust. Workers are described as vile, vulgar, slimy wretches. These are not people that Davis, her narrators, or her readers would regard as peers. A clear *us* and *them* distinction is inscribed into each text, differentiating the middle-class author and the reader from both their working-class objects of sympathy and their upper-class targets of criticism. Davis famously invokes the commonplace in her labor novels, but she does not count herself among its inhabitants; she does not regard herself or her reader as mere commoners. Instead, she portrays middle-class white women as spiritual mothers who are tasked with the religious imperative to redeem the working-class, and capitalist society writ large, by employing the tactics of domestic maternal nurture in the public sphere. By naturalizing class difference and depicting middle-class white women as maternal saviors, Davis and Phelps perform the work of middle-class formation. Their maternalism is a literary expression of sacralized domesticity. By sacralizing middle-class norms and depicting domesticity as the pathway to salvation, Davis and Phelps advance the formation of the middle-class and help to secure its cultural authority.

The Exalted Mother: Mid-Century Maternalism

In their labor novels, Davis and Phelps applied the middle-class theology of domesticity and its views on Christian nurture to the social problems caused by industrialism. In accord with the ethos of domesticity, which held that it was women's duty to act as the primary agents of salvation, these authors contended that mothers were charged with the spiritual formation of the nation just as the middle-class mother had been tasked with the moral formation of her children. As such, they sought to remedy the ills of industrialism by promoting the values and social roles prescribed by domesticity, not by advocating for systemic social reform. Therefore, Davis and Phelps worked, if inadvertently, to reproduce a social order that depended on unequal classes and gender roles.

Stowe well-exemplifies the ethos of maternalism in *The Minister's Wooing* (1859), where she writes that women are

> God's real priests... soul artists, who go through this world looking among their fellows with reverence, as one looks amid the dust and rubbish of old shops for hidden works of Titian and Leonardo, and, finding them, however cracked or torn or painted over with tawdry daubs of pretenders, immediately recognize the divine original, and set themselves to cleanse and restore.
>
> (131)

This is Davis and Phelps's approach to the poor and working-class. Sentimental writers, those women chosen to be the agents of God's will on earth and impelled by a soteriological calling, look on the commonplace "rubbish" of this world with pious sympathy and feel a duty—the duty of a white middle-class mother— to "set themselves to cleanse and restore" the working-class, to save them through maternal nurture. That is the true significance of Davis's invocation of the commonplace, to which she descends or stoops. It is the gesture of one who is willing to cross class boundaries but who has no interest in eliminating those boundaries. On the contrary, it is the crossing that makes the boundary more stable and secure.

The domestic "doctrine of women's influence" held that middle-class women wielded immense "but indirect power in society, as mediated through their relations to husbands, children, or brothers"[21] (Ryan, *Womanhood* 91–92). Middle-class women who had been newly endowed with religious authority during the Second Great Awakening were taught that they had the power to influence society through the affective formation of the family. Sentimental fiction endorsed the belief that women's influence was not limited to the home, but could "do considerable work in healing and perfecting the world" (Stokes 17). We recall that sentimentalists generally "embraced the growth of market culture" but believed that the values of domesticity had to be further reproduced to restrain the excessive individualism caused by capitalism[22] (Nelson 8). For example, as Jean Pfaelzer has ably shown, Davis's *Margret Howth* is a sustained sentimentalist attack on masculine, romantic individualism.[23] Davis and Phelps's maternalism exemplified the doctrine of women's influence by proposing that domestic affective norms, spread nationally, could moralize capitalism. They

---

[21] See also Ryan, *Cradle of the Middle Class*, 190.
[22] See also Ryan, *Womanhood in America*, 77.
[23] See Pfaelzer, *Parlor*, 54–75.

suggest that individualism and overriding self-interest arise from a lack of sympathy and failure to recognize mutual dependence. They forward sentimental maternalism as a method of cultivating feelings in the American populace that will restrain selfishness and promote social harmony. Davis and Phelps do not call for direct action, systemic change, or the abolition of class society. Instead, they maintain that the role of the social reformer is an extension of the role of the mother, who has the power to redeem American society one heart at a time.

Like other contributors to the canons of domesticity and sentimentalism, Phelps and Davis forward a discourse of interdependency that conserves economic inequality. As Amy Schrager Lang explains, sentimentalism's

> doctrine of the harmony of interests was expounded not only as economic theory but as spiritual principle. The consummate emblem of that harmony, bridging the economic and the spiritual, was the idealized middle-class home... Nowhere is this image more clearly drawn than in domestic fiction, where the problem of class is neither resolved nor repressed but rather displaced, and where harmony—spiritual, familial, and social—is the highest good.
>
> (Lang 129)

Through their sentimental maternalism, Davis and Phelps present a sacralized model of middle-class domestic harmony as the answer to class antagonism. They regard social harmony to be the felicitous organization and relation of unequal parties. Sentimentalists argue that by establishing the proper affective relations or structure of feeling between the classes, a moral and indeed sacred social harmony can be achieved in America—a nationwide social harmony that will replicate the domestic bliss of the middle-class home. Merish writes that

> sympathy [in sentimental literature] conventionally operates across a status divide: typical objects of sympathy in these narratives are children, slaves, the poor, the disabled; and in these sentimental narratives, it is the sympathy of the empowered for the disempowered, the "strong" for the "weak," the fully human for the dehumanized, that is enlisted as socially and ethically salient.
>
> (3)

Sentimental maternalists are not fighting for the emancipation of the poor, for economic equality, or for social equality, but for a kind of hierarchical interdependency modeled on domestic ideology. Just as the child is not equal to the parent, Davis and Phelps's objects of sympathy—the worker, the poor, the disabled, children—are not equal to the spiritual mother, who either appears as a character or a Virgilian narrator and who is more empowered socially and economically. In both Davis and Phelps, sympathy "operates across a status divide," but these authors do not call for the elimination of that divide. Instead, they endorse affective relations that support, reproduce, and mask existent industrial power relations.

Sentimental fiction legitimates and strengthens socioeconomic hierarchy by recasting interdependency as a sanctified affective relation, which masks the true relations of power it entails. The rhetoric of the harmony of interests was about conserving and further establishing boundaries between the classes in a new way, namely, by transforming class difference into a virtuous and necessary mode of emotional comportment that was said to be modeled on divine behavior. Elizabeth White Nelson explains that the sentimental structure of feeling "suggested the possibilities of mutuality, even as it insisted on the reestablishment of traditional hierarchies" (15). Because Davis and Phelps promoted "Christian community without erasing the hierarchy implicit in benevolence, the love of Christ could be extended without jeopardizing the social distinctions [between the classes] ... Readers could contemplate the ideal of social harmony without jeopardizing the social hierarchy" (Nelson 49–50). The affective imperatives that Davis and Phelps promoted through their sentimental maternalism were such that one could seemingly attain salvation without changing socioeconomic conditions in America. In their view, redemption is achievable through the restoration of social harmony. However, they maintain that social harmony is an outcome of right feeling, not systemic economic change.

3

The American Fetish: Religious Economics in the Novels of William Dean Howells

After having a profound conversion experience in 1887,[1] William Dean Howells vowed to renounce his former quietism and to begin writing about the injustices inherent to industrial capitalism. Like a prophet of the Gilded Age, he decried a national condition of mass idolatry, arguing that capitalism had been consecrated and established as the new, dominant American religion, superseding Christianity as the source of the sacred norms guiding Americans' thought and behavior. Over the next decade, he composed a series of "economic novels"—*Annie Kilburn* (1888), *A Hazard of New Fortunes* (1890), *The Quality of Mercy* (1891), *The World of Chance* (1893), and *A Traveler from Altruria* (1894)—in which he developed the most sophisticated literary critique of American capitalism to date (Taylor 103; Walsh 143). The social theory Howells advanced in these novels was consistent with recent trends in liberal Protestant theology. For example, his approach to reform was founded on the belief that sin is a function of social conditions rather than the essential depravity of human nature. Therefore, he argued that Americans must privilege collective, "social salvation" over the personal salvation of individuals. Perhaps most notably, Howells developed an insightful take on apotheosis aimed at demystifying how the attributes and aims of capitalism had been exalted and imbued with divine significance, effectively enshrining values that are antithetical to democracy.

---

[1] There has been a great deal of debate over the specific catalyst of Howells's conversion. Some argue that it was initiated by the events surrounding the Haymarket Riot (Parrish 1994; Kirk 1969), others contend that it began with his reading of Tolstoy (Budd 1950), while still others claim that it originated with his involvement in William Dwight Porter Bliss's Society of Christian Socialists (Kirk 1959). A thorough investigation into this question is beyond the scope of this chapter. Given what we know about Howells's upbringing, it is clear that Christian socialism had long been a part of his life. It is probable that a confluence of events and new influences combined with his early education and family history ultimately led to his conversion experience in the late 1880s. In any case, none of these factors was the sole constituent of Howells's mature theology and social theory. However, while we may not be able to say with certainty what initiated Howells's conversion, we can pinpoint the time that it began to occur.

Conversion and Complicity

By the late 1880s, Howells had established himself as one of the nation's most trusted gatekeepers of bourgeois culture. In the years following the Civil War, he was an unwavering defender of the economic system that had given him the opportunity to rise from the impoverished grandson of an immigrant printer to a wealthy and famous steward of high culture. In the early stage of his career, Howells became the de facto literary spokesman of the leisure class by distinguishing himself as a tastemaker, a critic of charity, and an invariable supporter of managerial interests in cases of labor conflict (Crider 410). Perhaps most famously, in September 1886, Howells denied the existence of social strife in Gilded Age America, writing,

> in a land where journeyman carpenters and plumbers strike for four dollars a day the sum of hunger and cold is certainly very small, and the wrong from class to class is inappreciable. We invite our novelists therefore to concern themselves with the more smiling aspects of life, which are the more American, and seek the universal in the individual rather than the social interests. It is worth while... to be true to our well to do actualities... The race here enjoys conditions in which most of the ills that have darkened the annals may be averted by honest work and unselfish behavior.
>
> (CF 128–9)

However, within just a year of expressing this sentiment Howells would undergo a radical conversion experience, transforming himself, to the dismay of friends and colleagues, from an apologist for free-market individualism to an outspoken Christian socialist. Howells, the Dean of American letters, who had recently advised American authors to focus their creative attentions on "the individual rather than the social interests" turned his own sights on social, ethical, and religious concerns; now he would write novels that satirized the "smiling aspects of life" to reveal the injustice and misery they concealed. Over the next ten years, he produced a series of novels that urged readers to regard "Christianity as a system of economics as well as a religion," and to see that capitalism had displaced Christianity as Americans' dominant confession of faith (HNF 277). In these books, he contends that authentic Christianity necessarily entails socialism, and that capitalism is an idolatrous faith predicated on values wholly at odds with America's democratic ideals.

This dramatic shift in political allegiance was an enormous risk for Howells, professionally and personally, one that scandalized his Brahmin peers. He weathered the initial storm and by the end of the nineteenth century was America's most widely read advocate for Christian socialism. However, it would be hyperbolic to call Howells a radical. Timothy Parrish argues that Howells was the "most politically radical writer"[2] of his generation, and he is right if we parse this claim a bit (25). Howells's writing in the decade following 1887 was radical, critically incisive, and immensely provocative but he did not live the life of a radical. Ultimately, Howells was a champagne socialist who failed to bring his lifestyle into conformity with his conscience. For the compulsively self-conscious Howells, this was a source of shame and depression. In a letter of January 15, 1888, to Hamlin Garland, Howells writes, "I am reading and thinking about questions that carry me beyond myself and my miserable literary idolatries of the past; perhaps you'll find that I've been writing about them. I am still the slave of selfishness, but I am no longer content to be so. That's as far as I can honestly say I've got" (*Letters* I, 407–408). Nine months later, though his disillusionment with America's capitalist culture continued apace, he despaired over having gotten no further in altering his personal practice. On October 10, 1888, he writes to Henry James:

> I am not in a very good humor with "America" myself. It seems to be the most grotesquely illogical thing under the sun... I should hardly like to trust pen and ink with all the audacity of my social ideas; but after fifty years of optimistic content with "civilization" and its ability to come out alright in the end, I now abhor it, and feel that it is coming out all wrong in the end unless it bases itself on a new equality. Meanwhile, I wear a fur-lined overcoat and live in all the luxury money could buy.
>
> (*Letters* I, 417)

Similarly, two weeks later he writes to Edward Everett Hale, "I am neither an example nor an incentive, meanwhile in my own way of living; I am a creature of the past; only I do believe that I see the light of the future, and that it is this which shows me my ugliness and fatuity and feebleness—Words, words, words! How to make them things, deeds" (*Letters* I, 419). Howells's own fraught awakening is reflected in the economic novels which feature "fur-lined" socialists like Annie Kilburn and Matt Hilary, members of the leisure-class who remain complicit in the very order they criticize, characters plagued by a recognition of their hypocrisy. These figures, like Howells, condemn America's idolatrous

---

[2] See also Taylor, Walter Fuller. "William Dean Howells and the Economic Novel," *American Literature* 4.2 (1932): 103–13.

civilization and pledge their solidarity with the working-class, while, at the same time, living "in all the luxury money could buy." Not all of the novels' protagonists become socialists, but each work features an affluent lead who is shaken from their complacent endorsement of Gilded Age materialism as a result of their relationship with a Christian socialist character. Like Howells himself, their redemptive conversion is never instantaneous or complete; it is, instead, incremental, imperfect, and unfinished—an apotheotic projection of Fabian gradualism. At the end of each book, the lead's conversion has only just begun; they are "no longer content," but that is as far as they have got. They have yet to fully bring their actions, their deeds, into conformity with their new beliefs.

Howells's progressive position—at once too extreme for the liberals and too moderate for the radicals—was a precursor to the middle-class religious anti-capitalism that would characterize the coming Social Gospel. Though he demurred from the kind of ascetic renunciation modeled by his beloved Tolstoy, Howells crafted the most refined literary indictment of capitalism that had so far appeared in the United States. He did not resort to the polemics of the radicals and tract writers who philosophized with a hammer, nor to the facile sentimentality and moralism of reformers, and he did not offer up the arid and artless worlds built by the utopians. Instead, Howells developed a social theory on the basis of a theological perspective and translated it into an aesthetic that conveyed how all Americans were harmed by industrial capitalism. He did not romanticize class antagonism by turning it into a conflict between starkly drawn heroes and villains. The narrator of Rebecca Harding Davis's *Margret Howth* remarks, "I never saw a full-blooded saint or sinner in my life" (102). Similarly, Howells did not ascribe pure vice to one class and unsullied virtue to another, he did not demonize or revere any station or occupation, but rather sought to paint a panoramic image of a nation whose citizens were variously, but inescapably, damaged by the social system they inhabited. Howells believed that the American economic system was the locus of sin, and that people of all social classes were the victims of this profane order. As such, it was not individuals who were blameworthy and in need of salvation, but the very structures of society that had to be redeemed. Howells's theory of social salvation was the bedrock of his realist aesthetic, which looked charitably on the pitiable "half-and-half characters" that people his economic novels, figures each touched, to a greater or lesser degree, by the corrupting influence of capitalism (Davis 101–2).

Just as the case had been for Transcendentalists and antebellum labor activists in the pre-Marxian era of American socialism, the foundation of radical social thought in America in the 1880s and 1890s was religious rather than secular-materialist. Though American socialists were often well versed in theories of political economy, they advanced their cause in primarily theological and moral terms; their reading of economic conditions was determined by those conditions' relative adherence to or transgression of religious principles of justice. For these believers, the sins of individuals were merely a symptom of an underlying social ailment, and therefore it was society itself that needed salvation. Social salvation, that is, liberation from the inequality produced by industrialism, necessitated the abolition of capitalism and the creation of a just economic system which they believed would be socialistic. Adherents of "social Christianity" argued that an equitable economic system could be achieved only by literally and concretely emulating the life and ethical teachings of Jesus. The theology of "practical Christianity" was built upon socialist economics and the belief that democracy would be realized through conformity to this ethos. Because of the intersectional nature of the sacred, Howells's conversion was at once religious and political. By taking up this cause, Howells put himself directly at odds with the culture and class he had long championed, but by doing so, he knowingly joined ranks with a line of social Christians that extends to the very origins of the American literary tradition. The religious philosophy and theory of redemption he began to endorse after his conversion formed the basis of his mature aesthetics. Howells's realism is the product of his attempt to translate the economic theology of practical Christianity into fictional form.

A Realist Hamartiology

Rather than forwarding a one-sided indictment of affluent culture, Howells offers a holistic, panoramic view of Gilded Age America and the manifold experiences, commitments, and perspectives of its citizenry. He never simply demonizes capitalists. For instance, in *A Hazard of New Fortunes* he draws the morally fallen speculator Dryfoos with as much compassion as he does Dryfoos's Christian socialist son, Conrad, declaring that the father is as much a victim of America's degraded capitalist society as his son, who is accidentally killed during a labor conflict modeled on the Haymarket demonstration of 1886. Similarly, in *A Quality of Mercy*, the wealthy embezzler Northwick, another tragic figure who elicits readers' pity, is described as merely the latest in a long line of businessmen who have been victimized by a value system that necessarily tempts and deforms the mind. Characters like Northwick and Dryfoos are never represented as two-dimensional villains with purely vicious motives; rather, they are unwitting victims of their social conditions. The moral fall of these affluent characters is depicted as an effect of a prior, systemic cause, namely, the culture-wide transvaluation of values initiated by industrial capitalism. Neither is essentially corrupt but is "the victim of circumstances" (QM 460). Howells writes, "Northwick isn't the disease; he's merely the symptom... It's the whole social body that's sick" (QM 166). Their pathology is anything but exceptional; rather, Northwick is "a kind of—incident; and a pretty common kind. He was a mere creature of circumstances—like the rest of us! His environment made him rich, and his environment made him a rogue" (QM 474). In these novels, Howells conveys "the slow and long decay of a moral nature" that necessarily occurs under capitalism in an effort to show the insufficiency of curing individuals and the need to redeem the entire system (QM 272). That is, he takes pains to show that the conversion or reformation of individuals is an inadequate remedy for current social ills and demonstrates, instead, that it is the economic infrastructure of society that requires salvation. Figures like Northwick and Dryfoos are not inherently depraved; their fall is caused by their economic conditions and the new social orthodoxy that they are obliged to honor. Howells and his more fatalistic naturalist successors will continually return to a simple refrain to explain this phenomenon: "conditions make character" (HNF 397). In one of the most important speeches in *A Hazard of New Fortunes* Basil March proclaims,

> conditions make character; and people are greedy and foolish, and wish to shine, because having and shining are held up to them by civilization as the chief good of life. We all know they are not the chief good, perhaps not good at all; but if someone ventures to say so, all the rest of us call him a fraud and a crank.
> (HNF 397)

Howells contends that America's acquisitive culture has caused the moral degradation of the populace and installed an ideal way of life that is antithetical to Christian ethics. Because this new national ideal has been sanctified and upheld as the basis of American identity, dissent is labeled heresy and treason. In Howells's economic novels, both the captain of industry and the common laborer, though estranged from one another, share a common plight; they are equally embroiled in a morally degrading system from which they must be emancipated. Their shared state causes both the bourgeois and proletarian characters to be objects of the reader's empathy. True to the social soteriology of his forebears, Howells communicates the exigent need to redeem institutions and social structures, and to deliver individuals from them, rather than to redeem individuals themselves.

Howells is concerned with showing how modern business reshapes American culture and the way people relate to one another. In *A Hazard of New Fortunes* Colonel Woodburn states, "it is very difficult, in a thoroughly commercialized society, like yours, to have the feelings of a gentleman," that is, to behave ethically (HNF 154). "How can a businessman, whose prosperity, whose earthly salvation, necessarily lies in the adversity of someone else, be delicate and chivalrous, or even honest?... The virus of commercialism... is on the whole country; the dollar is the measure of every value" (HNF 154–155). Howells argues that capitalism has become the sacred model against which all forms of value are measured. This has led Americans to believe that salvation is accomplished through competition and the subjugation of others, rather than through liberation.

In *A Traveler from Altruria*, we read that the new "American ideal" is "for each to rise above the rest," "not to change the conditions for all" (41). Howells argues that the nation's dominant salvation ethic is constituted by the values of laissez-faire individualism, which are directly at odds with Christian neighbor-love and the freedom of all. In the industrial social formation, Americans' "earthly salvation" is believed to be contingent on the subjugation of others. The individual must "rise above the rest" while ensuring the "conditions for all" remain unchanged. The novel's banker explains that "business is the national ideal, and the successful business man is the American type. It is a business man's country" (TA 117). He continues, "the millionaire is now the American ideal," and it is he who is revered more so than "the greatest statesman, the greatest poet, or the greatest soldier, we ever had" (TA 120). He is the moral exemplar in modern America and it is his values—"every man... for himself" and "each... above the rest"—which guide the actions of the average American (TA 118). The banker concludes,

> This is a business man's country. We are a purely commercial people; money is absolutely to the fore; and business, which is the means of getting the most money, is the American ideal. If you like, you may call it the American fetish; I don't mind calling it so myself. The fact that business is our ideal, our fetish, will account for the popular faith in business men, who form its priesthood [...] business is our national ideal [and therefore] the business man is honored above all other men among us.
>
> (TA 123)

For Howells, the process of fetishization or apotheosis has caused capitalism to become the new American religion; the business-class constitutes its priesthood and commerce its sacramental rite. Because capitalism and Christianity's respective systems of value are antithetical in his view, the transvaluation accompanying the rise of capitalism entails the moral devolution of Americans. For Howells, the exaltation of capitalism has necessarily resulted in the moral fall of modern America. In order for Americans to be redeemed from this condition, they must be liberated from its systemic cause.

Earlier examples of Christian literary activism in America dealt primarily with the superficial effects of a morally degraded society rather than with their underlying causes. Howells was the first American novelist to offer a sophisticated and artful critique of the "fundamental causes of economic unrest and [to call] into question the individualistic basis of American economy" (Taylor 108). Whereas previous fiction had dealt only with symptoms, Howells diagnosed "the disease" by taking an objective view of Gilded Age America that effectively encompassed multiple class perspectives and criticized the economic conditions that gave rise to harmful social effects. This paved the way for later economic novelists like Theodore Dreiser and Frank Norris who became famous for their macroscopic critiques of American capitalism. As a result of Howells's pioneering work, and that of others, Gilded Age Americans began to realize that the social ills they suffered from were outcomes of an economic system rather than the product of individual depravity. They were increasingly attracted to the era's many social theorists and, in particular, to Christians who argued that redemption required liberation from capitalism rather than the reform of personal behavior. Social salvation was the doctrine upon which Christian socialists' religious philosophy was built, and their creative works were an attempt to put that philosophy into symbolic form.

An Allegory of Apotheosis

One of Howells's principal aims in the economic novels is to demystify apotheosis, both analytically, in terms of its basic features and operation, and sociologically, in terms of its historical ubiquity, political function, and effects. In the modern American context, apotheosis appeared as a bidirectional leveling process that conflated religion and economy, and this phenomenon enabled America to be transformed from a theocratic city on a hill to a "business civilization" (Fried 84). Protestant Christianity was recreated in terms conducive to the reproduction of

The American Fetish 97

Figure 3.1 "The Godhead of America" by Art Young, *The Masses*, February 1911.

capitalist society, while, at the same time, commercial institutions and values were exalted and regarded as earthly embodiments of metaphysical laws. That is, the economization of Christianity and the sacralization of capitalism were two modalities of a unified process. Howells sought to show that this process of accommodation served an ideological function, namely, to legitimate unequal and exploitative group relations.

Howells recognized that humans have a tendency to deify the status quo and that this habit is a universal aspect of social experience. In *The World of Chance* we read, "there is something very curious in our relation to the divine. God is where we believe He is" (WC 307). Howells understood that this is largely how apotheosis works; we see God wherever we choose, wherever the exigencies of history make God's presence the most expedient to our interests. We find God wherever He can best serve our needs but, Howells warns, this has potentially dire ethical consequences. In the context of modern capitalism, someone may choose to "see His hand in a... deal, which prospered them, though it ruined others" (WC 307). That is, we choose to "see His hand" in an exploitative economic relationship in order to legitimate a culture of self-interest, where success can only be had at another's expense. Apotheosis is the alchemy that turns wrong into right. Howells is acutely aware of the apotheotic process and the injustices it has historically been used to defend. In particular, he is critical of naturalization, or the projection of social conditions onto "the unseen order of existence." This practice often leads to the essentialization of unethical behavior. In "Equality as the Basis of Good Society" (1895) Howells writes, "It seems to me that we are always mistaking our conditions for our natures, and saying that human nature is greedy and mean and false and cruel, when only our conditions are so" (67). Ultimately, Howells argues that the sacralization of capitalism is a modern form of idolatry that is antagonistic to liberty, equality, and fraternity, and must therefore be overcome. In "Are We a Plutocracy?" (1894) he writes, "if we have ceased to be a democracy and have become a plutocracy, it is because the immense majority of the American people have no god before Mammon" (191). In his work of utopian Christian socialism, *A Traveler from Altruria*, Howells develops a superb critique of economic naturalization and the recreation of human ontology in the image of liberal individualism.

For ideology to work, it cannot appear as ideology, but must be seen as a reflection of the eternal Truth that exists independent of historically contingent human interests. In *A Traveler from Altruria*, Howells deftly satirizes the ideological naturalization of capitalist economy and the value system that maintains it. In the novel, Twelvemough explains that Americans "regard [our economic conditions] as final, and as indestructibly based in human nature itself" (TA 16). The manufacturer in the novel contends that laissez-faire economics, which endorses the single-minded pursuit of self-interest, is the earthly incarnation of Natural Law: "the good of Number One first, last, and all the time… That seems to be the first law of nature, as well as the first law of business" (TA 48). Perhaps most importantly, the minister, who represents the Protestant establishment and its theology, contends that capitalism is an eternal element of God's creation. He explains that the social conditions and hierarchical distinctions produced by industrialism "must be, and always have been, and always will be" (TA 39). Ideology is not a matter of building consensus by demonstrating that a given practice or state of affairs is beneficial or reasonable; it is about transforming culture into nature by proclaiming that a particular social formation and set of mores is correlative to the ontological order designed and loved by God. Ideologues impose these norms through coercion, by extending a promise, and through force, by making a threat. They promise that, if you act in conformity to the rules deemed holy, then you will earn God's favor and ultimately salvation. If, however, you fail or refuse to reproduce the social formation, then you are not merely transgressing custom but are actively opposing God and perverting nature and will be punished accordingly. In this novel, Howells shows how the elite class—each faction of which is personified by someone at the resort—seeks to naturalize and sanctify capitalism by conflating it with the eternal "law of nature" created by God. It is this process, he argues, that has caused "property" and "business" to become "the two absolutely sacred things in the American religion" (TA 128).

Howells claims that it is not enough for the Gilded Age elite to sanctify the economic status quo; they also have to develop a theodicy to justify the inequality and suffering the system produces. Twelvemough recounts, " 'we believe [our conditions are] the best in the best of all possible worlds', I said devoutly; and it struck me that if ever we came to have a national church, some such affirmation as that concerning our economic conditions ought to be in the confession of faith" (TA 64). Rather than resorting to the moralism of the jeremiad, Howells opts for sardonic humor to mock the absurdity and irrationality of exalting the existent order. Twelvemough continues,

> I felt that it ought to have been self-evident to [Homos] that when a commonwealth of 60,000,000 Americans based itself upon the great principle of self-seeking, self-seeking was the best thing, and whatever hardship it seemed to work, it must carry with it unseen blessings in ten-fold measure. If a few hundred thousand favored Americans enjoyed the privilege of socially condemning all the rest, it was as clearly right and just that they should do so, as that 4000 American millionaires should be richer than all the other Americans put together. Such a status, growing out of our political equality and our material prosperity must evince a divine purpose to anyone intimate with the designs of providence, and it seemed a kind of impiety to doubt its perfection.
>
> (TA 71)

Howells recognizes that apotheosis is the engine of social reproduction, that it establishes necessity, legitimates norms, manufactures consent, and forestalls opposition by transforming the mundane into the metaphysical. Once capitalism is sacralized and deemed the embodiment of God's will, resistance becomes "a kind of impiety"; to oppose capitalism is to transgress divine law.

The novel ends with Homos's lengthy account of how Altruria came to be a "Christian republic" (TA 162). The tale functions as an allegory of the Altrurians' submission to a deified economic system and their eventual emancipation from it. Homos's account of Altruria prior to its adoption of Christian socialism is an analogous description of Gilded Age America. The main character in this story is "the Accumulation," a personified rendering of capitalism as a hostile, god-like entity that rules over the people. We read, "the Accumulation began to act upon its new consciousness" and

> it called itself prosperity, and wealth, and the public good, and it said that it gave bread, and it impudently bade the toiling myriads consider what would become of them, if it took away their means of wearing themselves out in its service. It demanded of the state absolute immunity and absolute impunity, the right to do its will wherever and however it would, without question from the people who were the final law. It had its way, and under its rule we became the richest people under the sun.
>
> (TA 149, 147–8)

This *mise en abyme* gives Howells an opportunity to explain how the apotheosis of capitalism works. In the tale, the economic system is imbued with autonomous being and alienated from the populace, making it appear to be a hostile supernatural agency rather than an assemblage of human relations and the product of human activity. Homos explains that the exaltation of the economy entailed an inversion of power and ontological status. While the Accumulation was invested with an agency it did not truly possess, humanity was stripped of its agency. We read, "by a logic irresistible and inexorable, the Accumulation *was*, and we were *not*" (TA 152). Apotheosis, we recall, simultaneously bestows and deprives of being; it ontologizes and deontologizes. A subject becomes an object, and an object is endowed with subjectivity. In the process of conferring power to their creation, the people divested themselves of sovereignty and became servants of their false god, on who they projected their own desire for adoration and obedience.

Homos's account of Altruria's salvation is the story of the republic's deliverance from fetishized capitalism. Just as Homos employs storytelling to help his listeners recognize the destructive process at work around them, and to awaken them to other forms of social organization, Howells attempts to convert his readers by exposing the mechanics of apotheosis.

Social Estrangement and the Ontology of Class

In addition to making industry and commerce sacred, Howells argues that the apotheosis of capitalism is characterized by the transformation of social rank into a state of ontological difference. By proclaiming that inequality is a feature of Being, the ruling class establishes a universal ground for an imbalance of power, making holy the master–slave or owner–worker relation. By convincing themselves that inequality is a cosmological necessity, the leisure class can alleviate the guilt caused by possessing wealth amid vast poverty and powerlessness. Further, when social hierarchy is considered a product of God's will, docile submission becomes an attribute of piety. For example, Annie Kilburn initially believes that it would be mere folly to challenge "the inequalities that there always must be in the world" (798). She ontologizes class, arguing that inequality is an eternal feature of Being itself; it "always had been" and "always must be" (AK 798). Similarly, Mrs. Camp, the working-class invalid in *A Traveler from Altruria*, resigns herself to the belief that "some are poor, and some are rich. That's the way the world has to be made up" (86). The wealthy Mrs. Makely exclaims, "There *must* be rich and there *must* be poor. There always have been, and there always will be. [...] Didn't Christ himself say, 'The poor ye have always with you'?" (TA 70, 87–88). Later, Twelvemough attempts to prove to Homos that class-based "subordination [is] a part of human nature, and that a principle which pervade[s] our civilization... must be divinely implanted" (TA 145). By converting culture into nature, and by ascribing sacred origins to the established social order, these characters illustrate how dominant groups use apotheosis to legitimate and reinforce their power.

In *The Minster's Charge* (1886), Reverend Sewell inveighs against the seemingly insurmountable alienation of the classes. We read:

> If only I could have reached the poor boy... But do what I would, I couldn't find any common ground where we could stand together. We were as unlike as if we were of two different species. I saw that everything I said bewildered him more and more; he couldn't understand me! Our education is unchristian, our civilization is pagan. They both ought to bring us in closer relations with our fellow-creatures, and they both only put us more widely apart! Every one of us dwells in an impenetrable solitude! We understand each other a little if our circumstances are similar, but if they are different all our words leave us dumb and unintelligible.
>
> (MC 37)

Here, Sewell argues that profane capitalist society and the rejection of Christianity's true ethical obligations are the cause of class estrangement. Rather than creating national solidarity, commercial mores "put us more widely apart." By claiming that alienation is caused by the "unchristian" aspects of American society, Sewell suggests that an authentically Christian social order would reconcile the classes. In this way, Howells claims that combating the exaltation of capitalism is the path to social solidarity and thus to America's redemption.

Because they are from different classes and are therefore "two different species," Sewell is unable to communicate with Barker (RSL 210). The classes are incomprehensible to one another and as a result remain isolated in "impenetrable solitude." Howells uses the novel of manners as a means of dramatizing the disintegration of American society that he attributes to capitalism. In numerous works, both comedic and tragic, characters from different classes struggle to communicate. Sewell's exclamation, "he couldn't understand me!" echoes Silas Lapham's despairing declaration to Tom Corey, "I don't understand you." Howells uses this technique to show that "economic barriers are immediately transformed into social barriers," and as a result, the "intermingling between the rich and the poor becomes impossible" (Taylor 110). This motif also serves as a refutation of sentimentalism's faith in the potential for sympathy to initiate social reform. For Howells, capitalism inhibits sympathy. For example, in *Annie Kilburn* the citizens of Hatboro find that, despite their calculated efforts to overcome alienation, social "union in our present condition of things, with its division of classes, is impossible" (797). The reconciliation of society, Howells argues, would require the abolition of classes and therefore, of capitalism itself.

In *A Traveler from Altruria*, the visiting Christian socialist, Homos, functions as a foil who exposes the hypocrisies of American society. Homos points out that, despite our pretensions to social unification and equality, "the severance of the man who works... from the man who does not... is so complete, and apparently so final, that nobody even imagines anything else, not even in fiction" (TA 40). In post-Civil War America, this is a damning indictment indeed. Howells suggests that, though the war is over, a civil war continues to rend the nation. The North and South have made peace but capital and labor remain locked in a battle over the fate of a disempowered class of Americans. In *Annie Kilburn* we read, "We live in an age of seeming preparation for indefinite war. The lines are drawn harder and faster between the rich and the poor, and on either side the forces are embattled" (804). He implies that, as long as the alienation of the classes persists, the Civil War rages on. Therefore, for Howells, the struggle for the liberation of the working-class is a form of postwar abolitionism. He sets out to show that the segregation of the classes, the essentialization of class difference, and the subordination of those ensnared in a system of wage slavery replicates in a more civilized manner the chattel slavery of antebellum America.

Homos asks, "Am I right in supposing that the effect of your economy is to establish insuperable inequalities among you, and to forbid the hope of the brotherhood which your polity proclaims?" (TA 59). Howells contends that economic inequality makes political equality impossible, and therefore undermines America's most fundamental principles. The gospels, like America's polity, proclaim "the hope of... brotherhood." However, the inequality wrought by capitalism prevents both the realization of God's promise and that of the constitution. Therefore this form of economy, in Howells's view, is contrary to both authentic Christianity and democracy. In order to redeem America, capitalism and class must be abolished. Until that occurs, the nation will remain estranged from itself, divided into two Americas, with each group perceiving the other as a hostile enemy.

Altruria's young farmer and Christian radical Reuben Camp, in conversation with the wealthy Mrs. Makely, opines:

> I don't believe we all have the same country. America is one thing for you, and it's quite another thing for us. America means ease, and comfort, and amusement for you... and if it means work, it's work that you *wish* to do. For us, America means work that we *have* to do, and hard work, all the time, if we're going to make both ends meet. It means liberty for you; but what liberty has a man got who doesn't know where his next meal is coming from?... I've seen men come and give up their liberty for a chance to earn their family's living... Yes, we are all Americans, but I guess we haven't all got the same country, Mrs. Makely. What sort of a country has a black-listed man got?
>
> (TA 100)

Similarly, in *A Hazard of New Fortunes* Lindau asks, "What gountry hass a poor man got, Mr. Marge?" (80). Howells contends that industrialism has "divided the nation into two camps" (TA 49). Workers' experience of disenfranchisement and social subordination makes them feel as though they comprise a different nation altogether, and the prevailing ideology confirms this intuition. The leisure class ontologizes class difference to naturalize workers' second-class citizenship and to imbue existent power relations with transcendent legitimacy. The naturalization of class causes each group to see the other as a "different species," furthering the impression that two separate Americas enjoy an increasingly unstable and antagonistic coexistence. Howells contends that the foundational ideals of fraternity, equality, and liberty, which define both Christianity and American democracy, are wholly incompatible with the values and social order entailed by modern capitalism, which necessarily alienates the citizenry and leads the nation into a condition of civil war.

Howells demonstrates that institutional Christianity plays an integral role in the apotheosis of class. In a key exchange between the banker and the minister in *A Traveler from Altruria*, Howells critiques the role of the church in the segregation of the classes. The banker asks the reverend, who is said to have the largest congregation in "one of the principle cities of the east," "how many of the lower classes are there in [your congregation], people who work for a living with their hands?" (TA 126). The minister hesitantly responds: "They—I suppose—they have their own churches" (TA 126). Feigning disbelief, the banker replies, "do you mean there are *no* working-people in your congregation?" (TA 126). "I cannot think of any" (TA 126). Here, Howells addresses the post-disestablishment classing of the denominations to show that capitalist society has reconstituted religious institutions as well as doctrines and practices. He chooses to make his minister immensely popular—he "preach[es] to more people than any other pulpit in the city"—to call attention to the fact that the most prominent churches in the nation's "principal cities" exclude the working-class (TA 126). This is meant to be emblematic of the state of religious affairs in America, where the classes have "their own churches," each disseminating theologies that lend divine approval to the group's defining traits and interests. Howells calls attention to this aspect of apotheosis to show that the nation's most powerful and popular denominations reinforce class antagonism. Far from being immune to the vicissitudes of secular society, the church is shown to be sensitive to changes in material conditions, and ultimately to be the cultural site where an economic ideology acquires the kind of authoritative justification that enables it to gain dominance. By projecting class difference into the heavens, and by altering theology to target a specific market, the church plays a pivotal role in the formation and alienation of two Americas.

In *Annie Kilburn*'s enigmatic Reverend Peck, Howells creates a figure who disrupts this status quo by attempting to practically emulate the ethics of Jesus. The novel's William Gerrish, the token of small-town America's business-class, objects to Peck's fraternization with laborers. Peck, who embodies Howells's early, Tolstoyan Christian socialism, advocates for a preferential concern for the poor and working-class. Gerrish cannot directly oppose Peck's practical Christianity because its precepts, he admits, are found "between the leds of the Bible," but he can charge that Peck is insubordinate (AK 726). Gerrish complains that Peck "walks too much with the poor, and converses too much with the poor, and converses too much with the lowly. He says he thinks that the pew-owners in Mr. Peck's church and the people who pay his salary have some rights to his company that he's bound to respect" (AK 726). Gerrish believes that Peck is beholden to "the pew-owners" and "the people who pay his salary," which is to say the town's middle-class, more so than to the poor and working-class with whom Peck spends most of his time and energy. Peck is considered a mere instrument whose function is to uphold and further sacralize the market morality that serves the interests of the town's merchants. Because they "pay his salary," Gerrish and his peers feel that they have a right to determine where Peck's sympathies lie, and the values he will affirm from the pulpit. In this way, Howells exposes the fundamental conflict of interest that shapes the doctrines of Protestant denominations in post-disestablishment America; ultimately, the concerns which determine theology are economic rather than ethical or biblical. Because Peck transgresses the socially mandated alienation of the classes, which is such a vital part of capitalist orthodoxy, he is branded a heretic. As a result, he is pilloried by the middle-class community and eventually resigns his office, determining, in Tolstoyan fashion, to return to the ranks of the industrial peasantry before he can be formally dismissed by the financiers who dictate the church's dogma. In novels like *Annie Kilburn*, Howells examines how religion and the economic interests that determine church doctrine contribute to the alienation of the classes and turn the nation against itself.

From Rural Utopianism to Urban Agitation

For Howells, antebellum abolitionism, the early labor movement, and the literary activism and communal experiments of the Transcendentalists were all part of a unified American tradition that was impelled by fierce religious commitment and dedicated to the liberation of all oppressed and exploited people. After 1887, he begins to see his work as the newest stage of that tradition, adapted to the exigencies of Gilded Age America. However, while he has the utmost respect for these former movements, Howells believes their tactics were fundamentally flawed. To repair this, he develops a socialist theology that builds on the tradition while pushing it in new directions that he believes will more effectively lead to the redemption of American society.

In *The World of Chance* Howells advances a sustained critique of the utopianism that had dominated socialism for the last half-century. Just as *A Hazard of New Fortunes* had largely been about how the young, bourgeois Basil March's social and religious horizons are broadened by his relationship with the older radical Lindau, *The World of Chance* charts the conversion that Shelley Ray experiences as a result of his relationship with David Hughes, "an old-time Brook Farmer" who has spent his entire adult life in utopian Christian communities (WC 287). Much like Howells in his youth, Ray is a provincial author who admires Hawthorne's fiction, particularly *The Blithedale Romance*, Hawthorne's account of his time at the Transcendentalist commune, Brook Farm. Howells contrives the encounter between Ray and Hughes to not only stage the young man's religious and political awakening, but also to renounce the Tolstoyan socialism that he had recently endorsed in *Annie Kilburn*.

In the course of his development as a Christian socialist, Howells began to find Tolstoy's religious ethic to be an unacceptable path to salvation insofar as it remained in thrall to liberal individualism. He writes that Tolstoy "gropes for a hopeless reversion to innocence through individual renunciation of society instead of pressing forward to social redemption"[3] ("Lyof N. Tolstoy" 851). After his initial conversion, during which time "Tolstoy had furnished him with the demand for literal obedience to Christian ethics," Howells moved on to socially oriented plans for holistic reform (Budd 300). This transition is given form in *The World of Chance* with David Hughes's decision to reenter society. Hughes's attempt to explain this change of heart to his old friend Mr. Chapley, an avowed Tolstoyan, gives Howells an occasion to convey his critique of the utopian, separatist phase of Christian socialism. Howells writes,

> Tolstoi is mistaken. I don't object to his theories of non-resistance; the Quakers have found them perfectly practicable for more than two centuries; but I say that in quitting the scene of the moral struggle, and in simplifying himself into a mere peasant, he begs the question as completely as if he had gone into a monastery. He has struck out some tremendous truths, I don't deny that, and his examination of the conditions of civilization is one of the most terrifically searching studies of the facts that have ever been contributed to the science of sociology; but his conclusions are as wrong as his premises are right. If I had back the years that I have wasted in a perfectly futile effort to deal with the problem of the race at a distance where I couldn't touch it, I would have nothing to do with eremitism in any of its forms, either collectively as we have had it in our various communistic experiments, or individually on the terms which Tolstoi apparently advises.
>
> (WC 90)

While Howells continues to affirm Tolstoy's pacifism and his analysis of competitive society, he objects to all forms of utopian "comeouterism"

---

[3] See also Howells, William Dean. *My Literary Passions*. New York: Harper, 1895, 252; *The World of Chance*, 90–1, 306–7.

because adherents simply quit "the scene of the moral struggle" without attempting to change the structures of society that codify the exploitation of the working-class. Such eremitism, Howells argues, evinces an implicit politics of self-interest that is still too concerned with individual rather than social redemption. Rather than attempting to concretely alter the conditions that lead to social sin, utopians simply absent themselves from society and thus eschew their responsibility for the poor. Howells's critique of utopianism marks a clear ideological transition from the romanticized return to the soil that he had formerly endorsed through such characters as Silas Lapham, Matt Hilary, and Annie Kilburn. He begins to renounce the agrarian, separatist ethics of the communitarian Christian socialists of the antebellum period like Bronson Alcott, George Ripley, and John Humphrey Noyes in favor of more direct forms of political action.

In addition to claiming that utopians relinquish their responsibility for the poor, Hughes argues that their accommodation of capitalism is a kind of hypocrisy that betrays a residual individualism. Howells writes,

> If anything in the world has thoroughly failed, it is communities. They have failed all the more lamentably when they have succeeded financially, because that sort of success comes from competition with the world outside. A community is an aggrandized individual; it is the extension of the egoistic motive to a large family, which looks out for its own good against other families, just as the small family does. I have had enough of communities.
>
> (WC 121–2)

Utopianism is, for Howells, competitive individualism on a smaller scale. The communitarians fail to fully transcend their economic context; the communities they create retain many of the values, aims, and practices of capitalist society, such as social exclusivity, competition, and the pursuit of self-interest. Whatever measure of freedom they enjoyed was bought at the expense of abandoning the exploited masses. Howells writes, "the community saved itself... by shutting out the rest of the world. It was selfish... The Family must include the whole world" (WC 184). Similarly, Ray remarks, "the experiment of emancipation is tried on too small a scale in a community" (WC 186). For Howells, it is insufficient for a small group of Christians to liberate themselves from capitalist society instead of attempting to free the whole nation. The liberation achieved in these communities was provisional, if not entirely illusory, and left the underlying problems they wished to escape unchanged. Howells writes that Tolstoy, and those like him, "would have us withdraw from the world, as if, where any man was, the world was not there in the midst of him!" (WC 91). It is "impossible... for a man to rid himself of his environment... [Tolstoy is] a monumental warning of the futility of any individual attempt to escape from conditions" (WC 208). After all, "conditions make character," therefore, those who attempt to escape capitalist society inevitably end up replicating its deficiencies in their own communities; they carry "the virus of commercialism" with them. The individual Christian socialist, Howells argues, cannot be redeemed by simply coming out of society, but must attempt to redeem the world by remaining in it. While Tolstoy was one of the influences that initiated Howells's conversion, *The World of Chance* represents his departure from Tolstoy's brand of separatist, communitarian socialism in favor of a more immersive, democratic socialism.

By the 1890s, Howells was advocating a political theology that rejected both radical insurrection and utopian separatism. He believed that the redemption of the nation could be accomplished only by peaceful, democratic means. However, he also emphasized the importance of establishing forms of active praxis in solidarity with the marginalized. The lapsed utopian David Hughes is a literary expression of Howells's quarrel with antebellum strategies for social reform. We read, "at sixty-nine [Hughes] discovered that his efforts to oblige his fellow-beings ever since he was twenty have been misdirected... He sees now that the right way to universal prosperity and peace is the political way" (WC 88). Hughes explains,

> We shall never redeem the world by eschewing it. Society is not to be saved by self-outlawry. The body politic is to be healed politically. The way to have the golden age is to elect it... The people must vote themselves into possession of their own business, and intrust their economic affairs to the same faculty that makes war and peace, that frames laws, and that does justice.
>
> (WC 91)

Howells contends that utopian Christian socialists ultimately remain passive, theorizing and eloquently advocating for change from the sidelines without attempting to produce it on the front lines of the struggle. Hughes states, "I abhor dreamers; they have no place in a world of thinking and acting" (WC 92). Howells thought that speculative social engineering and idealistic posturing, his dreaded "words, words, words!" would never redeem America. The nation's salvation could only be won through "deeds," through concrete, peaceful political action.

These principles also apply to Howells's stance on labor activism. He saw forms of destructive and violent action as counterproductive and, instead, advocated the use of politics as the means to secure change. This is why Basil March objects to Lindau's tactics in *A Hazard of New Fortunes* and why Hughes rejects Denton's call for revolt in *The World of Chance*.[4] Hughes states, "we must have the true America in the true American way, by reasons, by votes, by laws, and not otherwise" (WC 125). Conversely, Denton wants immediate social redemption: "I ask myself how they shall be saved, not some other time, but now" (WC 124). For Howells, the desire for revolution is one more expression of American Arminianism, that is, the capitalistic notion that redemption—a complete transformation—can occur immediately, as though paradigmatic social change resembles the momentary choice of a consumer. Howells argues, instead, in favor of a democratic social salvation that attempts to redeem society progressively. Howells's concept of salvation is Fabian in that he assumes that the redemption of humanity will occur over generations and in increments, just as the redemption history of humanity is staged in Judeo-Christian scripture.

The democratic Christian socialism that Howells develops in the economic novels signals a reorientation of social Christian norms which were shifting from the rural, agrarian comeouterism of the utopians to the concrete, urban political activism of the Social Gospel. The tactics, principles, and aims that Howells endorses in these novels will later characterize the work of Progressive Era reform movements in the first decades of the twentieth century. Howells understood a fundamental truth that the leaders of the Social Gospel would popularize in the years to come, namely, that "Christianity [is] a system of economics as well as a religion" (HNF 277). Though Howells is critical of the apotheosis of capitalism, it is notable that he never calls for a thoroughgoing separation of religion and economics. He acknowledges that they are inextricable. The question he grapples with is not whether we ought to combine the two, but rather, which system of economics is consistent with Jesus's ethics. As we will see in the next chapter, American authors will continue to debate this question by creating competing interpretations of Jesus that are determined by the economic interests of conflicting groups. Like Howells and those he regards as idolaters, these authors will insist that the salvation of American society depends on the economic model we choose to make sacred.

---

[4] See also *A Traveler from Altruria*, where Howells writes: "the socialists are the only fellows among [labor activists] who propose to vote their ideas into laws, and nothing can be more American than that" (TA 129).

4

Mistaking "Shadows for Gods": Class and the Christ Novel in the Progressive Era

Amid the rapid social changes of the Progressive era, fiction served as a vital medium of conflict between competing groups. Authors in both camps of the escalating class war strategically used religion in their literature to legitimate their respective economic positions. As we have seen, literature—or more generally, the symbolic—mediates the apotheotic process. Literary representatives of capital and labor made their class interests and objectives sacred by projecting the defining attributes and mores of their group onto a reimagined concept of God. In the generation after the Civil War, a new kind of novel, one focused on the life of Jesus Christ, became the most popular literary genre in America. These books functioned to reframe Americans' conception of authentic Christian values and practices in light of changing economic relations. The nation's most celebrated authors, such as Harriet Beecher Stowe and Elizabeth Stuart Phelps, contributed to the genre. By examining works of Christological fiction by three of the most best-selling authors of the early 1900s—Jack London, Upton Sinclair, and Bruce Barton—we can observe the integral role of apotheosis in machine age class conflict.

Post–Civil War Hagiography: Competing Christologies in *Fin de Siècle* America

The development of a proletarian Christology was the cornerstone of the socialist movement's effort to sacralize its ethos and economics. Walter Rideout aptly summarizes the Christology imparted in early-twentieth-century radical fiction, writing that Jesus is depicted "as the 'first Socialist' " by "authors who emphasize, not his divinity, but his carpentry. To them he is a revolutionary worker" (77–78). A brief look at three novels by Upton Sinclair will confirm

Rideout's account. As with his mentor Jack London, "the image of Jesus as a revolutionary leader" was at "the core of Sinclair's Christian doctrine" (Arthur 179). In *Samuel the Seeker* (1910), the young hero of the novel represents Jesus as a poor worker who was executed for being a revolutionary agitator:

> I don't believe that [Jesus] was God... He was a man, like you and me! He was a poor man, who suffered and starved! And the rich men of His time despised Him and spit upon Him and crucified Him!... The church cast out Jesus!... And it was the rich and powerful in the church who did it... And if he were here tonight He would be on my side–and the rich evil-doers who sit on this board would cast Him out again!
>
> (*Samuel* 258)

Not only does Sinclair argue that the leading lights of the modern church are the progeny of Jesus's moneyed executioners, but, most importantly, that Jesus is on the side of the socialists; their economic and political doctrines, he argues, are sanctioned by God, they are sanctified.

Similarly, in *The Jungle* (1906), Reverend Lucas insists that upper-class churches have perverted the true image of Jesus. "Our society churches," he argues, have transformed Jesus, "the man of sorrow and pain, the outcast, despised of the world... this class-conscious working-man! This union carpenter! This agitator, law-breaker, firebrand, anarchist!" into an "elegant prince," a "jewelled idol," "a divinity of the respectable inane" (*Jungle* 375, 374, *Carpenter* 3). By way of apotheosis, socialists like Sinclair reassign the predicates attributed to modern radicals—"outcast," "working-man," unionist, "agitator," "anarchist"—to God, thus indirectly divinizing their projects and values, even as they criticize capitalists for doing very same thing. The same blind spot is evident in Rev. Lucas's claim that Jesus

> was the world's first revolutionist, the true founder of the Socialist movement; a man whose whole being was one flame of hatred for wealth, and all that wealth stands for—for the pride of wealth, and the luxury of wealth, and the tyranny of wealth; who was Himself a beggar and a tramp, a man of the people, an associate of saloon-keepers and women of the town; who again and again, in the most explicit language, denounced wealth and the holding of wealth... Who drove out the businessmen and brokers from the temple with a whip! Who was crucified— think of it—for an incendiary and a disturber of the social order! And this man they have made into the high priest of property and smug respectability, a divine sanction of all the horrors and abominations of modern commercial civilization!
>
> (374–5)

Just as the bourgeoisie collectively represents Jesus as "the high priest of property" in order to legitimate commercial culture and its modes of domination, the working-class imagines Jesus to be the founder of socialism in order to lend "divine sanction" to their oppositional politics.

These kinds of assertions were not only found in socialist fiction but reflect the typical discourse of the labor movement. For example, a contributor to the *Railway Times* (1897) called Jesus "an agitator such as the world has never seen before or since… despised and finally murdered to appease the wrath of the ruling class of His time" (qtd. in Gutman 95). Similarly, Terence Powderly, leader of the Knights of Labor from 1879 to 1893, called Jesus "the world's greatest, most sublime agitator" (qtd. in McKanan 113). In 1899, William Mahon, president of the motorman's union, announced that unions were "fighting for the very principles laid down by Jesus Christ" (qtd. in Gutman 95). As Patrick Allitt has noted, "socialist magazines such as *The Masses* ran cartoons of Jesus wearing overalls and carrying his carpenter's tools, speaking at union meetings and participating in the life of the working class" (139). In their April 1914 issue, *The Masses* published Sarah N. Cleghorn's emblematic poem "Comrade Jesus." In a 1916 issue of *Solidarity*, a member of the I.W.W. remarked,

> The modern militant of the labor movement may without hypocrisy pause to do homage to the humble yet heroic carpenter of Nazareth. Despised as we are despised; hunted as we are hunted—he seems like one of our kind, with whom we may clasp fraternal hands across the centuries and bid to be of good cheer, since his ideal of universal brotherhood based upon toil is not forgotten–and it is about to be realized.
>
> (qtd. in Winters 126)

Perhaps the best example of the proletarian Christology promoted by American socialists was penned two years earlier by co-founder of the I.W.W. and leader of the Socialist Party of America, Eugene Debs, in his essay "Jesus, the Supreme Leader" (1914). There, Debs succinctly states the principles of proletarian Christology, arguing that Jesus was a "master proletarian revolutionist" who led a "campaign of agitation and revolt" (24). He stressed the anti-capitalist, "economic basis of his doctrine" and claimed that Jesus "was of the working class and loyal to it… to the very hour of his death" (Debs 26, 25). He writes that "pure communism was the economic and social gospel preached by Jesus Christ… Private property was to his elevated mind and exalted soul a sacrilege and a horror; an insult to God and a crime against man" (Debs 26). In an editorial for the *Railroad Trainmen's Journal* (1893), Debs writes that "the true spirit of Christianity [can] be found in the labor movement as every blow organized labor strikes for the emancipation of labor has the endorsement of Christ. It is... in alliance with Christ" (qtd. in Johnston 141n55). Echoing the contention of Sinclair's Rev. Lucas that the image of Jesus has been altered to make him "into the high priest of property" in order to lend "divine sanction" to "the horrors and abominations of modern commercial civilization," Debs writes that Jesus "has been disfigured and distorted by cunning priests to serve their knavish ends and by ignorant idolators to give godly sanction to" capitalism (Debs 23). Christian socialists were keenly aware of the apotheosis of capitalist mores and the way this led to a reformation of the image of God, but they were blind to their own practice of apotheosizing socialism to garner divine sanction for their aims. Debs writes, "Christ was metamorphosed from the master revolutionist who was ignominiously slain, a martyr to his class, into the pious abstraction, the harmless theological divinity who died that John Pierpont Morgan could be 'washed in the blood of the lamb' " (Debs 28). Richard Fox has argued that "the malleable figure of Jesus helped American Protestants *of all stripes* move into the modern age *together*" (qtd. in Moody 161, my emphasis). While the figure of Jesus was certainly malleable, evidence shows us that competing, class-based images of God were deployed by antagonistic groups within American Protestantism, and that these antithetical images were wielded as weapons of class warfare. However, as Dan McKanan has argued, the proletarian refashioning of Jesus did help to unify the labor movement. He writes that the creation of a working-class Jesus helped "to mediate between socialist factions" and to "bridge the divides separating radicals from liberals, workers from middle-class reformers, and immigrants from native-born Protestants" (McKanan 142, 120).

The plasticity of the god-image was made most evident in the modern era when many of the nation's most widely read authors began writing biographies of Jesus, creating an immensely popular new genre of religious fiction. These "lives-of-Jesus biographies" emerged as a new form of literary discourse in the years following the Civil War to acclimate Americans to the economy of industrialism and the new social relations it entailed[1] (Moody 158). Authors acting as envoys of their respective classes adapted the image of Jesus to new material relations, appropriating biblical authority to legitimate their social and political aims. Lisa Moody has identified Henry Ward Beecher—"the most visible American clergyman in the late nineteenth

---

[1] For a representative list of the numerous lives of Christ produced at this time, see Curtis, Susan. *A Consuming Faith: The Social Gospel and Modern American Culture*. Baltimore: The Johns Hopkins UP, 1991, 293n25.

century"—as the first to contribute to this genre with his *The Life of Jesus, the Christ* (1871) (qtd. in Moody 174). He was joined by other celebrity authors like Harriet Beecher Stowe with *Footsteps of the Master* (1877), Elizabeth Stuart Phelps with *The Story of Jesus Christ: An Interpretation* (1898), Jack London in *The Star Rover* (1915), and Upton Sinclair with *They Call Me Carpenter* (1922) and, later, *A Personal Jesus: Portrait and Interpretation* (1952). Stowe's *Uncle Tom's Cabin* (1852) and Phelps's *The Gates Ajar* (1868) were two of the most popular novels of the nineteenth century; London was "the most famous and most highly paid writer in the country" when he was writing about Jesus, and Sinclair had attained recent fame with *The Jungle* (Silet 49). These authors' immense, ready-made, established readerships allowed them to disseminate their ideological reimaginings of Jesus throughout American popular culture. Meanwhile, other previously unknown authors gained national fame by writing Jesus biographies, most notably, Lew Wallace with his best-selling *Ben-Hur: A Tale of the Christ* (1880). Other examples of the genre include Howard Pyle's *Rejected of Men* (1903), Bouck White's *The Call of the Carpenter*[2] (1911), and Mary Austin's *The Man Jesus* (1915). Some, like Sinclair, employed "the subjunctive" device of placing Jesus in modern America to suggest how he would respond to current social conditions, such as W. T. Stead in *If Christ Came to Chicago* (1894) and W. E. B. Du Bois in "Jesus Christ in Georgia" (1911) (Jackson 642). Others, rather than recounting the events of Jesus's life, used "the subjunctive mood" to suggest how Jesus's ethics should be applied in the everyday lives of modern Americans (Jackson 642). Examples of this kind include Archibald McCowan's *Christ, the Socialist* (1894), Elizabeth Stuart Phelps's *A Singular Life* (1895), and, most importantly, Charles M. Sheldon's *In His Steps: What Would Jesus Do?* (1896). Wallace's *Ben-Hur* and Sheldon's *In His Steps* were the "two most popular novels in nineteenth-century America," together selling "more than ten million copies" (Allitt 128). These lives of Christ, arguably the most popular genre of post–Civil War American fiction, constituted "a powerful form of mass media" that functioned as religious propaganda aimed at reframing Americans' conception of authentic Christian values and practices in light of a changing economic culture (Jackson 642). Not only did these works aim to alter Americans' values and practices, but, as Gregory Jackson has argued, they encouraged activism, "social engagement," and the creation of "communities of action" (Jackson 643–4). The lives novels were potent ideological tools that functioned to realign Americans'

---

[2] Soon after publishing *The Call of the Carpenter* White went on to found "The Church of the Social Revolution" and to pen a manifesto explaining and promoting its doctrines in, *Church of the Social Revolution: A Message to the World* (1914). For an account of the popularity and content of White's *Call*, and a history of his church, see Burns, David. *The Life and Death of the Radical Historical Jesus.* Oxford: Oxford UP, 2013, 87–132, 123–46.

relation to the new economic order. The god-image each promoted entailed a new salvation ethic—a set of values, practices, and social norms that were thought to be guarantors of redemption—that was predicated on the class-oriented interests of its author. By "rewriting an image of Jesus," Moody writes, these works functioned "as a rewriting of theology and social ethics" (161, 158). She continues: "by offering a model of behavior that presumes to reflect the anterior world outside of the text, these writers combine a metaphysical concept of authority" with their "visions for dealing with the conditions and concerns of… industrial culture" (Moody 179). The authorial representatives of each social class "invariably described a Jesus sympathetic to their own concerns," creating an image of God that was ultimately an "idealized vision of themselves" (Allitt 128, 130). As Shirley Case recognized in 1925, each class "depicts Jesus in accordance with its own immediate interests and ideals" (qtd. in Moody 169). Mary Austin cheekily referred to this widespread process of apotheosis as founding "the Church-of-Whatever-Makes-You-Most-Comfortable" (Austin 4). However, these works did not simply function to console Americans troubled by rapid social change. They were ideological texts that sought to legitimate antagonistic positions in the conflict of capital and labor by sacralizing the ethos of each faction. Moody writes that "each writer appropriates the authority of Jesus to sanction [their] moral concerns allowing these new ethics to be labeled as Christian principles" (161). While many critics have described the proliferation of the lives genre, most have failed to diagnose and explain why this phenomenon emerged and the political function it served. If we take a closer look at two emblematic examples of the genre, we can clearly observe the ideological function of god-making and the role it played in class conflict at the turn of the century.

In *They Call Me Carpenter: A Tale of the Second Coming* (1922), Upton Sinclair gives readers a particularly stark expression of radicals' desire to sanctify socialism. In an attempt to show what, according to Christian socialists, Jesus would do about the labor question, Sinclair contrives a story that makes use of the well-worn device employed by Edward Bellamy in *Looking Backward* (1887) where "the hero wakes up in the end, and we realize that we have been watching a dream" (*Carpenter* 7). After being struck on the head during an anti-German riot, the protagonist, Billy, escapes into a church, falls into a reverie, and sees Jesus walk out of a stained glass window and into 1920s America. Sinclair offers a literary embodiment of the social gospel's call to Christianize the social order[3] by taking Jesus out of the church and into the streets. When Jesus begins to leave

---

[3] E.g., Rauschenbusch, Walter. *Christianizing the Social Order*. New York: The Macmillan Company, 1913.

the church Billy asks, "I thought you belonged in the church?" to which Jesus replies, "Do I?... Am I not more needed in the world?" (*Carpenter* 13). Sinclair then replicates Jesus's ministry in the context of modern America in an effort to prove that Jesus was a working-class revolutionary whose message, identical to that of socialists, would make him as much an enemy of the established order today as it had in antiquity. He describes the novel as "a literal translation of the life of the world's greatest revolutionary martyr, the founder of the world's first proletarian party" (*Carpenter* 224). We read that the sermons Jesus delivers in the novel are "merely a translation [of the gospel] into modern American... a free adaptation of those ancient words to present day practices and conditions" (*Carpenter* 140). The result of this adaptation is a Christ whose teaching sounds as though it were issued from atop a soapbox. The novel is essentially an answer to the plea of liberal Christians like Walter Rauschenbusch to adapt old Christian doctrines to new economic and social conditions. It even includes an appendix that cross-references sixty-eight passages in the novel with the corresponding verses in the gospels from which they are adapted.

Shortly after beginning his "fight with modern civilization," at one point intervening on behalf of a striking restaurant worker who is being clubbed by a policeman, Jesus becomes a reluctant leader of local labor activists (*Carpenter* 44). When Billy first asks his name, Jesus simply replies, "call me Carpenter"; now a comrade among the socialists, Jesus becomes "fellow-worker Carpenter" (*Carpenter* 19, 148). In response to the distress and suffering caused by extreme economic inequality and industrial exploitation, Carpenter preaches a "new gospel of deliverance" among the workers: "I have walked about the streets of your city, and I know myself in the presence of a people wandering in a wilderness. My children!—broken-hearted, desolate, and betrayed... I call you into the way of salvation!" (*Carpenter* 119). In keeping with the procedure of apotheosis, Sinclair first offers working-class readers a god remade in their image, a proletarianized Christ who then prescribes a new salvation ethic, proclaiming that the path to redemption requires the establishment of a socialist society, a process that must begin with the creation of "One Big Union" (*Carpenter* 180). After preaching his syndicalist gospel, Carpenter is accused of being "a Goddamn Bolshevik"; the novel then culminates in a kind of proletarian Passion when an attempt is made to lynch Carpenter, now dubbed the "Red Prophet" (*Carpenter* 117, 215). Red paint is poured over his head and he is paraded through the streets, humiliated. Ultimately, Carpenter escapes, returns to the stained glass window, and Billy awakens from his dream.

With the proletarian Christology Sinclair develops in this novel—as well as in *The Jungle* (1906), *Samuel the Seeker* (1909), *The Profits of Religion*[4] (1917), *Hell* (1923), *What God Means to Me* (1936), *Our Lady* (1938), and *A Personal Jesus* (1952)—he attempts to prove that authentic Christian belief requires conversion to socialism and active engagement in its political mission, for the labor movement is simply "the fulfillment of the old religion, since it implied but the literal application of all the teachings of Christ" (*Jungle* 353). By performing the apotheotic act of conflating Christianity and socialism, Sinclair bestows divine sanction on the values, objectives, and institutions of the labor movement.

However, just as those in favor of labor's cause sought to reinterpret Christianity in order to bring it into conformity with labor's doctrines and forms of life, apologists for capitalism worked diligently to adapt the faith to the newly established economic order. For example, in Robert Norwood's life of Christ, *The Man Who Dared to Be God* (1929), Jesus plies his carpentry trade to become a petit bourgeois boat builder. In Sheldon's *In His Steps*, readers find that, when a dry-goods merchant begins to apply Jesus's ethics in his everyday life, his business thrives. While Norwood refashions Jesus into an archetypical small businessman, Sheldon suggests that Christianity and capitalism are not only compatible, but that practicing the faith will result in material prosperity and the growth of small businesses. Allitt notes that readers of Wallace's *Ben-Hur* "found reassuring the coexistence of Christianity with immense wealth" (136). Katherine Pearson Woods employs a different tactic in her *Metzerott, Shoemaker* (1899), where she "characterizes socialism as fully incompatible with Christianity," and thus indirectly attests to the congruity of Christianity and capitalism (Stokes 182). Examples of this sort abound but undoubtedly the foremost literary embodiment of bourgeois Christology published during the Progressive Era was Bruce Barton's runaway bestseller, *The Man Nobody Knows: A Discovery of the Real Jesus* (1925).

Though largely forgotten today, Bruce Barton was a cultural icon in the 1920s. Barton, the son of a Congregationalist minister, co-founded the era's most prominent advertising agency, Batten, Barton, Durstine & Osborn, and served as a public relations advisor for the nation's most elite conservatives. As the country's leading PR man, Barton not only promoted his clients' products but also acted as an apologist for American capitalism itself. In 1925, Barton wrote *The Man Nobody Knows: A Discovery of the Real Jesus,* a life that portrayed Jesus as "the founder of modern business" (np). The book became an immediate "publishing

---

[4] Particularly in "Book Seven: The Church of the Social Revolution."

phenomenon" (Fried ix). More widely read than Fitzgerald's *The Great Gatsby* (1925), Dos Passos's *Manhattan Transfer* (1925), or Hemingway's *In Our Time* (1925), the novel spent eighty weeks on the *Publishers Weekly* bestseller list, reaching number one among non-fiction bestsellers in 1926 (Fried 102). More than 250,000 copies were sold in the first eighteen months alone, and 487,000 copies were in print by 1944, with sales totaling 726,890 by 1959 (Fried 102). The book, as Barton's biographer Richard M. Fried put it, became "a defining sign" of the times, "the symbol for an age" that ultimately helped "to canonize business in the 1920s" (Fried 84, 85). The period of Barton's ascension to celebrity was "an era of flux," when America was transitioning "from a producer-driven society... to a consumer-driven society" (Fried 10, Prothero 90). A major part of Barton's appeal lied in his ability to help Americans navigate this period of transition, when the cultural paradigm shifted to that of a "business civilization," a time epitomized by Calvin Coolidge's 1925 statement that "the chief business of the American people is business." Fried suggests that, by linking "the realms of religion and business," by reconciling Christianity and Madison Avenue, Barton comforted Americans, reassuring them that "God smiled upon" the new "imperatives of the modern age," such as mass consumption, the ascendency of business culture, and the desire for leisure and self-gratification (Fried x, Prothero 90). However, despite its immense popularity, *The Man Nobody Knows* was the source of a great deal of controversy. Many saw the book as a mere "tract for consumer capitalism," wholly bereft of religious value, and driven by self-serving motives (Prothero 98). One New York City Presbyterian pastor charged Barton with "making of religion a sanctified commercialism with Jesus a Big Business Man and Christianity a Babbitt cult" (qtd. in Fried 100). Ultimately though, as we have seen, Barton was simply the most visible among "a long line of Jesus experts who saw in the man from Nazareth a reflection of themselves" (Prothero 100).

Like London and Sinclair, though Barton is able to recognize how the class interests of others influence their conceptions of Jesus, he is incapable of seeing the very same process at work in his own thinking. He writes, "every man sees the side of [Jesus's] nature which appeals most to himself... The agitator remembers only that he denounced the rich; and the communist that his disciples carried a common purse" (Barton 124). Barton's intent with *The Man* is, ostensibly, to rectify this error; he argues that early theologians sacralized their own traits when creating their image of God and thus "robbed the world" of "*the Real Jesus*." However, though Barton claims to correct this "distortion," his remedy consists entirely of projecting onto Jesus the traits, ideals, and interests of his own class and vocation.

Barton seeks to refute the notion that Jesus was a "sad-faced" social outcast, arguing instead that he typified the traits of a member of the leisure class (Barton 134). Never an outsider, Jesus was immensely sociable and became the darling of high society. He was "the most popular dinner guest in Jerusalem" and moved primarily among the elite. He was no pariah; rather, "his associates [were] among the socially elect" (Barton 71). Barton claims that Jesus expressed greater solidarity with the middle-class than with the poor, arguing that his social circle consisted of "pharisees... merchants... tax collectors [and] cultivated women" (Barton 71). Moreover, he insists that Jesus was not the self-sacrificing ascetic that tradition portrays him as, but was rather an exemplar of the leisurely, hedonic life, a joyful, jocose man who enjoyed a good banquet and proclaimed that "life is a gift to be enjoyed" (Barton 88). According to Barton, Jesus was not "the man of sorrow and pain, the outcast, despised of the world" described by those like Sinclair; he was not the "class-conscious working-man" or "union carpenter" of radical Christologies, but was, instead, an ebullient man about town and progenitor of the modern corporate executive (*Jungle* 375, 374; *Carpenter* 3).

Ultimately, the aim of *The Man Nobody Knows* is to prove that Jesus Christ was "the founder of modern business" (Barton np). While radicals sought to portray Jesus as the original opponent of capitalism, Barton contended that Jesus preached a gospel synonymous with "the spirit of modern business" (165). Through his ministry, Jesus revealed the "principles of modern salesmanship," crafting parables and slogans that remain "the most powerful advertisements of all time" (Barton 104, 107). Adopting the subjunctive mood often found in the lives novels, Barton insists that if Jesus were alive today he "would be a national advertiser... as he was the great advertiser of his own day" (140). Despite Francis Greenwood Peabody's assertion that "hardly any problem of exegesis is more difficult than to discover in the gospels an administrative or organizing... Christ," Barton does precisely that, claiming that Jesus "picked up twelve men from the bottom ranks of business and forged them into an organization that conquered the world!" (Peabody 89, Barton np). Barton paints a portrait not of Christ the Redeemer, but of Christ the Executive, the great organization-builder who managed a vast marketing endeavor and whose genius lied in his ability to persuade the masses to buy a product that they did not want or need. Barton marvels at Jesus's ability to conjure new markets by "creating desire" for a soteriological product that he and his disciples were poised to supply (Barton 99). He writes that, at the time of Jesus ministry, "there was no demand for a new religion; the world was already over-supplied," and yet Jesus managed to create demand, convincing "prospective believers" to "inves[t] in a new religion" despite the surplus present in an already glutted religious marketplace (Barton 92, 97, 102). By Barton's account, the great revelation of the gospels are methods for producing consumer demand. While radicals were busy imagining a savior who fulfills the economic needs of the people by abolishing want, the bourgeoisie were designing a god who manufactures evermore needs and desires.

However, Barton is not only concerned with depicting Jesus as the exemplar of corporate mores, but wishes to sanctify business and capitalism in general. He writes that Jesus is "the silent partner in every modern business" and that "all business is his Father's business" (Barton 188, 180). Barton seeks to inscribe capitalism onto the ontological order, arguing that Being itself is "the great [business] enterprise which He has initiated" (Barton 180). By reproducing the capitalist social formation we contribute to the realization of that holy endeavor "which He can never finish without the help of men" (Barton 180). Perfectly exemplifying the apotheosis of modern capitalism, Barton recreates the universe in the image of American commercial culture, imagining it to be a cosmic business enterprise where God presides as the divine executive and humanity acts as the middle-managers charged with realizing the boss's vision.

"We Know How Gods Are Made": Anthropotheism and the Politics of Salvation

Amid the cultural upheaval caused by industrialization, upper- and working-class thinkers alike invested their economic and social philosophies with sacred import, elevating their material interests to the level of divine necessity. Among the leisure-class, this gave rise to a salvation ethic which buttressed the economic status quo, while the working-classes produced a soteriology of the disprivileged that portrayed socialism as the means to society's salvation. The radical fiction of the period illustrates the apotheosis of socialism and its transformation into a salvation ethic, as well as the crucial cultural role played by literature in propagating that soteriology. These works, as well as those that sought to sanctify commercial mores by similar means, bear witness to the centrality of religion in the conflict of capital and labor at the turn of the century and demonstrate that literature was a vital site where each faction endeavored to syncretize Christianity and their respective economic models.

More than any other author who contributed to the lives genre or made Christology a key strategic armament on either side of the cultural front, Jack London was alive to the ideological power of god-making and its historical role in social dynamics.[5] The period of London's most fervid interest in socialism, 1899–1908, coincided with the time when he was engrossed in the study of Christianity and the figure of Jesus in particular. Throughout this period, he compiled notes and research for a grand Christ novel he planned to write. In the early days of planning his Christ novel, London had already chosen its epigraph, one that reveals a great deal about the political theology so central to his fiction and activism. It was to read, "There is only one thing more wonderful than the reality of Christ, and that is, Christ never existing, that the imagination of man should have created him" (Tavernier-Courbin 259). Many years later, just prior to his death, London wrote in his introduction for Sinclair's *The Cry of Justice* (1915), "We know how gods are made" (11). London was not primarily interested in Jesus as a supernatural being, rather, "he was interested in how people had created a Christ out of Jesus of Nazareth" (Williams 34). He was compelled by the process of transforming a man into a god and by the social-political function of this process. For London, "Jesus was neither fraud nor Christ"; rather, he was an all too human individual whose "teachings represent a stage in the moral development of mankind" (Williams 37, 31). London's conception of history and humanity's social development owed more to Hegel than to Marx. He fused his vestigial Christianity with a utopian evolutionary humanism derived from a Hegelian model of salvation history. For London, the history of all hitherto existing society is the history of humanity's struggle to achieve salvation by becoming conscious of its freedom. Salvation history is the drama of humanity coming into consciousness of its inborn freedom, but this is a process that must pass through successive stages of apotheosis. He concurred with Sinclair who wrote, "my God is the process of my being… My God… says to men: 'I am still making you, and you are still making Me' " (*Autobiography* 283, 284). Williams writes that in London's work, " 'Freedom' has become a substitute for 'redemption,' but they have nearly interchangeable meanings" (25). In his notes for *The Iron Heel* (1908), one finds that, for London, "Freedom became a religion, [the] expression of the religious sentiment or religious nature of man—so that the [proletarian] struggle for freedom… resembled the early Christians of the first century" (qtd. in Williams 24). Along these lines, London proclaimed in his homiletic essay "Revolution" that "the revolutionist… sings

---

[5] See Bembridge, Steven. "Jesus as a Cultural Weapon in the Work of Jack London," *Studies in American Naturalism* 10.1 (2015): 22–40.

the eternal song of human freedom—a song of all lands and all tongues and all time" (Foner 502).

London believed that god-making and the perennial reimagining of existent concepts of God play an integral part in a dialectical realization of human freedom. Antithetical images of God and the ethics each sanctions are ideological tools continually employed by humanity in an ongoing historical struggle, an evolutionary conflict that, in London's view, will ultimately lead to the redemption of humankind. *The Iron Heel* is a narrative predicated on this concept of apotheosis and its role in salvation history. Ernest Everhard is a prophetic figure who is undoubtedly presented in Christ-like terms and whose actions often replicate the stages of the Christ story, but ultimately Everhard is all man, merely one phase in the salvation history of humanity, the culmination of which is represented in the frame story set in a utopian future where Everhard is regarded as a founding father or saint but not as a god. In 1911, London began planning a series of novels that would tell the story of humanity's salvation history. The series would be a comprehensive, coherent, interconnected narrative ultimately leading to social salvation. In his notes, we read: "No. 1, — *Before Adam*; No. 2 — Christ Novel; No. 3, — The Middle Ages; No. 4, some great proletarian-bourgeois conflict story of the present; No. 5, *The Iron Heel*; No. 6, — The Far Future, the perfected and perishing human race" ("Authorial" 29-30). For London, god-figures like Everhard or Jesus—whether he is portrayed as worker or merchant—represent humanity's need to create deified embodiments of evolving stages of moral and material development. These are not supernatural beings, but are the means of legitimating dialectically competing ethics through a process of apotheosis, a process that will eventually lead to the liberation of humanity.

In his early essays, London shows that he concurs with the young Hegelians' view of how god-images are created and the ideological function they perform. He writes, "all social codes"—such as those regarding the path to salvation—"are but reflexes of existing economic conditions" ("Wanted" 439). Elsewhere he writes, "A people must have some standard by which to measure itself and its individuals; then it must shape its institutions in such manner as will permit its attaining this standard" ("Communities" 430). A god-image is (re)created when a social class deifies its "existing economic conditions" and defining traits. This sacralized self-reflection then functions as an ideal standard of comportment or an ethic that sanctions and legitimates the class's interests. For the ruling-class, this functions to reproduce the existent order and to justify their position of mastery. For the subordinate class, this functions to console by sanctifying their suffering and to authorize the negation of the established economic order.

Fittingly, readers are first introduced to Earnest Everhard "in the midst of... churchmen," during John Cunningham's "preacher's night," a weekly dinner party composed of eminent clerics (*Iron* 11). Here, Everhard claims that the mainstream churches' failure to engage the working-class stems from the nature of the ministers' "metaphysical thinking." The doctrines of the bourgeois church, he argues, are anathema to workers because they are projections of the subjectivity of the ruling-class. They function to lend divine sanction to the mores of this class, to legitimate their dominance, and to justify their exploitation of labor. Everhard claims that clerics are "cosmos-makers. Each of you dwells in a cosmos of his own making, created out of his own fancies and desires... Each of you goes into his own consciousness to explain himself and the universe" (*Iron* 14-15). This tendency toward apotheosis, he explains, leads them to mistake "their own shadows for gods" (*Iron* 16). While "the scientist explains himself by the universe," "the metaphysician explains the universe by himself" (*Iron* 15). Theologians, bourgeois or otherwise, are mere "shadow-projectors" (*Iron* 16). Ultimately, Everhard explains, there is little difference between the ruling-class minister who imagines a god that affirms laissez-faire capitalism "and the Eskimo who makes a fur-clad blubber-eating god" (*Iron* 16). Each creates "gods in their own shapes and out of their own desires" (*Iron* 16).

Here, London evinces a self-awareness and theoretical understanding of the politics of apotheosis that is lacking among his peers. As his account of modern shadow-casting makes clear, he understands that both the working and ruling-classes manufacture, by way of the apotheotic process, a divine sanction for their economic and political priorities and design a salvation ethic that imbues the conduct necessary to realize those ends with redemptive power. The evidence assembled here shows us that the religion of each class, and the code of conduct each believed necessary to attain salvation, were shaped by the material conditions of the Industrial Age. This reveals that class conflict in the first decades of the twentieth century was a matter of clashing economies of redemption. Each side in the conflict of capital and labor believed that it was not merely engaged in a power struggle, but that it was fighting for the salvation of humanity.

"Salvation through Socialism": Conversion in the Work of London and Sinclair

The most common motif in early-twentieth-century radical literature is the conversion narrative. Rideout has observed that the conversion story is a central element in one-third of all the labor novels written in the first three decades of the twentieth century. A variation on the bildungsroman, these works feature techniques used by evangelical revivalists and depict conversions to socialism or to the labor movement that are modeled on religious experience. Here, a character's salvation is achieved through the acquisition of class consciousness, which is described as a kind of rebirth, awakening, or recognition of revelation (Rideout 58). The most widely read and emblematic radical authors to consistently employ this trope were Jack London and his protégé Upton Sinclair. Not only did London and Sinclair use the conversion story in their fiction and nonfiction time and again, they both described their own discovery of socialism as a religious conversion. In their work, both authors seek to conflate Christianity and socialism, to prove that the two are compatible, and to show that conformity to Christian principles demands the endorsement of socialism. London and Sinclair use their writing as an instrument of evangelism that aims to convince their audience that socialism is a religious enterprise and a means to salvation.

Evangelists for the Church of the Revolution

Jack London's fervent devotion to socialism is well known, but he is not typically remembered as a Christian socialist. However, in both his essays and his fiction, as Jay Williams puts it, "socialism and Christianity" run "in the same stream bed" (304). Though London's "deeply spiritual" interpretation of socialism is most overt in the work he produced from 1899 to 1906, "the religious element in London's rhetoric is never lost" and remained "a constant for him throughout his life" (*Sail*, 444; James Williams, "Authorial" 25). "Christian imagery and rhetoric abounds" in London's early essays, where he first begins to present socialism as a religion that is synonymous with authentic Christianity ("Authorial" 25). Biographer Carolyn Johnston argues that London not only believed he had found "salvation through socialism" but that it "could provide salvation" for all Americans as well (63, 85).

London's identification of Christianity and socialism can be traced back to his early tutelage under Frederick Irons Bamford, a reference librarian at the Oakland public library and proponent of the Social Gospel who endorsed the Christian socialism of minister-activists George Herron and Walter Rauschenbusch. Bamford acted as a mentor to young London in the 1890s, guiding the reading that would ultimately lead London to champion socialism and to persistently interpret it through the lens of Christianity. Joan London writes that her father's early acquaintance with Bamford "was destined to dictate the course of his life," and Williams notes that while "London was too radical to be called a Social Gospeler, he did agree with its major tenets" (95; "Authorial" 27). The sustained influence of this early study of the Social Gospel is evident in that, in the years to come, long after he had outgrown Bamford and become versed in Marxist theory and scientific socialism, London continued to approach socialism as a moral imperative.

Throughout the period of his serious interest in socialism, 1899-1908, London publicly represented the cause as a religious endeavor while privately compiling notes for the Christ novel. Johnston explains that London was both "a socialist minister" and an "evangelist for socialism" who engaged in a tireless "crusade" to spread the "revolutionary gospel," effectively making him "the Charles Finney" or "the Billy Sunday of the socialist movement" (65, 109, 113, 112). Prior to his famous 1905-6 lecture tour, London's "preaching" was confined to print (Johnston 71). In 1899, London entered *Cosmopolitan* editor John Brisbane Walker's essay contest and won with his essay "What Communities Lose by the Competitive System." Walker, a millionaire and would-be preacher "who wrote Christian sociological essays," was sympathetic to the religious tone of London's entry in which he insists that capitalism is "soulless" and antithetical to Christianity, as "altruism and industrial competition...cannot exist together" (*Sail* 302; Foner 428). In his 1902 essay "Wanted: A New Law of Development," London calls socialism "the passionate gospel of the dispossessed," and in July of that year, he sailed to London to research and compose *The People of the Abyss*, his study of the city's underclass (Foner 442). As Williams has noted, this work relies on a "faith-based" examination of economics and uses quotations from scripture to forward "a biblical argument" against the capitalist system (*Sail* 444). Here, London maintains that England's relief efforts have failed because reformers do not "understand the simple sociology of Christ" (*Abyss* 306). In his 1903 essay "How I Became a Socialist," London describes his discovery of socialism as a kind of religious "conversion," claiming, "I had been reborn" (362, 365). The following year, in his "Explanation of the Great Socialist Vote of 1904," London contends that socialism is "a religious movement" that "preaches the passionate gospel of the brotherhood of man" (Foner 405). A year later, in "What Life Means to Me," he offered his most impassioned synthesis of Christianity and socialism to date, explaining that in socialism, he found "a spiritual paradise":

> I found...warm faith in the human, glowing idealism, sweetness of unselfishness, renunciation, and martyrdom,—all the splendid, stinging things of the spirit...
> I was in touch with great souls who exalted flesh and spirit over dollars and

cents... All about me were nobleness of purpose and heroism of effort, and my days and nights were sunshine and starshine, all fire and dew, with before my eyes, ever burning and blazing the Holy Grail, Christ's own Grail, the warm human, long-suffering and maltreated, but to be rescued and saved at the last.

(*No Mentor* 93, 91)

Finally, in "Revolution," London's most famous essay and the text that served as the "sermon" he delivered on his 1905-06 lecture tour, we find his most strident endorsement of Christian socialism (Johnston 110). In the essay, London employs several forms of Christian suasion. First, he assumes a prophetic register, exhorting his listeners to disavow capitalist idolatry—to "cast off allegiance to the bourgeois gods" (Foner 493). He then assumes the role of a socialist apologist to demonstrate that socialism and authentic Christianity are one and the same. He explains that "the revolutionist... preaches righteousness" and "service, unselfishness, sacrifice, martyrdom—the things that sting awake the imagination of the people, touching their hearts with the fervor that arises out of the impulse toward good and which is essentially religious in its nature" (Foner 502). He ends with an appeal to new converts to take up the mantle of evangelism themselves. He proclaims that "preaching the revolution—that passionate gospel," is "in essence a religious propaganda with a fervor in it of Paul and Christ" (Foner 504). Ultimately, as Johnston has recognized, the essay was intended to initiate a conversion experience by employing the tactics of "a Christian sermon in which the minister tries to convince his audience of the evils of sin so that the sinner will accept salvation" (110). In "What Life Means to Me," also written in 1905, London argues that to be complicit in the injustices of capitalism is to "sin passively" (Foner 93). Here, he once more condemns "the sins of capitalism" and presents socialism as the means to salvation (Johnston 110).

After completing his essay for Walker, London wrote to Cloudsley Johns on August 10, 1899 to tell his friend that he had decided to write a "Christ novel" (*Letters* 104). It would be his first foray into the form. However, though London was engrossed in research for it, he chose to write *The Daughter of the Snows* (1902) first, as the commissioned novel would provide him with much-needed funds immediately and could be written quickly. London would go on to compile sources and compose notes for his Christ novel from 1899 to 1915, a period spanning nearly the entirety of his literary career, and would ultimately incorporate this material into *The Iron Heel* and *The Star Rover*. His early notes on the novel indicate that he originally planned to "show Christ partly and largely a labor-leader" and to demonstrate that Christianity and socialism were founded on identical principles (Tavernier-Courbin 260). London "clipped, saved, and marked at the top 'Christ Novel' " a review of Karl Kautsky's *Der Ursprung der Christentumus* entitled "A Socialist View of the Origin of Christianity" ("Authorial" 25). He was particularly interested in the passage where the reviewer writes that in Kautsky's view, "Jesus was an agitator, a revolutionary, a rebel, and felt a strong class hatred of the rich," and he underlined a sentence in which the reviewer indicated that Kautsky saw Jesus as a "working class messiah" ("Authorial" 25). He also collected relevant texts, such as an article entitled "Economic of Jesus" and a pamphlet called "The Socialism of Jesus" that presented a "socialist portrayal of Jesus as a proletariat working to undermine the ruling classes" ("Authorial" 26, 28). He made notes instructing himself to revisit the work of Walter Rauschenbusch, to "see POLITICAL ECONOMY OF CHRIST," and to refer to Howard Pyle's *Rejected of Men* (Tavernier-Courbin 260). In the novel, Pyle "describes the events of Jesus's life as if they had happened in New York, 1903. Jesus is portrayed as a leader of the oppressed poor" and is "executed by the ruling church body" ("Authorial" 25). Williams writes that "London, like other socialists, was attracted to the idea that the organization of men behind Jesus was communistic in nature. Jesus's followers, the theory postulated, were the first to form an urban working class collective [whose]... immediate goal was to overthrow Roman rule" ("Authorial" 25). London was compelled by Christianity's ethics and economic philosophy, by "the socialistic nature of Jesus's message" ("Authorial" 27). But most importantly, he was interested in "the organization of men" who had made Jesus into a god. As he demonstrates in "Revolution," London was keenly aware of the power of "religious propaganda" and wanted his Christ novel—in whatever form it would take—to show that "the task of all socialists was like the task of the early Christians: to overthrow the corrupted institutions" that constituted capitalism ("Authorial" 25).

Though it would not be published by Macmillan until 1908, London composed *The Iron Heel* from August to December 1906, just months after completing his evangelistic lecture tour. London's research into ancient Jerusalem and the crucifixion of Jesus would not be translated into fiction until he composed *The Star Rover* between 1913 and 1914, but it was here, in *The Iron Heel*, that London incorporated the bulk of his forgoing work on the Christ novel; this was the culmination of the work on Christianity and socialism that he had been crafting and refining over the previous seven years.

As in his earlier essays, in *The Iron Heel*, London characterizes revolutionism as a religious enterprise led by zealots, ascetics, and martyrs.[6] The novel's Avis Everhard recalls that "the Revolution took on largely the character of religion. We worshipped at the shrine of the Revolution, which was the shrine of liberty. It was the divine flashing through us. Men and women devoted their lives to the Cause, and newborn babes were sealed to it as of old they had been sealed to the service of God" (179). London suggests that the revolutionists are fulfilling God's plan and adhering to His will, depicting those who perform this holy task as saintly figures intent on the salvation of humanity. He reuses a passage from "What Life Means to Me," written just months earlier, to describe the novel's socialist combatants as martyrs whose eyes were set on "Christ's own Grail" and their "ardent idealism" as directed toward the "maltreated" who were "to be... saved" by the revolution. Like so many of his peers in the movement, London exalted labor activists, imbuing them with a saintly aura, and sacralized socialism, depicting it as redemptive return to authentic Christianity.

The Iron Heel is essentially a hagiographical text that documents the final days of a Christ figure—Ernest Everhard—covering his evangelism, his recruitment of disciples, and the early stages of the revolutionary movement that would ultimately lead to his martyrdom. Throughout the novel, Ernest is by turns characterized as a prophet, oracle, teacher, "father confessor," and evangelist, "one of God's own lovers" (5, 56, 44, 133). While it is clear that Everhard is modeled on London's interpretation of Jesus, we must recall that London did not regard Jesus as a god but as an integral figure in the progressive salvation history of humanity, a person who possessed a preternatural command of the divinity inherent in all people. Therefore, Everhard is depicted as a messianic figure or proletarian savior but not as a deity: "All his lifetime [Everhard] toiled for others... And all his life he sang the song of man. And he did it out of sheer love of man, and for man he gave his life and was crucified" (132). London's use of Jesus as the template for his socialist hero is perhaps most explicit in his account of the transfiguration of Ernest Everhard. Avis recounts,

> Ernest rose before me transfigured, the apostle of truth, with shining brows and the fearlessness of one of God's own angels, battling for the truth and the right, and battling for the succor of the poor and lonely and oppressed. And then there arose before me another figure, the Christ! He, too, had taken the part of the

---

[6] Frederick Engels noted the commonality of the two movements, particularly with respect to the promise of salvation. He writes, "Both Christianity and workers' socialism preach forthcoming salvation from bondage and misery; Christianity places this salvation in a life beyond, after death, in heaven; socialism places it in this world, in a transformation of society." Engels, Frederick. "On the History of Early Christianity," *Die Neue Zeit*, 1894–95. Translated by the Institute of Marxism-Leninism, 1957.

lowly and oppressed, and against all the established power of priest and pharisee. And I remembered his end upon the cross, and my heart contracted with a pang as I thought of Ernest. Was he too, destined for a cross?

(49)

On a subsequent occasion, Avis notes that "as before I had seen him transfigured, so now he stood transfigured before me. His brows were bright with the divine that was in him, and brighter yet shone his eyes from the midst of the radiance that seemed to envelop him as a mantle" (61). We recall, of course, that the Transfiguration is the culminating event of Jesus's life as an evangelist, related in each of the synoptic gospels. Here, Everhard takes the place of Christ and is imbued with divine light that shone from his brow, surrounding him as it had Jesus.

Conversion to the Religion of Socialism

An alternative title for *The Iron Heel* could be *The Gospel according to Avis* as it consists of her account of Ernest's ministry and martyrdom and the establishment of the church of the revolution. By preaching the gospel of socialism, Everhard provokes a conversion experience in many of his interlocutors, who receive his teaching as revelation and are born again after attaining class consciousness. *The Iron Heel* is a prime example of a common type of conversion narrative, one that concerns the redemption of a member of the leisure class. As is standard with this type, the novel recounts a young, wealthy woman's "conversion into a revolutionist" upon meeting and falling in love with a charismatic socialist hero who opens her eyes to economic injustice and her class's complicity in the sins of modern industry (200). Avis's conversion experience occurs when Ernest awakens her class consciousness, which she describes in decidedly religious terms: "It was as though I were about to see a new and awful revelation... My whole world was turning over" (48-49). The word "conversion," of course, literally means "turning over." Hearing Ernest's socialist gospel leads Avis to be born again, to become his leading disciple and to become a member of the church of the revolution. In this way, Avis joins the ranks of numerous middle-class women in radical fiction whose conversions are provoked by saintly socialist men, such as the namesake of William Dean Howells's *Annie Kilburn* (1888), Margaret Vance in his *A Hazard of New Fortunes* (1890), Evelith Strange in his *Through the Eye of the Needle* (1907), Freda Hartwell in Charlotte Teller's *The Cage* (1907), and Mary Magna in Sinclair's *They Call Me Carpenter*, to name but a few.

Moreover, this literary motif corresponds to the real-world experience of many radicals at the turn of the century. Many socialists of the era described their experience of the movement in terms reminiscent of revival conversions. For example, Henry George reported that his awakening to the "social problem" in 1869 came to him as a "conversion after the pattern of evangelical Protestantism" (Gutman 106n9). George writes, "Once, in daylight, and in a city street, there came to me a thought, a vision, a call—give it what name you please. But every nerve quivered. And there and then I made a vow" (Gutman 106n9). Autobiographical conversion stories were a staple element of the radical publications of the time. Numerous papers and journals featured articles written by prominent socialists in which they recounted how they were called to the movement. These testimonials of political rebirth were invariably written in the idiom of the Christian conversion story and were pervaded by allusions to their religious analog.[7] By conflating these two forms of conversion, radical authors suggest that salvation is to be achieved through the endorsement of socialist norms.

Perhaps the most widely read of the Progressive Era's radical conversion novels is Sinclair's *The Jungle*. The extent to which Christianity pervades Sinclair's conception of socialism is observable in its climactic pages. Before his ultimate conversion to socialism, Jurgis Rudkus joins a labor union, which Sinclair equates to a religion:

> Jurgis had always been a member of the church, because it was the right thing to be, but the church had never touched him... Here, however, was a new religion—one that did touch him, that took hold of every fibre of him; and with all the zeal and fury of a convert he went out as a missionary... after the fashion of all crusaders since the original ones, who set out to spread the gospel of Brotherhood.
>
> (100)

Not only does Jurgis undergo a conversion, he becomes an evangelist for his newfound faith. Later, disillusioned with his trade union and in despair, Jurgis inadvertently stumbles into a meeting where he hears what can only be described as a sermon. The speaker offers a "message of salvation," a gospel of "deliverance" (338, 339). At times, the speaker's words are indistinguishable from those of a revivalist who beckons unrepentant sinners to the mourner's bench with the

---

[7] For example, see Debs, Eugene. "How I Became a Socialist," *New York Comrade* 1 (April 1902): 146–8; Keller, Helen. "How I Became a Socialist," *New York Call*, November 3, 1912; and London, Jack. "How I Became a Socialist," *Comrade* 2.6 (1903): 122–3.

promise of redemption: "There will be some one man whom pain and suffering have made desperate... and to him my words will come like a sudden flash of lightening to one who travels in darkness—revealing the way before him, the perils and the obstacles—solving all problems, making all difficulties clear!" (340). Through conversion to socialism, the speaker promises, the believer will become "a free man at last! A man delivered" (340). This message produces a "supernatural experience" for Jurgis, causing him to feel as though he'd been born again (353). The speaker's words

> rang through the chambers of his soul... with a sense of things not of earth, of mysteries never spoken before, of presences of awe and terror! There was an unfolding of vistas before him, a breaking of the ground beneath him, an upheaving, a stirring, a trembling; he felt himself suddenly a mere man no longer–there were powers within him undreamed of, there were demon forces contending, age-long wonders struggling to be born, and he sat oppressed with pain and joy, while a tingling stole down into his fingertips, and his breath came hard and fast... There was a falling in of all the pillars of his soul, the sky seemed to split above him—he stood there, with his clenched hands upraised, his eyes bloodshot, and the veins standing out purple in his face, roaring in the voice of a wild beast, frantic, incoherent, maniacal. And when he could shout no more he still stood there, gasping, and whispering hoarsely to himself: "By God! By God! By God!"
>
> (344, 345)

Jurgis's emotionally fraught experience is clearly reminiscent of a revival conversion, where one finds salvation and is reborn through the acceptance of a new revelation: "A miracle... had been wrought in him... [H]e knew that in the mighty upheaval that had taken place in his soul a new man had been born... [H]e had been delivered... [H]e was free" (346).

Given Upton Sinclair's personal history, it should come as no surprise that he described his own discovery of socialism in religious terms, as "a conversion" or "a visitation by angels" (qtd. in Gottesman xxi). Religion had been an ever-present and immensely significant part of Sinclair's youth. He had, he explains in his autobiography, "been brought up as a very religious little boy"; he was "a devout little Episcopalian" whose mother "decided that [he] was to become a bishop," and he went to church consistently, taught Sunday school as a teen, and "could recite every prayer and sing every hymn" (288, 30, 31, 30). However, when the young Sinclair, who had attained class consciousness at an early age, was unable to reconcile his religion with the economic inequality he witnessed and suffered firsthand, his faith was thrown into crisis. Sinclair was mentored during this period by Reverend William Wilmerding Moir, who "became a foster father" to the young man; later, Sinclair described Moir as having "more influence upon me than any other man" (*Autobiography* 30). Though Sinclair had become disenchanted with the church, that had not shaken his faith in Christianity: "My quarrel with the churches is a lover's quarrel. I do not want to destroy them but to... drive out the money changers from the front pews" (*Autobiography* 31). This is an exemplary expression of a sentiment shared by many Christian socialists of the era, whose vocal anticlericalism did not preclude a pious devotion to the faith and, in particular, to the figure of Jesus.

Though Francis Lacassin contends that it was Jack London who converted Sinclair to socialism in 1902, Sinclair attributes his turn to radicalism to "the Protestant Episcopal Church" (Lacassin 3, *Autobiography* 99). Sinclair explains, "I really took the words of Jesus seriously"; by converting to socialism, he writes, "I thought I was helping to glorify the rebel carpenter, the friend of the poor and lowly, the symbol of human brotherhood" (*Autobiography* 99). In 1901, nearly on the eve of his fortuitous discovery of socialism, Sinclair writes to Edwin Markham that he wants "to give every second of my time and of my thought, every ounce of my energy to the worship of my God and to the uttering of the unspeakable message that I know he has given me" (qtd. in Arthur 178) In 1902, Sinclair found the language with which to utter that "unspeakable message," when, as he was "dropping off an article for consideration at *The Literary Digest*," he met a young man named Leonard D. Abbott, "an active socialist" (Arthur 20). Abbott gave Sinclair a copy of *Wilshire's* and some socialist pamphlets, including one authored by the preeminent Christian socialist George Herron. Sinclair was so moved by what he read that he wrote Herron "an admiring letter" (Arthur 20). Herron quickly replied and invited Sinclair to a dinner that, as Sinclair learned upon arriving, was being hosted by Gaylord Wilshire himself, who, at the threshold of an "apartment of extreme elegance... introduced himself as 'Comrade Wilshire' " (*Autobiography* 101). It was this triumvirate of Christian socialists, Abbott, Wilshire, and Herron, who "opened his eyes to socialism," an experience Sinclair describes in terms reminiscent of an effervescent revival conversion: it was "like the falling down of prison walls about my mind" (*Autobiography* 101).[8] Herron would become Sinclair's chief benefactor, supporting the young writer while he completed *Manassas* in 1903. Meanwhile, the Sinclairs and the

---

[8] Wilshire would publish his treatise on Christian socialism, *Socialism: A Religion*, in 1906, the same year *The Jungle* was published.

Wilshires became "intimate friends" (*Autobiography* 104). Like Herron, Wilshire was eager to support the burgeoning writer and printed a picture of Sinclair in his magazine, introducing him to the socialist movement as "a coming novelist" before Sinclair had even begun work on *The Jungle* (*Autobiography* 104). In 1904, after completing *Manassas*, Sinclair began his study of socialism in earnest under the direction of Herron and Wilshire, reading Marx, Kautsky, and Veblen, among others. Sinclair met this coterie in a time of personal and professional crisis. His long-held faith was shaken, and he was failing as a writer. "What saved Sinclair," explains biographer Anthony Arthur, was "being converted to the religion of socialism" (324). Sinclair was "searching for the true path to salvation. Socialism gave him that path" (Arthur 324) Like London, Sinclair had been grasping for a means to reconcile his faith and his opposition to capitalism. Like London, he found his answer in Christian socialism.

Though Sinclair did not attribute his conversion to London, it is incontestable that London's Christian socialism had an immense influence on Sinclair. In 1902, Sinclair began to write "reverential letters to London," who was a "boyhood hero" (Silet 49, 51). London kindly responded and so began a friendship that, though conducted "entirely by mail" continued, as Sinclair put it, "all our lives" (qtd. in Allatt 78). Though their personal lifestyles were incompatible, Sinclair continued to see London as a kind of "guru" and he often went to him for advice and aid (Lacassin 5). Sinclair recalls that after their first meeting in January 1906, he "was prepared to give my hero the admiration of a slave" (*Mammonart* 364). Throughout the years of their relationship, London remained generous to his protégé, and by Sinclair's own account he was largely responsible for the success of *The Jungle* and the fame it brought its young author. After *The Jungle* had been rejected by several publishers, London intervened and sent a synopsis of the novel to his publisher, Macmillan, who gave Sinclair a $500 advance but ultimately declined to published the book (Lacassin 1; Silet 26-27). Fred Warren finally agreed to serialize the novel in the *Appeal to Reason* from February 25 to November 4, 1905, but only with the stipulation that London, now the favorite son of the socialist movement, write a favorable review of the book in a major newspaper or magazine. London not only obliged Warren by writing a glowing review for the *Appeal to Reason* in November 1905 but also improved on Warren's request by writing similar reviews for *Wilshire's* and the New York *Evening Journal* in August 1906, just as he was beginning to write *The Iron Heel*. Sinclair later maintained that "if that book went all over the world, it was Jack London's push that started it" (*Mammonart* 372). One year after completing *The Star Rover* and just one year before his death, London performed a final favor for his devotee, composing an introduction to Sinclair's anthology *The Cry of Justice* in which he writes that when a person comes to understand socialism and its ethical imperatives, they are "converted to the gospel of service" (*No Mentor* 155). On March 22, 1915, Sinclair wrote London to thank him for the introduction, describing it as "a really quite religious utterance—written to organ music" (qtd. in Lacassin 5). This underscores that from 1899 until the time of his death, for Jack London socialism was synonymous with authentic Christianity and that this was a sentiment shared by his disciple, Upton Sinclair.

The conversion trope was the most common among numerous methods that radical and progressive activists used to conflate socialism and Christianity. Evangelical rhetoric, biblical allusions, and Christian virtues pervade leftist American literature at the turn of the century. Popular Christian motifs in the period's radical discourse include identification of the poor with the enslaved Jews of the Old Testament, the celebration of acts of self-sacrifice and martyrdom, messianism, millennialism, the rejection of dominant economic norms, and references to the unification of a community of the righteous who are socially subordinate but divinely favored. In this respect, London and Sinclair's personal experience and rhetorical tactics were not unusual. Their attempt to integrate socialism and Christianity is particularly significant because it is emblematic of a widespread practice, a practice, moreover, that was not limited to the members and allies of the working-class. Advocates of laissez-faire capitalism took part in an equally vigorous campaign to convince the American populace that capitalism was the earthly embodiment of God's will. While scholars have mined the archive to gather examples of capital and labor's respective appropriations of religious authority and expression, the cause and function of these epiphenomena have remained largely unexamined.

Properly understanding how apotheosis works and the outcomes it produces sheds a great deal of light on the modes of sacralization employed by capital and labor in the first decades of the twentieth century. The efforts of Barton, London, and Sinclair, among others, potently exemplify the centrality of apotheosis in class conflict at the turn of the century. The pervasive conflation of religion and economy in their work poses a significant challenge to the prevailing Weberian conception of modernity as an era of disenchantment and secularization. This archive of collective representations proves that the domestic political battles of the period were waged in largely soteriological terms, in service to concepts of redemption that were implicitly based in opposing systems of political economy. Moreover, having a clear understanding of apotheosis will help us to recognize the ways it continues to fundamentally shape American culture today.

5

"Christianity Incorporated": Sinclair Lewis and the Taylorization of American Protestantism

Frederick Winslow Taylor is the forgotten engineer of modern American culture. In the first decades of the twentieth century, he revolutionized industrial production by creating an efficiency system that was adopted nationwide. Though his system of "scientific management" originated in the factory, Taylor's ultimate goal was to reengineer every facet of American society and after an intense campaign of proselytizing he achieved that aim when popular interest in Taylorism reached a fever pitch, initiating an efficiency craze that gripped the nation and grew into what Samuel Haber likened to a "Great Awakening" (ix). Taylor's system of scientific management soon went from being a method of industrial production to being a new set of norms that infused and restructured every institution in American society: the church, the school, the government, the military, the world of commerce, and even the domestic sphere with the invention of home economics. Haber's term is not merely analogical as a determining factor in the immense success of Taylor, and his system was a result of their being invested, from the very start, with the sacred. Taylor was portrayed as a messianic figure and his system was promoted as the means to the nation's redemption. As Taylorism was increasingly transformed from a system of industrial efficiency into the nation's prevailing salvation ethic, Protestant institutions and doctrines were modified to accommodate the new dogma.

This was the cultural milieu Sinclair Lewis inhabited at the pinnacle of his literary prowess. Lewis's finest satirical novels, written at the height of the efficiency craze, are a sustained indictment of Taylorism and its sacralization. In these works, Lewis argues that Taylorism has been recast as divine truth, allowing it to transcend the factory to become the dominant system of norms operative in American society. Lewis found that, as American society became increasingly retooled to Taylor's specifications, Americans were redefining the sacred by projecting the characteristics of Taylorist industry onto their theological ideas, reformulating them on the basis of their new economic conditions. Lewis insisted that religion and economy were being unduly conflated; as a result, Taylorism was abstracted and made metaphysical, causing the church to adopt the priorities and procedures of the modern factory, while, at the same time, industry and commerce began to assume the trappings of religion. Lewis recognized that the Taylorist mode of production mandated standardization and a new division of labor that codified rigidly asymmetrical power relations as well as disciplinary forms of control and normalization. He feared that the sacralization of Taylorism and its reproduction throughout American society was giving rise to an authoritarian political and religious fundamentalism that demanded total cultural homogeneity. Lewis argued that, by converting Taylor's principles of scientific management into a set of holy commandments and by deriving a salvation ethic from them, modern Americans conferred divine legitimation to a system of exploitative and undemocratic relations. He believed that the apotheosis of Taylorism had given rise to a fascistic popular piety that severely threatened the existence of democracy and freedom in America. In this chapter, I will examine the critique of Taylorism that Lewis developed in his novels of the 1920s. We will find that, in *Main Street* (1920), Lewis contends that the effort to rationalize American culture is a result of exalting Taylor's principles of scientific management. We will see that Lewis further elaborates his critique in *Elmer Gantry* (1927)—his analysis of Protestantism's thoroughgoing adoption of Taylorist structures, values, and ends—and in *Babbitt* (1922), where Lewis satirizes the sanctification of business culture and the emerging managerial middle-class.

In order to properly recognize the nuanced and often implicit satirization of Taylorism in Lewis's novels, we must first review the defining characteristics and aims of scientific management. To that end, I have devoted the first half of this chapter to giving an account of Taylor's philosophy, to its diffusion throughout American culture in the 1910s and 1920s, and to the sanctification of Taylor and his doctrines. In the second half of the chapter, we turn to an examination of Lewis's fiction, paying particular attention to his critique of Taylor's influence on American Protestantism and to the way he derides the apotheosis of modern industry and commerce.

The Gospel of Efficiency

When future Supreme Court justice Louis Brandeis made Frederick Winslow Taylor's system of scientific management the cornerstone of his argument in the Eastern Rate Case, argued before the Interstate Commerce Commission in 1910,

Taylor and his philosophy were catapulted, almost overnight, from obscurity to the front pages of newspapers across the nation, making Taylor and scientific management household names. Brandeis argued that if railroads adopted Taylor's principles of efficient management, they could save one million dollars a day and would have no need to raise freight costs. Such an outlandish claim made an even bigger splash than Brandeis had hoped. Though Taylor's ideas were relatively well known among American engineers, the publicity generated by Brandeis's million-dollar claim sparked nationwide interest in scientific management and, in short order, snowballed into an efficiency craze that would grip the country for a decade and ultimately come to wholly transform modern American culture.

Though Frederick Winslow Taylor is synonymous with modern industrialism, he did not invent any new machine, tool, or material apparatus; rather, his contribution to industry was a new mode of human engineering. The Taylor System, as it came to be called, was a new apparatus of power and knowledge implemented in American industries in order, ostensibly, "to secure the maximum prosperity" for all, for both the management and for workers (Taylor 9). Taylor believed that by rationalizing industry to maximize productivity and minimize waste, greater profits would be generated which would then translate into higher wages for the workers and lower prices for consumers. Moreover, Taylor and his disciples were convinced that by enabling the reconciliation of capital and labor through higher wages and shorter hours, the system would resolve endemic class conflict. During the "great diffusion" of scientific management from 1910 to 1920, Taylor succeeded in popularizing a new ethos that would come to inhere in sectors well beyond the confines of the factory and would ultimately constitute the dominant system of norms operative in American society.

Scientific management was a system that sought to replace the "mere traditional or rule-of-thumb" practices employed by mechanics with standardized processes to facilitate the most efficient production methods possible (103). This system was predicated on new relations of production that revised the status of industrial agents, and upon a new division of labor that separated thought from action. Taylor contended that modes of production based on the traditional trade and craft knowledge of industrial workers—arguably their sole asset—were irrational and inefficient and were therefore to be eliminated and replaced by procedures designed by college-educated planners and managers who used science to determine best practices. Taylor writes that this new class of experts are charged with rationalizing the "haphazard" knowledge of craftsmen by "classifying, tabulating, and reducing this knowledge to rules, laws, and formulae" which would then "replace the judgement of the individual workman" (36, 37). Workers were no longer permitted to use their own thought or craft knowledge in the performance of their work; they were now required to act in strict accordance with instructions issued by managers and newly formed planning departments.

Despite the fact that Taylor dealt primarily with skilled craftsmen, one of the fundamental principles of scientific management was the presumed ignorance of the worker. Taylor maintained that the industrial worker "is so stupid... that he more nearly resembles in his mental make-up the ox than any other type" (59). He writes that "it would be possible to train an intelligent gorilla so as to become a more efficient [worker] than any man can be" (40). Because the worker is "so stupid," he is "unable to understand the real science" of doing his work efficiently and cannot "properly... train himself"; therefore, he must be controlled and disciplined "by a man more intelligent than himself" until he "habitually works in accordance with scientific laws, which have been developed by some one else" (Taylor 59, 63).

Taylor's endeavor to replace inconsistent trade customs with rationalized laws and formulae entailed the standardization of tools, procedures, and most importantly, the standardization of the industrial worker. Taylor employed time and motion studies to determine the precise movements of the body required to work at the most efficient and prolific rate, essentially reducing workers to standardized mechanisms of production calibrated by the management. This new division of labor was characterized by radically asymmetrical power relations that thoroughly disempowered workers by dictating that their actions, down to the most minute motions of their body, were to be determined for them, by managers, whose orders were to be carried out without question or recourse to one's own judgment. Taylor believed that too much freedom among the working-classes was a bad thing and openly endorsed the use of force in normalizing their behavior. He writes, "too great liberty results in a large number of people going wrong who would be right if they had been forced into good habits" (qtd. in Haber 20). He contends that "it is only through *enforced* standardization... and *enforced* cooperation that this faster work can be assured" (Taylor 83). Taylor revolutionized industry not by retooling existent means of production, but by reengineering American workers to generate maximum productivity and docility. For Taylor, scientific management was not only a system for increasing industrial efficiency and profitability but was also a mechanism for generating social efficiency; that is, it was an instrument of social control that was calculated to reduce the freedom of the working-class in order to forcibly inculcate "habits" approved by the managerial class.

In contrast to his image of doltish workers, Taylor conceived of managers as a kind of industrial priesthood, a coterie of educated, middle-class experts who were agents of God's will. "The way of management," Taylorists evangelized, is "the way of the Lord" (Banta 302). As Robert Kanigel put it, for Taylor, "the priests of efficiency, in their temples of formula and rule, seemed to possess science's secrets" (516). Technocrats were the "elect," the ordained mediators of a "special knowledge," a rational revelation, who were charged with disseminating the gospel among the "unredeemed mass of the labor force" (Taylor 104, Banta 94). Taylor maintained that "the duty of enforcing the adoption of standards and of enforcing this cooperation rests with the *management* alone" (83). It was the manager's calling to standardize the worker, "to train and to make" him into a "ready-made... man," to transform him into a docile, obedient, and maximally prolific producer (Taylor 103).

Taylor's new regime of knowledge—led by a newly created technocracy of middle-class managers, planners, and record keepers—codified a new matrix of power relations as well. But it wasn't just the working-class who needed to be transformed, rather, Taylor sought nothing less than "a complete revolution in the mental attitude and the habits" of all Americans (Taylor 43). This goal was to be attained by the implementation of "a single standard" of thought and action in every aspect of American life (Taylor 118). The professed aim of this revolution, then, was the general reproduction of Taylorist norms throughout American society.

Long before Taylor's star had risen, he dreamed of applying "Scientific Management principles and ideas, not only to every industrial activity but to every conceivable human activity" (qtd. in Haber 29). One of the explicit, primary aims of *The Principles of Scientific Management* (1911)—Taylorism's holy book—is to advocate for "the general adoption of these principles" in every mode of individual and social endeavor (Taylor 141). Taylorism was always a social philosophy as well as a program for industrial rationalization. Taylor writes,

> the fundamental principles of scientific management are applicable to all kinds of human activities, from our simplest individual acts to the work of our greatest corporations... the same principles can be applied with equal force to all social activities: to the management of our homes; the management of farms; the management of the business of our tradesman, large and small; of our

churches, our philanthropic institutions, our universities, and our governmental departments.

(Taylor 7–8)

In 1903 Taylor announced that scientific management would "not be true until its truth abides everywhere" (Banta 120). In the following years, Taylor saw this dream realized. The new norms of production he designed were gradually reproduced socially as the standardized "rules, laws, and formulae" that governed permissible thought and behavior generally, not just in the workshop.

Samuel Haber writes that "the progressive era gave rise to an efficiency craze—a secular Great Awakening, an outpouring of ideas and emotions in which a gospel of efficiency was preached without embarrassment to businessmen, workers, doctors, housewives, and teachers, and yes, preached even to preachers" (ix). During this time—the period Kanigel calls "the great diffusion" of Taylorism—efficiency became synonymous with the Good. The spread of this craze was made possible by recasting Taylor's system of industrial efficiency into a form of morality. The Taylorist norms governing industry and later commerce became the norms determining social behavior. As a result, efficiency became "the cardinal virtue of American culture" (Rifkin 106).

Taylor contended that the aim of scientific management was to discern the eternal laws that constitute the divine, moral order of reason, and to bring our industrial processes into conformity to those laws. For Taylor, "the object of mechanical knowledge is… unchanging natural law" (Royce 217). It was the task of the engineer-manager "to be the hierophant of the new society," to discover what William James called the "unseen order of existence," and to bring our conduct into conformity with that order (Bell 135). Taylor believed that the principles of scientific management corresponded to immutable laws of nature and therefore conflated his industrial norms of production with "moral codes and ethical systems" (Banta 28). Martha Banta writes that "Taylor originally justified his scientism as a program of ethics. Taylor contended that production procedures become moral acts through the agency of science and the engineers in charge of the machine process" (81). This apotheotic process of superimposing mundane economic norms onto conceptions of a divine order led Taylor to believe in the inherent "morality of efficiency" and to see the dictates of his system as a code of moral conduct (Banta 98). Therefore, Taylor and his technocratic disciples maintained that "efficiency would bring moral rightness" to society (Banta 42). The good life was now equated with "the efficient life," "the managed life" (Banta 4).

This conflation of Taylorism with God's cosmological plan served an important function. The apotheosis of Taylorism was necessary to invest it with normative authority and enable its reproduction throughout American society. As Engels put it, "on the pretext that the moral world... has its permanent principles which stand above history," the managerial class was able to impose the "moral dogma" of Taylorism on the American people by proclaiming that it corresponded to "an eternal, ultimate and forever immutable ethical law" (Engels 726).

The height of the efficiency craze spanned from 1910 to 1915[1] but with America's entry into the First World War in 1917 the diffusion of scientific management increased exponentially. In the context of America's war effort and the need for increased production, Taylor appeared to be a veritable savior. During the war, even Taylor's most vehement detractors were converted, becoming advocates of the system. Amid calls for unified effort and purpose, and for America to become "a single machine," an "efficient, democratic autocracy," Taylorism was endorsed as the ethos that would lead to the nation's salvation (Kendall 18, 19). During the First World War, "efficiency became a patriotic duty" and was made synonymous with Americanism (Haber 119). To be an opponent of Taylorism became taboo, at once a sin and an act of treason.

As America's "secular Great Awakening" progressed, Taylorism was applied, as its creator had hoped, to every sector of American life. Efficiency societies and periodicals sprung up all over the nation which "helped to sanctify the... master's efficiency system" and to promote its adoption in schools, the home, government, business, and the church (Banta 174). The reproduction of Taylorism in the domestic sphere gave rise to the field of home economics. Christine Frederick promoted the introduction of Taylorism into the home with her book *The New Housekeeping: Efficiency Studies in Home Management* (1914), a work "written with missionary fervor" in the idiom of the conversion story, in which Frederick sought to spread the gospel of efficiency by recounting her rebirth in Taylorism (Banta 235). In her book *The Business of Home Management: The Principles of Domestic Engineering* (1918), Mary Pattison taught readers how to rationalize the home and to raise "housework to the plane of Scientific Engineering," for the home was now considered "part of a great factory for the production of citizens"

---

[1] In March 1914, Lenin published his indictment of Taylorism, "The Taylor System—Man's Enslavement by the Machine." However, he and other radicals did not oppose rationalization or scientific management as such. Indeed, Lenin argued that Taylor's system was not efficient enough, and that it was calculated to benefit capitalists alone. The efficiency system Lenin proposed, by contrast, promised "to cut by three-fourths the working time of the organised workers and make them four times better off than they are today" (154).

(Pattison 1).² In his exceptional work *Education and the Cult of Efficiency*, Raymond Callahan gives a thorough account of the Taylorization of American public schools and the administrative bureaucracies that were created as a result. With America's entry into the First World War, Taylor's closest disciples and the nation's leading consultants on industrial efficiency were recruited by the US government to set about Taylorizing the nation's bureaucracies and military arsenals, leading America's political infrastructure to bear Taylor's design.³ Moreover, from the beginning of the efficiency craze, Taylorism began to be thoroughly "institutionalized in corporate America" (Kanigel 19). Figures like Harlow S. Person, who served both as the dean of Dartmouth's Amos Tuck School of Administration and Finance and as president of the Taylor Society from 1913 to 1919, introduced Taylorism into America's leading business schools, effectively shaping the nation's commercial and financial philosophy for generations. Further, "student branches of the Taylor Society at the best business schools introduced scientific management to the future officialdom of the large corporations" (Haber 163-4). Particularly in the 1920s, when "the gospel of production... gave way to a new interest in sales," corporate America flocked to Taylorism and before long newly converted Taylorites filled the ranks of "the vanguard of American business thought" (Haber 164). Following in the footsteps of the business community, Protestant clerics argued that the modern church must be conceived of as "a business establishment"; therefore, it was incumbent upon them to adopt "business methods of efficiency" and to accommodate the new "division of labor determined by our changing order" if the church was to continue to be "a dynamic force in the modern world" (Mathews 58, 46-47, v). Along with the rest of American civil society, the Protestant Church began to apply "the philosophy of efficiency... to the working of churches" (Mathews 12-13). Guides for the application of scientific management to religious institutions, like those pertaining to its adoption in the home, the office, and in schools, became commonplace during this Great Taylorist Awakening.⁴

---

[2] See also Bruere, Martha B. and Robert W. Bruere. *Increasing Home Efficiency*. New York: Macmillan, 1912; Frederick, Christine. *Household Engineering: Scientific Management in the Home*. Chicago: American School of Economics, 1915; Leupp, Francis E. "Scientific Management in the Family," *Outlook*, August 1911; "A Brandeis for the Kitchen," *Boston Evening Transcript*, January 23, 1911.

[3] See Haber, *Efficiency and Uplift*, 68-9, 108-16.

[4] See also Andrews, George Arthur. *Efficient Religion*. New York: George H. Doran, 1912; Barbour, Clarence Augustus, ed., *Making Religion Efficient*. New York: Association Press, 1912. Camp, Eugene M. "Better Church Methods," *Journal of the Efficiency Society* 4 (April 1915); Rev. Greul, Frederick B. "Organizing the Church for Efficient Economic Service: A Present Day Necessity," *Journal of the Efficiency Society* 3 (March 1913); Peterson, Peter B. "Scientific Management in American Protestant Churches," *Proceedings of Eastern Academy of Management* (May 1988); Rev. Stelzle, Charles. "Efficiency in Church Work," *Journal of the Efficiency Society* 3 (March 1913).

In the first decades of the twentieth century Taylorism transcended the confines of the factory and began to reshape the American social order, encompassing "every aspect of cultural existence" (Banta 4). As Thorstein Veblen put it, the cultural reproduction of Taylorism caused "the routine of the machine industry... and its discipline [to] extend beyond the mechanical operations as such, so as in great part to determine the habits of all members of the modern community" (311). Scientific management went beyond codifying new laws of industrial labor to codify new laws of social life; the norms governing a Taylorized factory permeated civil society and were established as the moral norms governing everyday American life. Such a state of affairs was exemplified in 1924 when Edward Eyre Hunt, an aide to Herbert Hoover, remarked that Taylorism had become "part of our moral inheritance" (Hunt xiv). As Mary Nolan put it in *Visions of Modernity*, Taylor's "rationalized factory... became the model for everyday life" (213).

Taylor succeeded to this degree because he proposed more than a program of industrial reform; he offered a millennial utopianism for the machine age. Taylor dreamed of creating a rationally planned and managed society, a "control society" that would transform America into "a New Jerusalem" (Banta 5, 119). He invested his system with salvific power, proselytizing that the Taylorized "machine process" is "the redemptive process that turns earthly flaws into heavenly perfection" (Banta 37, 302). Taylor promised that America would be "redeemed by good management," that "the evils of waste and the chaos of class tensions will cease in the society governed by his principles; worker and manager will be joined together as the lion lies down with the lamb on the factory floor" (Banta 77, 81). Daniel Bell writes that "Taylor was more than an engineer. In his own mind's eye, he was a prophet who felt that he had discovered the scientific principles that would settle all social conflicts" (Bell 133). Taylor proclaimed that his system was not only the means to resolving class conflict, but that once it was reproduced throughout American culture, it would bring about the redemption of society. "Taylor the Good Shepherd" transformed his program of economic reform into a salvation ethic, promising that salvation and social harmony "would come to all people if they would but live according to the principles of scientific management" (Bell 58). However, in order to fulfill the "redemptive task" of Taylorism, he would have to supersede the established Protestant salvation ethic (Bell 97). Accordingly, and in keeping with his system, Taylor denied "the ideals of personal redemption," regarding the Arminian concept of salvation to be analogous to the rule-of-thumb craft knowledge he was eliminating in industry.

In its place, he advocated for a technocratic soteriology—a doctrine of salvation that is discerned, deployed, and enforced by a managerial elite.

However, the general reproduction of Taylorism in American society had dire consequences. When his model was diffused throughout the culture at large, it threatened to subvert the democratic basis of American society, and this is precisely what Sinclair Lewis attempted to reveal in the novels he wrote in the 1920s. When the principles of scientific management—such as the centralization of authentic knowledge among an elite middle-class, the elimination of free thought and action among a disempowered working-class, the enforced standardization of all behavior and belief, and the radical asymmetry of power relations—are adopted as divinely sanctioned norms, a fascistic social order is the necessary result.

Industrial Messiahs and the Cult of the Machine

Lewis's major novels of the 1920s form a taxonomy of apotheosis that addresses how all levels of the new economic order were undergoing a process of sacralization. Not only were the dominant class of industrialists and managers as well as new modes and means of production being exalted in popular and religious culture, but the world of business was being sanctified as well. Lewis makes this phenomenon a central motif in his fiction to underscore its vital role in the development of modern American culture. Modern America, he claims, is characterized by the deification of the industrial process, and, like a prophet decrying idolatry, he laments the fate of a nation where the machine is made god.

It is misleading when Haber calls the national popularization of Taylorism a secular Great Awakening because Taylor and his supporters had described their program for a new social order in religious terms long before its meteoric rise. For years prior, when Taylor and his followers tirelessly promoted the system, they perceived the endeavor as a kind of evangelism. One follower, Robert T. Kent, remembered these early evangelists as "crusaders" who were sustained in battle by their immense "faith" in the movement and in Taylor (Kent 23). When Taylor published a series of articles in *American Magazine* from March to May 1911 that promised to be "the first authoritative presentation" of his system—before Harper & Brothers published *The Principles of Scientific Management* later that year[5]—he chose the title, "The Gospel of Efficiency: A New Science of Business

---

[5] For a detailed account of the embattled publication history of *The Principles of Scientific Management*, see Dean, Carol Carlson. "The Principles of Scientific Management by Frederick W. Taylor: The Private Printing," *Journal of Management History* 3.1 (1997): 18–30.

Management" (563).⁶ In the works and later remembrances of his followers, religious language and imagery abound; "words like creed, cult, gospel, dogma, faith, and prophet" are pervasive in the literature (Kanigel 412). In his *History of Technology* Glenn Porter writes that "scientific management took on some of the trappings of a kind of secular religion; Taylor was the messiah, and his followers, who spread the word, were (and still are) commonly referred to as 'disciples' " (513). Carl Barth, for example, was proud to be called Taylor's "most orthodox disciple" (1204). Another of Taylor's followers, Jim Dodge, stated that "Taylor in this movement is comparable to the Almighty. There are a few apostles, Gantt and Barth and some others. There are a number of disciples, such as myself… The rest are all members of the church" (qtd. in Haber 34). As with any other emergent sect, the integrity of Taylorism's dogma was fiercely protected. When Gantt and Gilbreth, two of Taylor's "direct disciples" introduced heterodox ideas into "Taylorite doctrine," "both were cast out of the church" (Kanigel 412, 503). In 1914, the poet Berton Braley wrote a hymn for the church of Taylorism published in *American Machinist* called "The Spirit of Management." It reads in part,

> We've done with the days of "hit or miss"
> When we blundered along in careless bliss…
> So here's the gospel—…
> We must show the Worker the work to do,
> The WAY to do it, until he KNOWS;
> We must give him the mighty spirit, too,
> By which the World in its wonder grows;
> For the Spirit of Modern Progress comes
> From men with bodies and minds kept strong,
> Not puny weaklings from out the throng
> Who swarm in ghettoes and fetid slums!"
>
> (34)

Braley alludes to the "muscular Christianity" popular among evangelicals at the time and suggests a nativist interpretation of Taylor's principle of selecting the right kind of worker.

Historians find religious language apt to describe Taylorism as well. Callahan refers to Taylorism as a "cult" and calls its leader "the great preacher of the gospel

---

[6] Following the appearance of the three-part series in its March, April, and May issues, *American Magazine* published a rebuttal by Upton Sinclair as well as a response by Taylor in June. Later, after the First World War, Sinclair apotheosized his critique of Taylor's gospel and published a competing religious text, *Hell: A Verse Drama and Photo-Play* (1923). In the play, Satan tricks the angels, locks them in Heaven, and then turns control of the earth over to Mammon, his "business manager," who had "systematized the torturing of the damned." Mammon and his "efficiency-demons" start a world war "which is carried on by the latest efficiency methods brought up from Hell" but are ultimately thwarted by Wobblies who take over Hell, sow revolution on earth, and liberate "Comrade Jesus" (3).

of efficiency" (18). For Kanigel, Taylor was "the zealous purveyor of a new gospel" who would deliver "messianic, hours long monologues" sermonizing scientific management and spreading "the Good News of high wages, high profits, and low prices" (412, 2, 534). Martha Banta and Daniel Bell write that Taylor was "the prophet of scientific management" who, along with his "disciples," preached "the gospel of efficiency" with "missionary fervor" and a "sense of messianic mission" (Bell 135, 133, Banta 117, 235, 120). Ultimately, thanks to the international proselytization of these "missionaries," "the master's teachings spread" throughout the world (Kanigel 502).

Following the Eastern Rate Case and the First World War, Taylor and his system were increasingly sacralized and endowed with supernatural significance. His "missionaries" touted Taylor as the "industrial messiah" whose system would prove to be the salvation of class antagonism, it was "the one best way" to industrial peace, and in the eyes of the American people, Taylor's rational revelation seemed to "glow with an aura of spiritual certainty" (Kanigel 411). In 1929 a stained glass window depicting Taylor was installed in the Unitarian church his mother had helped to found. On it, Taylor is represented as a heroic, "muscled, blonde Adonis… clad in a flowing robe, strolling along a country road," sowing seeds from "a basket at his hip" (Kanigel 411). The inscription on the window reads, "Behold a sower went forth to sow. The sower soweth the word" (Kanigel 411). Here, Taylor is memorialized as the figure in the parable of the sower, found in the gospel of Mark, who Jesus said sowed "seeds of divine truth." From the very beginning of the efficiency craze, Taylor was canonized by the masses and his philosophy was conflated with divine truth. Moreover, in addition to sacralizing Taylorism, many began to interpret divinity through the lens of Taylorist dogma; for example, in 1914 the Parisian priest and theologian Père Sertillanges began a sermon by proclaiming, "The love of God is the Taylor system of our spiritual life" (Kanigel 493). The consecration of Taylorism and projection onto the metaphysical was an integral part of its widespread dissemination and its eventual reconstitution of modernity.

As Durkheim insightfully wrote,

> Let a man capture [society's] imagination and seem to embody its principal aspirations as well as the means to fulfill them, and this man will be set apart and considered nearly divine. Opinion will invest him with a majesty quite similar to the majesty that protects the gods… And proof that this sort of apotheosis is the work of society alone is that society has often consecrated men who did not deserve it.
>
> (160)

Whether Taylor's investment with the sacred was merited or not, it indisputably occurred. More broadly, the case of Taylor and scientific management wholly undermines Weber's theory of secularization. Here, rationalization and sacralization went hand in hand; indeed, it was the apotheosis of the system and its creator that enabled rationalization to become fully integrated into American culture. For Weber, rationalization was not a modern phenomenon; rather, it was a global, centuries-long process that he predicted would culminate in modernity and result in the disenchantment of society. Taylorism epitomized Weber's concept of rationalization and certainly represents its zenith in America. However, the success of the system was made possible by sacralization, not secularization.

The apotheosis of Taylorism, its transformation from a system of industrial rationalization into a salvation ethic, led industry in general to be imbued with redemptive power.[7] As Karen Lucic has noted, at the height of American industrialization, reverence for the machine "approached the dimensions of a cult... many spoke of the machine as the new religion of the twentieth century" (9). For example, in 1916, lieutenant governor of Massachusetts and future president Calvin Coolidge emblematically proclaimed that "the man who builds a factory builds a temple" and "the man who works there worships there" (Coolidge 14). Henry Ford, an early acolyte of Taylor who introduced scientific management into his automobile factories, further illustrated the sacralization of industry when he announced in 1928 that "Machinery" is "the New Messiah" (Ford 34). Robert Hughes writes that Ford "believed he had invented something like a new religion, based on industry" (385). Similarly, Banta reports that, for Ford, "God is the business enterprise, God's kingdom is Highland Park, and the Ford Motor Company's assembly line is the new messiah" (89). Ford affirmed the salvific promise of industry through his "merger of machine with the Christ who comes to save society from itself" (Banta 88). As a high priest of the new dispensation, Ford, like Taylor, was deified, while his philosophy and institutions were invested with redemptive import. In an issue published in 1928, *Vanity Fair* called Ford "almost Divine" and described the Ford Motor Company as "an American altar of the God-Objective of Mass Production." Here, his factory was deemed "America's Mecca, toward which the pious journey for prayer" (Jacob 15). American modernists also played a crucial role in "the cult of the machine" (Lucic 14). Charles Sheeler, whose photographs of Ford's River Rouge plant

---

[7] See also Callahan, Jr., Richard J., Kathryn Lofton, and Chad E. Seales. "Allegories of Progress: Industrial Religion in the United States," *Journal of the American Academy of Religion* 78.1 (2010): 1–39.

accompanied the *Vanity Fair* article—captioned "By Their Works Ye Shall Know Them"—regarded the factory with an attitude "akin to religious awe" (Lucic 14). Like many American modernists, Sheeler depicted the iconography of the machine age—industrial machines, factories, mass-produced commodities, and urban architecture—with pronounced reverence, believing these products of American engineering to be as sacrosanct as "the most celebrated cathedrals" (Lucic 28). Sheeler famously insisted that "our factories are our substitute for religious expression" (qtd. in Rourke 130). Similarly, the eminent modernist painter and American émigré Joseph Stella regarded the Brooklyn Bridge, the quintessential monument of the machine age, to be "the shrine" of "a new religion," the embodiment "of the new civilization of AMERICA" and all of its "efforts" at "APOTHEOSIS" (87–88). In works such as *Brooklyn Bridge* (1919–20) and *New York Interpreted (The Voice of the City)* (1922)—the latter created in the form of an altarpiece—Stella sought to depict his subject as "the presence of a new DIVINITY" (88). The salvific promise of industry was present in the literature of the period as well. For example, in her 1929 story "Flowering Judas," Katherine Anne Porter's revolutionary protagonist maintains that "the machine is sacred, and will be the salvation of the workers" (98).

The practical religion of Lewis's all-American men exemplifies the "cult of the machine." We read that Will Kennicott and George Babbitt are "devotees of the Great God Motor" who express their piety through "the worship of machinery" (*Babbitt* 22, 70). Like many Americans who had little contact with industry itself, they practiced their faith through the worship of its fetishes, household gods like consumer goods and, most importantly, Ford's automobile which had become "a sacralized thing" (Banta 273). For Kennicott and Babbitt, "motoring was a faith not to be questioned, a high-church cult, with electric sparks for candles, and piston-rings possessing the sanctity of altar vessels" (MS 228). Similarly, in *Main Street*, we read,

> The railroad was more than a means of transportation to Gopher Prairie. It was a new god... a deity created by man that he might keep himself respectful to Property, as elsewhere he had elevated and served as tribal gods the mines, the cotton-mills, motor-factories... If the town was in disfavor, the railroad could ignore it, cut it off from commerce, slay it. To Gopher Prairie the tracks were eternal verities, and boards of railroad directors an omnipotence.
>
> (MS 272–3)

Lewis's aim here is to offer a literary representation of apotheosis and its consequences. He explains that religious ideas are generated by sacralizing current material conditions. In an example of anthropotheism, Lewis's characters craft an image of god by deifying dominant material relations and modes of production. In the context of American modernity, apotheosis is observable when industrial institutions like Ford's factory and products like the automobile are abstracted, detached from their mundane moorings, and converted into supernatural agents who seem to possess mastery over their creators. As a consequence of this process, a factory becomes Mecca, a car becomes "a deity," and mass production becomes God's ultimate objective. Apotheosis is a mirroring, a specular inversion of subject and object. During the machine age, material objects and networks of relations like mills, mines, and factories were "elevated" and transformed into immaterial subjects, "tribal gods," just as free subjects were diminished and made the subordinate servants of "a new god." Lewis adeptly stages the processes of anthropotheism and sacralization that are necessary for the reproduction of the dominant economic order.

The Sanctification of Commerce

On Main Streets across America, Lewis observes, "the dollar-sign has chased the crucifix clean off the map" (MS 134). Commercial culture and the "worship of a good deal" had replaced Christianity as the nation's collective "confession of faith" (MS 233, 298). In 1920s America, Lewis remarks, "selling nails was considered as sacred as banking" (MS 58). Just as Calvin Coolidge had exemplified the nation's sanctification of industry, he also famously encapsulated the creed of "the New Era" when he proclaimed, two years after the publication of *Babbitt*, that "the chief business of the American people is business" ("Speech"). "But," Arthur Schlesinger notes, "for Coolidge, business was more than business; it was a religion" (57). With the widespread cultural reproduction of Taylorism throughout the 1920s, Taylor's sanctified ethos spread beyond the confines of the factory floor to redefine American commerce as well. By this time, Taylorism had been thoroughly sanctified and imbued with religious authority. To Taylorize commerce, therefore, was to invest business with religious significance. As Banta notes, Taylorism supplied a new "gospel for the modern office" (170). Similarly, in 1923, Anzia Yezierska wrote that, in America, "efficiency is the new religion of business" (164). In the first decades of the century, commerce was increasingly invested with the sacred. As a result, business became America's dominant religion. As the nation's pious exemplar of the "new faith," President Coolidge dutifully "worshipped business" (Schlesinger 57). In this context and with a prescient incisiveness that surpassed any other American author of the time, Lewis satirized the conflation of commerce and religion with the creation of George Babbitt and Elmer Gantry—the Janus faces who represented two modalities of a single social phenomenon. While Gantry embodied the commercialization of American religion, Babbitt personified the sanctification of commerce.

Just as Elmer Gantry would come to represent the new class of corporate clergymen, George Babbitt was the distillation of a new American type; "he was the modern business man" (*Babbitt* 12). In *Babbitt*, Lewis thematizes the conflation of commerce and religion by developing a portrait of "the business cult" and its priesthood, the emerging managerial class (Schlesinger 75). Lewis writes that Babbitt's office was "a steel chapel where loafing and laughing were raw sin"; it was "a temple-spire of the religion of business, a faith passionate, exalted, surpassing common men," where "he whistled the ballad 'Oh, by gee, by gosh, by jingo' as though it were a hymn melancholy and noble" (*Babbitt* 36, 16). Babbitt embodies "the true believer" in this "new faith," "the religion of business," "its sacrament the weekly lunches of fellowship at Kiwanis or Rotary, its ritual the collective chanting of cheerful songs, its theologian a New York advertising man named Bruce Barton" (Schlesinger 71). Like Gantry, Babbitt had answered "the calling of selling," and as a prominent realtor in Zenith he "function[ed] as a seer... a prophetic engineer" (*Babbitt* 6, 46). He and the rest of Zenith's managerial class, including its merchants, bankers, and businessmen, were regarded as a kind of priesthood of the new dispensation, "the pastors... of commerce" whose guiding norms had been "sanctified by precedent" (*Babbitt* 222, 49). In answer to the divine call, Babbitt had "devoted himself... to the cosmic purpose of Selling—not of selling anything in particular, for or to anybody in particular, but pure Selling" (*Babbitt* 143). Here, Lewis suggests that commercial exchange has been elevated to the ontological level of a Platonic Idea, to that of "pure Selling," and the earthly work of the modern businessman construed as the realization of a "cosmic purpose." As in the case of industry, commercial business was inscribed into cosmology and imbued with necessary, divinely ordained being. Accordingly, businessmen assumed the mantle of a clerical elite who occupied positions of authority in the new religion, overseeing the dissemination of its values, the growth of its institutions, and the clarification of a dogma that was meant to reveal the divinity of a Taylorized economy.

In *Babbitt*, Lewis unmasks the apotheosis of commerce and its investment with religious import. His critique, however, is not limited to lampooning the sanctification of sales and the newly anointed priesthood of merchants, but extends to their counterparts in exchange—consumption and the consumer. Much of the novel is devoted to a critique of nascent American consumerism and, in particular, the fetishization of consumer goods. Lewis writes that, for George Babbitt, the American everyman, "god was Modern Appliances" (*Babbitt* 9). "The contents of his pockets," we read, "were of eternal importance"; the objects they contained were talismans that signified his identity, his social rank, and his place among the elect (*Babbitt* 13). Moreover, in towns like Zenith and Gopher Prairie, those synecdoches of modern America, expenditure was "in itself a virtue" (*Babbitt* 37). The act of consumption was a redemptive rite that denoted piety and an adherence to social norms. T. J. Jackson Lears has noted that in the first decades of the century, America was undergoing a fundamental shift from being "a production-oriented society" to "a consumption-oriented society" (3). However, "to thrive and spread, a consumer culture required more than a national apparatus of marketing and distribution; it also needed a favorable moral climate" (Lears 4). The "crucial moral change" that prepared the way for a consumption-oriented society, he argues, was "a shift from a Protestant ethos of salvation through self-denial toward a therapeutic ethos stressing self-realization in this world" (Lears 4). Similarly, Schlesinger argues that, in the 1920s, "salvation was to be measured by success; and success thus became the visible evidence of spiritual merit" (72). That is, in the 1920s a shift occurred in dominant American mores in which the Protestant salvation ethic that mandated self-denial and restraint was superseded by one that demanded self-realization through consumption. An individual's righteousness was no longer measured by humility or frugality but by "the possession of... splendor," by a conspicuous show of reverence for the many fetishes and deities of modern capitalism (*Babbitt* 95). Through the figure of Babbitt, Lewis offers a timely and unmatched examination of a culture undergoing a fundamental shift in its dominant values and norms. Namely, an examination of a culture where the concept of salvation has been reformulated in accordance with the imperatives of capitalism, where consumption, competition, and material acquisition are no longer barriers to redemption, but have become the very means of achieving it.

The Commercialization of Religion

By the end of the nineteenth century, the ethos of business constituted the new national ideal, providing Americans with a novel system of norms by which to live their lives. Accordingly, the prosperous American businessman became our new moral exemplar, replacing the cleric as the model of virtue and the Good. Recognizing this, Sinclair Lewis creates the character of Elmer Gantry, a transitional figure that simultaneously occupies each of these cultural spheres, at once a clergyman and a successful businessman; though he enters the superseded vocation, the ministry, his theology, aims, and tactics are entirely those of the new dominant ideology. It is crucial to acknowledge that, for Lewis, Gantry is not simply a charlatan whose "reverent admiration" for money, fame, and power is antithetical to religious norms; rather, Gantry is a paragon of modern American Christendom, a character who typifies the general conflation of capitalism and Christianity (EG 220). Gantry's endorsement of a Taylorized business ethos is not exceptional but signifies American Protestantism's thoroughgoing adoption of Taylor's salvation ethic. Gantry is both a product of, and a contributor to, the process of accommodation that was causing Christianity to be retooled to meet the specifications of modern business, and capitalism to be endowed with divinity. Amid such a state of affairs it is fitting that a figure like Gantry would perform a dual social role, at once a merchant and a cleric.

Though it was apparent early in Gantry's life that he was destined to be a "business-man," possessing as he did the affectedly ingratiating demeanor of a "sewing-machine agent" and clearly more at home in "the stock-exchange" than the pulpit, he nevertheless chose to try his hand at "the gospel game," endeavoring to become a "Professional Good Man" (EG 35, 106, 9, 237, 292). The ministerial profession that Gantry enters is well suited to his entrepreneurial sensibility, having already undergone the transformation described by Donald Scott in *From Office to Profession*; that is, the church had become a model of Taylorist rationalization, possessing the attributes, tactics, and aims of America's commercial culture. The crass commercialism Gantry comes to employ in his calling, Lewis argues, epitomizes the ethos of the modern Protestant cleric and the culture he endorses. For example, prominent theologian and dean of the University of Chicago's Divinity School Shailer Mathews outlined a program for the Taylorization of churches and seminaries in his *Scientific Management in the Churches* (1912). Mathews argued that "the Christian spirit must be institutionalized if it is to prevail in an age of institutions" (Mathews v). Just as "business organizations" must "constantly... readapt themselves to changing conditions" in order to "out-class" their "competitors," the church must accommodate a new division of labor and new modes of production if it is to remain influential in "the new epoch upon which the church is entering" (Mathews 19-20, 66). Simply put, Mathews claimed that if the church was to survive in the age of business, it must begin to conceive of itself as a business enterprise, adopting the methods, mores, and rationalized modes of organization prevailing in the industrial and commercial sectors. He writes that churches must employ "business-like planning" and begin to be "organized in the business sense of the word"; which is to say, churches must adopt the Taylor System (27, 37). They must "replace haphazard, traditional methods" with "standardized operations" and embrace scientific management's division of labor (Mathews 1, 3). He writes that the church needs "a far more systematic division between the [...] management and those who perform tasks in accordance with plans worked out for them [...] Theoretically the church should be regarded as a body of workmen ready to perform definite tasks as these tasks are outlined for them by its committee of management" (Mathews 27, 33, 36). "Church workers" must be taught to perform standardized tasks "under the direction of those who have discovered such standards" (Mathews 37, 3-4). "If," Mathews writes, "this seems to make the church something of a business establishment it is precisely what should be the case" (58). The efficiency craze gripping American culture ushered in a new epoch of "rational ecclesiasticism," "Christian efficiency," "ministerial efficiency," and "spiritual efficiency," where the church was recast in the image of the Taylorist factory, department store, or corporation (Mathews 61, 39, 45, 57). This is the theological and institutional environment that Gantry enters and Lewis critiques. In 1927, the year *Elmer Gantry* was published, Taylorism was still at the height of its popularity and continued to shape the practical reason of the American people. That year Dexter Kimball, the dean of Cornell University's engineering school proclaimed, "at no time has the influence of Fred Taylor been so great or his memory so secure as at this moment" (307). In his novels of the 1920s, Lewis attempts to make apparent the high spiritual and political price of accommodating Taylorism into the organization, dogma, and practices of the Protestant Church. For Lewis, the ministry's attempt to "readapt themselves to changing conditions" was resulting in a reversal of the church's most fundamental values and commitments.

In seminary, though Gantry is a very poor student, wholly uninterested in the nuances of theology, he is adept at the business of religion, at making money and generating publicity, even winning a prize for his essay, "Sixteen Ways of Paying a Church Debt" (EG 83). Despite being entirely unconcerned with the spiritual well-being of his congregants and lacking more than a mere modicum of faith, Gantry succeeds in the ministry because he is an accomplished salesman. He typifies the new class of minister-managers who, during this time, began to receive their training in Taylorized seminaries. For example, Mathews—dean of one of the nation's leading seminaries—argued that "ministerial education must be changed to conform to the changing function of the church" (48). Rather than merely receiving theological training, pastors must be "trained in efficiency" and "trained to be chairmen of committees of management" (Mathews 45). For Mathews and those like him, seminary is the place where ministers are taught how to be managers of Taylorized business enterprises, rather than merely being schooled in the delivery of a good sermon. Gantry is the quintessential embodiment of this kind of Taylorized ecclesiasticism; for him, "religion is a... business" that is predicated on "selling the gospel" and he is willing, to that end, to "use every method that... will sell the goods" (EG 411, 333, 225). Lewis writes that revivalists like Gantry and his peers resemble "floor-walkers," that is, department store managers whose job is to "affectionately coerc[e] people into buying things they did not need" (EG 322, MS 304). Similarly, Mathews regarded as a sign of progress the fact that "revivals... are as carefully organized by the leading evangelists as is a department store" (15). For Gantry, referring to salvation as "the goods," to preachers as "salesmen," and to converts as "clients" is not merely metaphorical. In this way, Lewis argues that the Protestant clergy have wholly adopted the means and ends of modern industry and commerce; they see themselves as businessmen, the church as a corporate institution, and their occupation as predicated on selling the greatest amount of goods in the most efficient and profitable manner possible. One of Gantry's counterparts in *Babbitt*, Rev. John Jennison Drew, "often said that he was 'proud to be known as primarily a business man' " and writes editorials on "The Dollars and Sense Value of Christianity" (*Babbitt* 205). He boasts of his salesmanship, claiming to hold "the local record for conversions... an average of almost a hundred... per year" and wrings profits from his congregants by admonishing that "the real cheap skate is the man who won't lend to the Lord!" (*Babbitt* 205). Another, Mike Monday—Lewis's caricature of eminent evangelist Billy Sunday—publishes a kind of annual stock-holder report that shows "that he is the world's greatest salesman of salvation, and that by efficient organization the overhead of spiritual regeneration may be kept down to an unprecedented rock-bottom basis. He has converted over two hundred thousand lost and priceless souls at an average cost of less than ten dollars a head" (*Babbitt* 98). The church, Lewis argues, has been so utterly reconstituted by Taylorism that religion has simply become another business enterprise whose defining widget happens to be redemption. Ministers have become experts in the "salesmanship of salvation" and employ the strategies of modern commerce to coerce congregants into consuming redemption (EG 317).

In addition to adopting the promotional practices and organizational structure of corporate America, the institutional church embraces the aims of industry and commerce as its own; in doing so, the essential objectives of modern capitalism become the principles that Christian fundamentalists vehemently strive to conserve. In his depiction of Babbitt's attempt to redirect the priorities and commitments of his church, Lewis illustrates how the Protestant Church accommodates the economic conventions of the managerial class, consequently refashioning its doctrines and practices. In his work with a local church, Babbitt insists that in order for the institution to succeed, in order for it to be "a real virile hustling religion," it must be transformed into "Christianity Incorporated," an enterprise that epitomizes commercial virtues like efficiency, competition, and perpetual growth (*Babbitt* 211). Babbitt laments the failure of his church to lead the denominational pack in the local free religious market, complaining that its Sunday School "is the fourth largest in Zenith... We ought to be the first" (207). He claims that, to make the Sunday School more competitive, the endeavor must be approached as "a merchandizing problem, of course the one basic and fundamental need is growth... we won't be satisfied till we build up the biggest darn Sunday School in the whole state" (215). The truly righteous performance of "the Lord's business," argues Babbitt, requires congregants to be "he-hustling, getting out and drumming up customers" (221, 216). Here, Babbitt exemplifies Mathews's claim that "successful businessmen... can contribute much" to the education of task performers—like Sunday School teachers and students—in the most effective ways of Taylorizing their church programs (42). For the ministry to successfully perform God's evangelical imperative, Babbitt suggests, they must acquire more money and surpass the denominational competition by making their programs more efficient and by making their soteriological product attractive to potential "customers"; they must alter their theological doctrines, practices, and aims in response to market pressures and in accordance with commercial mores. In the process of instructing church leaders on how best to assume these values and practices, Babbitt learns that "Sunday School journals"— American Protestantism's trade magazines—feature articles on "Focusing Appeals" for more money and "Scouting for New Members." That is, he finds that American Protestantism has already fully embraced commercial culture. He learns from these publications "how scientifically the Sunday School could be organized" and that the majority of the nation's churches are "keyed to the top-notch of efficiency" (*Babbitt* 210, 221). Here Lewis wishes to emphasize that Taylorist principles of scientific management have been thoroughly assumed by Protestant denominations to make "the Lord's business" more efficient, cost effective, profitable, and competitive, resulting in a kind of standardized Taylorist Christianity that emulates modern modes of industrial production and corporate organization.

Through his depiction of characters like Babbitt, Gantry, Drew, and Monday, Lewis contends that modern American Protestantism has been entirely transformed by its adoption of the values, aims, and modes of organization championed by Frederick Winslow Taylor. The Taylorization of Christianity, Lewis argues, leads seminaries to be refashioned into "preacher-factories," churches to be governed by "efficiency-systems," and minsters to become "managers of factory-like institutional churches" (EG 157, MS 252, EG 127). For example, Gantry refers to his megachurch as "a bang-up plant" and we read that he "was like the new general manager of a factory" (EG 425, 334). Gantry wishes to follow the example of his mentor, Sharon Falconer—Lewis's caricature of Aimee Semple McPherson, megachurch pioneer and master of mass-media marketing—whose own revival enterprise Lewis describes as a Taylorized "factory" that is managed by a "foreman" who plans and directs the work of the "gospel crew" (EG 210, 223). Ultimately, Lewis maintains that when capitalism is made sacred, the church assumes the priorities and procedures of modern industry and commerce. When churches adopt the characteristics and objectives of Taylorism, salvation becomes a mere standardized, mass-produced commodity.

Standardizing Salvation: The New Orthodoxy

One of the cardinal virtues affirmed by Taylor was that of complete standardization. The sacralization of Taylorism, Lewis argues, causes a new standard to be established that is implemented and enforced as obligatory dogma, wholly reshaping Americans' way of life. Lewis's works from the 1920s are sustained analyses of the forced normalization that stemmed from the apotheosis of standardization. Taylorism, argues Lewis, was creating "a new type of civilization," one whose "shifting spiritual values" mandated a kind of "self-imposed discipline" that was geared toward managing citizens' adherence to norms designed to benefit industrial and commercial interests (*Babbitt* 167, 196, 60). The way of life and system of mores necessary for consumer society to flourish had been deemed "the way of the righteous" and, once Taylor's principles were adopted as the nation's dominant spiritual values, citizens who wished to safeguard their salvation were easily crafted into efficient producers and pious consumers (*Babbitt* 169). The result is the mass production of "right-thinking and regularized citizens," that is, "the Standardized American Citizen... fellows with hair on their chests and smiles in their eyes and adding-machines in their offices" (*Babbitt* 60, 166). Individuals and institutions alike are "Americanized into uniformity," resulting in the formation of homogeneous subjects and the "standardization of stores, offices, streets, hotels, clothes, and newspapers throughout the United States" (MS 309, *Babbitt* 167).

The citizens of Zenith incorporate standardization into their existent fundamentalism. As a result, they believe that, like the Word, "Standardization is excellent, *per se*," its truth is beyond question (*Babbitt* 92). However, Lewis argues, when rationalized measures for the production of uniform commodities are applied to the formation of subjects, the outcome is necessarily "the standardization of thought" (*Babbitt* 92). Martyn J. Lee explains, "in a mass-consumption economy, in order for value to remain in motion and for the accumulation process to proceed relatively smoothly, the agencies of capital require that the mass of ordinary people... both think and behave in a manner which is broadly supportive of the prevailing economic and political interest" (86). Market-friendly mores are, therefore, recast as religious norms, as the standard of "right-thinking" and respectable behavior (*Babbitt* 32). But, Lewis suggests that in such a system of standardization, freedom is a sin, it is untruth. In order to be rigidly maintained, the standard of acceptable thought and behavior requires vigilant regulation and management; this gives rise to modes of social and self-imposed discipline. Accordingly, the Protestant church and other sectors of civil society become "agencies of 'cultural regulation' " that employ modes of coercion to manage the production of "standardized minds" and to designate "what a whole nation should wear and eat and say and think" (Lee 86, *Babbitt* 92, EG 441).

The "orthodox opinions" of middle-class "Regular Guys" like Babbitt are entirely determined by these agencies of regulation and they, in turn, manage the ideas and behaviors of the masses (MS 350, *Babbitt* 109). Lewis writes that if no Republican, Presbyterian, or commercial "doctrine [is] laid down for him" concerning how he ought to regard a given event or state of affairs, Babbitt is entirely devoid of an opinion (*Babbitt* 20). These are the purveyors of his every notion; he does not think for himself in any way. Following Taylor's division of labor, the people are required to unquestioningly behave in accordance with a standard that has been devised for them, rather than think for themselves. Lewis writes,

> Just as he was an Elk, a Booster, and a member of the Chamber of Commerce, just as the priests of the Presbyterian Church determined his every religious belief and the senators who controlled the Republican Party decided... what he should think about disarmament, tariff, and Germany, so did the large national advertisers fix the surface of his life, fix what he believed to be his individuality. These standard advertised wares–toothpastes, socks, tires, cameras, instantaneous hot-water heaters–were his symbols and proofs of excellence; at first the signs, then the substitutes, for joy and passion and wisdom.
>
> (*Babbitt* 87)

Lewis suggests that, in a consumer society, the only choice we have is consumer choice, our only freedom, the freedom to buy.

He takes particular satirical aim at that quintessential American conceit, that the nation is the last bastion of true individualism. We read that Babbitt and his peers "all had the same ideas and expressed them" in the very same way; though they are fond of singing the praises of "personal liberty," they do so in hackneyed phrases, parroting pre-packaged, secondhand banalities (*Babbitt* 127, 104). For Lewis, America's cult of individualism sanctifies its antithesis: standardization, uniformity, homogeneity. Lewis argues that American individualism is ultimately about enforced uniformity, mediated by consumption. Rather than facilitating the exercise of one's freedom and individuality, as it promises, consumption represents the illusion of choice. Lewis claims that applying the strategies of scientific management to the governance of society requires the elimination of individuality. Variance of any kind is deemed error or inefficiency and is rectified accordingly. The apotheosis of Taylorist standardization, Lewis proposes, enshrines a market-friendly fundamentalism that is militantly enforced as the prevailing orthodoxy. Once Taylorist norms are perceived as the divine laws to which humanity is subject, deviation from that standard of thought and behavior is deemed heretical, and therefore merits normalization, exclusion, or elimination. The authentic expression of individuality in such a system is, quite literally, regarded as evil.

Lewis claims that, when a given standard is made sacred, opposing positions are no longer simply considered variant opinions, but are deemed wicked and heretical. Imbuing commercial values with divine significance establishes their perceived infallibility and permanence, elevating a system of economy from the realm of ongoing political controversy to the incontestable level of ontological necessity. In the prologue to *Main Street*, Lewis couches Gopher Prairie's small-town standardization in religious terms. He writes that, in Gopher Prairie, "whatsoever [Ezra Stowbody the banker] does not know and sanction, that thing is heresy, worthless for knowing and wicked to consider" (MS 2). Lewis suggests that sacralizing the established order is necessary to forestall opposition. Once the economic and political status quo is made sacred and transformed into dogma, all those who espouse opposing points of view are not perceived as dissidents, who are merely exercising their freedom, but as heretics, blasphemers, and evildoers.

Main Street and *Babbitt* are largely devoted to analyzing the processes of social inclusion and exclusion that stem from the apotheosis of standardization. In these novels, ideas that fail to conform to "orthodox opinions" are deemed "heresies"; those who conform to orthodoxy are counted among the "Ordinary People," while heretics make up "the Undesirable Element" that is open to social exclusion and communally sanctioned acts of violence (*Babbitt* 93, 308). An individual's normality, their respectability, indeed, their very sanity is determined by their willingness to adhere to the new dogma. Only the "Standardized Citizen" is a "Sane Citizen" or a truly "Solid American Citizen" (*Babbitt* 165, 58). "Critics of the sane and efficient life," on the other hand, are regarded as infidels whose Christianity, citizenship, and mental health are uncertain, at best. For instance, because Bjornstrom is such an outspoken opponent of Gopher Prairie's "sane standardization," he is labeled a "crank" and "considered slightly insane" (*Babbitt* 167, MS 95).

Lewis argues that American orthodoxy is at once religious, economic, psychological, and political. As a result, atheism, anti-capitalism, insanity, and treason are collapsed into a single mode of heresy. For example, Carol Kennicott's heterodoxy leads her to be labeled "an abnormal... traitor to the faith of Main Street"; she is simultaneously a mad, treasonous, apostate (MS 290). Similarly, the unconventional Bjornstram is branded "the Red Swede" and condemned as "a blasphemer and a traitor" (MS 95, 365). Likewise, when *Elmer Gantry*'s Frank Shallard dares to openly challenge the status quo, he is considered a "traitor," a "God damned atheist—and probably a damn socialist or I.W.W. too!" (EG 423, 422). As these examples demonstrate, "American," "capitalist," and "Christian" are mutually entailed categories of inclusion.

Lewis argues that the apotheosis of standardization and its conflation with fundamentalism gives rise to a form of authoritarian religiosity that seeks to impose dominant norms by force. Shallard gives a lecture, "Are the Fundamentalists Witch Hunters?" in which he argues that fundamentalists' anti-intellectualism and militant vice crusade amounts to "a new Inquisition, a new hunting of witches. We might live to see men burned to death for refusing to attend Protestant churches" (EG 420-421). As Lewis's mouthpiece, Shallard warns his audience that this is a fascistic trend that is leading toward disaster: "think how they would rule this nation!" (EG 421). Before Shallard can complete his lecture he is attacked, thrown into a car, and taken to the outskirts of town to be murdered. Though he overhears his inquisitors discussing his fate— "Let's hang him. Here's a swell tree"—they ultimately show mercy and blind him instead (EG 423). Through Shallard's story, Lewis argues that the penalty for heresy in America is normalization, exclusion, or execution. "Enforced standardization" has effectively been translated from an industrial norm into a religious obligation. To transgress the norm is taboo and must be expiated through sacrificial violence. Lewis insists that this kind of disciplinary action is an essential element of the dominant economic creed which openly condones normalizing violence: all atheists, traitors, and "labor agitators," we read, "should be hanged" (*Babbitt* 42).

Lewis shows that, when standardization is exalted, an emphasis on purity inevitably surfaces in areas beyond the economic. This gives rise to "homicidal and sides-taking" forms of militant nativism, nationalism, and racism; orthodox observance then becomes less about religion than about demonstrating one's whiteness or one's faithful allegiance to capitalism (*Babbitt* 140). For example, Lewis writes that fundamentalists like "Elmer admired [the Ku Klux Klan's] principle—to keep all foreigners, Jews, Catholics, and negroes in their place, which was no place at all, and let the country be led by native Protestants, like Elmer Gantry" (EG 393). Once it is apotheosized, Lewis argues, standardization doesn't end with the regulation of industry and commerce, but extends to practices of racial and ethnic cleansing. When racial, sexual, or civic purity is conflated with election or righteousness, individuals in minority groups are regarded as either essentially evil or as persons who require normalization.

Both *Babbitt* and *Elmer Gantry* culminate in the formation of secret police forces composed of standardized citizens who wage an attack on unorthodox individuals. Gantry's "Committee on Public Morals" endorses "personally marching down on these abominations, arresting the blood-guilty wretches," and does precisely that (EG 371, 375). In regard to the owner of a local speakeasy, the pious and respectable Dr. Zahn, "the Lutheran" asserts, "if I had my way, I'd burn the proprietor of that joint at the stake" (EG 374). Similarly, Babbitt is forced—by threat of excommunication—to join "the Good Citizens' League," a group devoted to forcing individuals "to conform to decent standards" and to putting "the kibosh on cranks" (EG 309). Their motto—"he that is not with me is against me"—is indicative of the perspective they represent; either one submits to standardization or is deemed a heretic who must be normalized, excommunicated, or burned at the stake. Lewis writes that the League, in its capacity as a citizen-led agency of cultural regulation which sought to implement the teachings of the fundamentalist church, had "the air of a Vigilante committee" that "stands for the suppression of free speech and free thought" (*Babbitt* 330, 332). When Babbitt objects to the methods and intentions of the League, his wife suggests that he sounds "like the German furnace-man," because voicing any opposition to the status quo is "like being a socialist!" (*Babbitt* 333, 115). In his portrayal of "the Good Citizens' League" and the "Committee on Public Morals," Lewis argues that America's reactionary moral organizations, which were led my prominent members of the business class, merely use the cause of virtue and Christian piety as a pre-text for the forcible imposition of values and practices that serve the interests of the ruling-class.

In *Main Street* and *Babbitt* Lewis portrays two characters' struggle with the American salvation ethic of the 1920s. Both novels are expressions of the characters' longing to be liberated or redeemed from Taylorism. For example, the citizens of Gopher Prairie believe that salvation is attainable through standardization but Carol Kennicott finds the Taylorization of the spirit to be alienating and stultifying. Therefore, her desire to reform Gopher Prairie is not entirely altruistic. Ultimately, this is a religious matter for Carol; she insists, "I am trying to save my soul" (MS 233). Similarly, *Babbitt* can be read as the story of George's desire to liberate himself from a Taylorized salvation ethic, and his failure to do so. Despite all of his boostering for Taylorized Christianity, Babbitt experiences a crisis of faith. This commercial priest begins to have doubts about the righteousness of middle-class piety, and this is the dramatic crux of the novel. He backslides into sin by openly opposing the "bullying" Good Citizens' League and by coming to the defense of strikers and immigrants but eventually returns to the fold. Despite his flirtation with heterodoxy, Babbitt chooses "repentance" and is born again—"he swore faith... to business efficiency... to the Booster's Club... to every faith of the Clan of Good Fellows" (*Babbitt* 344). Babbitt is seemingly redeemed by reaffirming his faith in American orthodoxy and "within two weeks no one in the League was more violent regarding the wickedness of Seneca Doane, the crimes of labor unions, the perils of immigration, and the delights of golf, morality, and bank-accounts than was George F. Babbitt" (*Babbitt* 346). Like Carol, Babbitt wants to save his soul but is unsure how that is to be achieved. He fears that, having "been led astray by [the] manifold temptations" of social heresy, "he had imperiled his salvation. He was not quite sure there was a Heaven to be attained, but Dr.

John Jennison Drew said there was, and Babbitt was not going to take a chance" (*Babbitt* 350, 349).

For Lewis, when it comes to the Taylorization of American society, "the trouble is spiritual" (MS 313). Lewis is concerned with the spiritual condition of the modern American, which extends beyond the confines of the church-house to the lived experience of the nation's communities. Though Taylorism brought material prosperity to the few, Lewis argues, it caused the spiritual impoverishment of the American people. Socially and politically, the apotheosis of Taylorism—sacralizing its mores, its prescribed power structure, and modes of relation—gives rise to a disciplinary society where forced homogeneity and the elimination of free thought and action are not only permissible but are also thought to be salvific. A Taylorized salvation ethic requires "a rigid ruling of the spirit" that amounts, for Lewis, to "slavery self-sought and self-defended. It is dullness made God" (MS 308). In his novels of the 1920s, Sinclair Lewis explores the aftermath of Frederick Winslow Taylor's revolution of the mind and the social consequences of making his economic model sacred.

6

Gastonia Revisited: Religion, Literature, and the Loray Mill Strike of 1929

In April 1929, textile workers in Gastonia, North Carolina, called a strike. Within just six months the strike was broken, combatants on both sides of the industrial conflict had been killed, and sixteen union organizers were tried for murder. Though labor strikes were commonplace in America at the time, the story of Gastonia captivated the nation and inspired six novels—Mary Heaton Vorse's *Strike!* (1930), Sherwood Anderson's *Beyond Desire* (1932), Olive Tilford Dargan's *Call Home the Heart* (1932), Grace Lumpkin's *To Make My Bread* (1932), Myra Page's *Gathering Storm* (1932), and William Rollins Jr.'s *The Shadow Before* (1934)—as well as Liston Pope's landmark sociological study, *Millhands and Preachers* (1942). No other labor dispute in US history has garnered this level of literary and public engagement, before or since. Perhaps one observation can illustrate the apparent peculiarity of the Loray Mill strike. Rather than the customary union songs, striking workers in Gastonia sang hymns on the picket line and in fellowship at their local headquarters. Similarly, however, the lynch mob that continually terrorized the strikers also sang hymns as they destroyed those headquarters, kidnapped three union organizers, and ruined the food stores intended for impoverished families, intoning "Praise God from Whom All Blessings Flow" as they poured flour into the street.[1] The Gastonia novels and the abundance of empirical evidence compiled by social scientists can help us to understand how these two groups, so diametrically opposed and fiercely dedicated to antithetical economic systems, could believe they were adhering to the same religion. The Gastonia novels accurately convey the vital role of religion on both sides of the battle between capital and labor, and, more broadly, provide insight into the relationship of religion and economy in modern America. With the exception of Liston Pope, this relation has been largely ignored in studies of

---

[1] See Dargan 319; Gray 317; Hall et al. 273; Pope 292; Salmond 123; *Storm* 331–2; Vorse 30, 86, 108, 116, 190, 198.

Depression-era southern culture; with respect to the literature on Gastonia, it has been overlooked entirely.

It would be useful to begin by briefly recounting the events of the strike. On April 1, 1929, over 2,000 members of the National Textile Workers' Union voted to strike from the Loray Mill in Gastonia, North Carolina, in protest of "the stretch-out," the millhands' term for the recently implemented Taylor System.[2] Two days later, Governor O. Max Gardner deployed five units of the National Guard to break the strike. That same day, the *Gaston Daily Gazette* began a vitriolic campaign that sanctioned antistrike violence, announcing that the unionists were "against all religion" and posed an immediate threat to Americans' "very way of life."[3] On April 18, a local lynch mob destroyed the union headquarters and the relief store that supplied food to the poorest workers. By the end of the month, 90 percent of the strikers had returned to work or moved on to another mill. On May 6, families of strikers who lived in the mill village, largely consisting of women and children workers, were evicted from their homes. One child suffering from smallpox was carried out in his bed by mill officials and set down in the rain and mud. The homeless workers then erected a tent colony at the edge of town. On the night of June 7, a lynch mob led by former and future congressman Alfred L. Bulwinkle descended on the tent colony and gunfire was exchanged. In the fray, many on both sides were injured and the chief of police, Orville Aderholt, was mortally wounded. Scores of union organizers and strikers were arrested; sixteen were charged with murder and conspiracy to commit murder.[4] Due to overzealous prosecutorial antics, a mistrial was called on September 9. The subsequent three weeks leading up to the second trial was a period of "unbroken mob terror," during which the union's balladeer and a mother of five, Ella May Wiggins, was shot to death in public (Garrison 229). Despite numerous witnesses, no one was convicted for her murder. In late September, the NTWU suspended all strike activities in Gastonia and one month later, the seven retried unionists were convicted. Pending sentencing, the seven were conveyed to Russia, escaping imprisonment. In 1938, the strike's leader, Fred Beal, became disillusioned with Russian communism and returned to the United States, where he surrendered and was jailed.

---

[2] On the faulty application of scientific management to the southern textile industry, see Rehn, Henry Joseph. *Scientific Management and the Cotton Textile Industry*. Chicago: The University of Chicago Libraries, 1934. For an extended literary depiction of the "stretch-out," see Page, *Gathering Storm*, Chapter 19.

[3] *Gaston Daily Gazette*, April 3, 1929.

[4] For more on the injuries and charges, see Dunne 7.

There was an abundance of southern strikes in 1929, with eighty-one in South Carolina alone, many of which were marked by higher death tolls and more violent strikebreaking tactics than those in Gastonia. The conflict there was not unique.[5] Yet, the Loray Mill strike became a cause célèbre in America that transfixed the national media and garnered the financial and PR support of the Communist Party. Within just five years, the strike served as the subject of six novels and, later, in-depth sociological studies.[6] Wiley Cash's recent book, *The Last Ballad* (2018), a new novel about the Loray Mill conflict, is a testament to the continuing relevance of the strike in the cultural memory of the South. No American strike has elicited that kind of sustained interest among artists and scholars.

But if Gastonia was not unique, then why was it so significant at the time? A number of explanations have been put forward; some argue that the strike gave Marxists the opportunity to test their theories about the ideological function of proletarian fiction and the chance to "employ art as a class weapon"[7] (Sowinska 122). Many others contend that Gastonia was received as proof of the Comintern's prediction that global capitalism was entering a phase of fundamental crisis, its "Third Period," a time when the spread of the Taylor System would cause an upsurge of radical agitation that would ultimately initiate full-scale revolution.[8] For example, Albert Weisbord, the secretary of the NTWU and spouse of Vera Buch, a Gastonia organizer and defendant in the subsequent murder trial, proclaimed, "This strike is the first shot in a battle which will be heard around the world. It will prove as important in transforming the social and political life of this country as the Civil War itself" (qtd. in Reilly 500). For leftist devotees, Gastonia proved "that revolution was at hand" (Garrison 217). By contrast, Pope averred that Gastonia was neither unusual with respect to southern industrial relations and modes of production, nor a portent of revolution. The strike was, however, a particularly stark exemplar of cultural conflict. He writes, "Seldom have two opposing economic philosophies and forces come into such clear opposition within a rather isolated social context" (Pope 208). The situational peculiarities of Gastonia make it "a remarkable laboratory" for examining the relation of religion and economics in the early twentieth century, as well as the integral role of religion in the conflict of capital and labor (Pope 208).

---

[5] See Hall et al. 271; Salmond 9.
[6] See also Earle, John R., Dean D. Knudsen, and Donald W. Shriver, Jr. *Spindles and Spires: A Re-study of Religion and Social Change in Gastonia*. Atlanta: John Knox Press, 1976.
[7] See also Cook 52.
[8] On Gastonia and the Third Period, see Ackerman 67, "Martyr" 33, *Tobacco* 86, Devinatz 261–2, Garrison 217, Pope 245, Reilly 500–1, Schreibersdorf 307, and Weisbord 240. On the Third Period and its relation to Taylorism, see Kozlov and Weitz, 387, 395–6.

A New Heaven: Religion and the Rise of the Textile Industry in the South

By 1929, the North Carolina piedmont had surpassed New England as the largest producer of cotton cloth in the United States,[9] largely as a consequence of paying workers half as much as their northern counterparts.[10] Textile industrialists operating in the South adopted the feudal structure of plantations in their design of the paternalistic mill village system. Under this regime, millhands were housed in planned communities adjacent to factories and provided, ostensibly, with all of the goods, services, and institutions they would need. While this readymade communal infrastructure was an attractive enticement to families migrating from their farms in the nearby Appalachian mountains, it was proffered in exchange for low wages and company scrip. The system was cloaked in the pretense of benevolence, but its true purpose was to give management control over every aspect of workers' lives. The social form of paternalism mirrored the new industrial division of labor and the class hierarchy it created by strictly segregating mill villages from adjoining towns populated by local professionals. The social dynamics of the paternalistic system in Gastonia, namely, the textile industry's control over all sectors of civil society, make it an ideal test case for examining how changing material conditions influence cultural institutions and norms, such as religion, morality, and law. In particular, Gastonia affords the opportunity to witness how the development of industrial capitalism changed Protestant Christianity over the course of the region's transition from an agrarian to a mass-production society. The cultural analyses of Gastonia conducted by novelists, social scientists, and historians show that, at the turn of the century, textile manufacturers conflated Christianity and capitalism to garner public support for the burgeoning industry and that, once established, the paternalistic system allowed textile mills to exert control over religious institutions. With their command of the religious establishment, mill owners sanctified industrial capitalism and demonized trade unions, thus utilizing the power of apotheosis to maintain and reproduce the new economic order.

 The development of textile industrialism in the South was made possible by "the early approval tendered by the churches" (Pope 27). That approval came in the form of apotheosis, that is, by identifying the growth of the industry with the will of God and by praising industrialists as the "redeemers" of the new South (Pope 21). For example, in an 1890 editorial in the *Raleigh Christian*

---

[9] See Eller 124, Salmond xi.
[10] See Eller 125, Rehn 166, and Salmond 2.

Advocate, we read, "Wherever they plant a mill they plant a church of God" (qtd. in Pope 23). A South Carolina minister summed up the prevailing thinking in a 1927 speech where he proclaimed that "It is imperative that we think of Southern industry as a spiritual movement and of ourselves as instruments in a Divine plan. Southern industry is the largest single opportunity the world has ever had to build a democracy upon the ethics of Christianity" (qtd. in Pope 24-25). Industrial capitalism was able to gain a foothold in the South only by making it a God-ordained phase in the salvation history of humanity. Sherwood Anderson begins *Beyond Desire* by depicting the instrumental role of apotheosis in the rise of the textile industry. In the fictional, but historically accurate, backstory Anderson gives Gastonia—here called Langdon—a local banker, Tom Shaw, enlists the help of a revivalist preacher to raise money and garner public support to build a cotton mill. The evangelist treats the campaign like a revival, delivering his message as he would a sermon, and espouses a new doctrine of salvation to persuade the townspeople to embrace the introduction of large-scale manufacturing. Rather than preaching on salvation in the afterlife, he holds out the promise of redemption in the present, through the growth of industrial capitalism. Anderson writes,

> Tom Shaw and the preacher had got together. There had been a new kind of revival in town and in the country communities about Langdon. Presently the revivalist dropped everything else and, instead of talking about a life after death, talked only of the present... of a new and glowing kind of life [...] There was a good deal of confusion. Although the preacher had got a new theme, was speaking now of a new Heaven men might enter, did not have to wait until death to enter, he still used the tone of a man delivering a sermon and, as he talked, often pounding some pulpit and running up and down before his audience, the audience became confused. There were shouts and groans at the mill meetings as there had been at the religious meeting... The preacher said that, because of the wonderful new life, brought into so many Eastern and Middle-Western towns by the factories, every one had suddenly become prosperous. Life was filled with new joys. Now, in such towns any man could own an automobile... "Yes, God," some one in the audience said fervently. "I want that. I want it. I want it," a woman's voice cried. It was a sharp plaintive voice... "Yes, God. Save us, God."
> (32-35)

Anderson's rendering of the integral role of religion in the early development of the industry is consistent with historical facts. His choice of words here is significant, because ultimately apotheosis is a kind of confusion, one characterized by the collapse of the material and the spiritual, the real and the ideal, of the profane and the sacred. It is this kind of misrecognition that causes a new economic model to be confused with a salvation ethic and a factory town to be regarded as "a new Heaven."

The church's early endorsement of the textile industry was predicated on its apotheosis, that is, on investing mills with divine agency. This misled workers, who were made to believe that mills were "a source of salvation" (Hall 17). Ronald Eller explains,

> From 1900 to 1930, thousands of mountaineers left their farms for the mill districts... After the turn of the century, when labor supplies began to diminish in the piedmont, many of the mill owners actively recruited workers in the mountain districts, sending agents into remote areas to tap what was believed to be an inexhaustible [sic] source of cheap labor. Life in the textile mills, the recruiters preached, would be "like heaven."
>
> (125)

Textile companies distributed brochures among mountain farmers depicting mill villages "as industrial Edens," ultimately convincing "over three-quarters of a million mountaineers" to migrate (Pope 14, Eller 126). The Gastonia novelists accurately represent this course of events. For example, in *To Make My Bread*, a mill recruiter assures the McClure family, "They say out there the rivers flow with milk and honey and money grows on trees. [...] They said I was to spread the news. It's the poor folks' time if they'll pick up and go" (Lumpkin 39). In an interview, the son of a migrant worker reported that his father moved their family from a North Carolina tobacco farm to a mill village in the 1890s because he "felt that all we had to do when we come to town was to reach up and pull the money off of the trees" (Hall et al. 249). In Page's *Gathering Storm*, Annie Totherow believes that a recruiter was sent by God to deliver "the good tidin's" and that the mill will be the family's salvation. Page writes, "the good Jehovah sent this stranger to us. I prayed, 'Lord, send some-one from Macedonia to helpen us. Your people is dying' here in the hills, 'n the stranger come, an answer to my prayer" (*Storm* 16, 17). When they leave for the mill, Annie is filled with the same exultation she feels at "revival meetin's" (*Storm* 19). Similarly, when the McClures begin their migration, Emma rejoices, "Hit's like the Israelites... a-going to the Promised Land" (Lumpkin 142).

We recall that apotheosis entails the false, specular reversal of subject and object. This phenomenon causes subjects to be divested of agency and subordinated to an object-made-Subject. In the context of industrial capitalism, apotheosis causes the factory to be regarded as a god, a divine Subject, while humans are merely worshipers of the omnipotent fetish, dispossessed of freedom. In the Gastonia novels, migrant workers deify the mill, initially regarding it as a benevolent savior, and, later, as a malevolent monster that consumes them; in each case, they believe their fate is determined by the will of the factory. In *Beyond Desire*, a worker considers the opening of a mill to be a "semi-religious occasion" and wonders why capitalism should not become a "new religion" and factories "a sacred thing... new churches—new sacred places?" (Anderson 30, 284). The mill inspires reverence in migrant workers who see it as holy. For example, when Ishma Waycaster begins to work in the mill, she approaches the looms "with wonder and respect" (Dargan 270). Similarly, when she first sees it, Emma McClure stands in awe of the mill. " 'Hit's the factory,' Emma said to Ora with a catch in her voice. [...] She spoke in a whisper as if she was afraid the factory would hear" (Lumpkin 147, 149). The factory was "superhuman" and "independent," capable of bestowing its "approval" or "remonstrance" upon workers (Anderson 50, 284, Dargan 270). Anderson writes, "The looms... seemed more and more to have a life of their own. The looms were outside the lives of the weavers" (Anderson 284). By contrast, in a self-objectifying remark, one worker explains, "We're only machines ourselves" (Anderson 95). In this clear example of apotheotic confusion, subjects consider themselves mere machines and see the factory as the divine Subject. As a consequence of the textile industry's control of the church, the factory was made sacred. For millhands, it functioned as a "totemic emblem" that was "like the visible body of the god" (Durkheim 184). One worker correctly reflects, "I'm a-getting to believe the factory's an idol that people worship" (Lumpkin 200).

In his rigorous study, *Millhands and Preachers*, Liston Pope collected a wealth of evidence which proved that economic factors had a major impact on "the genesis and growth of religious institutions" and theologies in Gaston County (Pope 126, 102). He and his team found that Protestants "adapted themselves to the emergence of social classes" and "to class segregation" by constructing "class churches" (Pope 69, 70). In response to class formation and the new social relations caused by industrialization, separate churches and theologies were created to reflect the qualities and needs of each class. The economic experience and interests of each group constituted the "imaginative pattern" that determined its theological concepts and norms (Reilly 503). Whereas religion in the mill villages offered the working-class an otherworldly theology that promised "escape from economic conditions" in the afterlife, religion in the "uptown churches" supplied the privileged class with a theological "sanction of prevailing economic arrangements" (Pope 92). Pope reports, "The role of the uptown minister, and his church, is not to transcend immediate cultural boundaries but to symbolize and sanction the rightness of things as they are" (Pope 95). The theology of the propertied class served to sacralize and legitimate the economic status quo. Similarly, "the religion of the mill worker is heavily conditioned by the economic and social environment in which he lives" (Pope 91). Pope continues,

> The forces which play upon the mill worker and isolate him into a separate social class operate through him upon his church. The structure and program of the mill church are conditioned in innumerable respects by the occupational requirements, wage levels, educational achievement, housing facilities, recreational needs, and psychological state of mill villagers. The timing and character of religious services, and attendance at them; the quality of lay leadership; the methods of raising money and the amount available; the ideas a preacher may expound and the routine by which he may make pastoral calls— all these and many more, are affected profoundly by the mode and levels of life among the constituency of the village church. If the mill worker is different, his church must be different too.
>
> (86, 84–85)

Pope is careful to acknowledge that "Gastonia is far from unique" (Pope xx). However, it provides a clear and concrete exemplification of the way economy shapes religious concepts, practices, and institutions, and the manner in which those forms of religion are weaponized for cultural conflict. In particular, Pope focuses on "the tie between the church and the dominant classes of society," or, as Weber would put it, religion "under the influence of the ruling classes" (Pope xx, SR 141).

The structure of industrial paternalism was such that textile mills controlled Gastonia churches and their ministers. Every mill in Gaston County built a church for their adjoining mill village and heavily subsidized the uptown churches attended by management. Area churches and their personnel were among the mills' assets. As a consequence, textile mills exercised direct and indirect forms of control over nearly all of the churches in the county. Churches' financial dependence on the mills made it impossible for them to oppose management's stance on economic or social matters. Churches were "inextricably bound" in fealty to the mills and were therefore "conscripted into the cause of management" in all labor disputes (Pope xx, xlvii). Ministers rationalized this "by equating paternalism... with Christian principles," that is, by apotheosizing industrial paternalism (Pope 161). Myra Page illustrates this dynamic in *Gathering Storm*, where she writes that "the village church [was] owned and operated by the company" (69). There, the Sunday school teacher held "forth on the Fatherhood of God and the Brotherhood of Man... She explained how the mill owners and workers were really one big family" (*Storm* 70). This gospel of paternalism suggests that workers' vassalage to mill management is determined by the chain of being and duplicates on earth humanity's relation to God. Here, the projection of prevailing relations of production into the heavens is reversed to portray the social order as a reflection of divine order.

The cotton mills' control of the churches was a means to dictate the behavioral norms of the working-class. Pope found that "Organized religion was a key instrument in creating a manipulable labor force" (xx). The salvation ethic espoused by mill ministers was composed of values that were conducive to the creation and maintenance of a docile labor force. As Cook put it, mill ministers "preached humility, hard work, sobriety, and rewards in heaven—virtues guaranteed to make malleable employees" (*Tobacco* 87). One Gastonia mill official explained, "Belonging to a church, and attending it, makes a man a better worker. It makes him more complacent... more resigned" (Pope 31). In short, the paternalistic system in Gastonia allowed the mills to use religion as a means of social control.

The churches in Gastonia remained indifferent to the problems faced by textile workers and focused instead on promoting an otherworldly soteriology. By diverting attention away from economic matters, the religious establishment indirectly sanctioned the mill system. After the Loray Mill strike began, ministers' silence in the face of continual mob violence, lynch parties, and show trials was even more significant than their overt opposition to the strike. For example, none of the Gastonia ministers commented publicly on the murder of Ella May Wiggins. Pope's seminal study of religion and economy in the region yielded the following conclusion:

> Gastonia ministers revealed that their economic ethicways were products of the economic system in which they lived, with no serious modification by any transcendent economic or religious standard. They were willing to allow the power of religious institutions to be used against those who challenged this economic system, and themselves assisted in such use. At no important point did they stand in opposition to the prevailing economic arrangements... In no significant respect was their role productive of change in economic life. By and large, they contributed unqualified and effective sanction to their economic culture.
>
> (330)

Further, Page reports that "in times of union agitation and strikes, [workers] have found pastors siding with the company and serving to undermine labor's solidarity" (*Cotton Mills* 51). This circumstance remained unchanged in 1929 when Gastonia's ministers supported the Loray Mill and made a concerted effort to break the strike.

All of the novels about Gastonia thematically prioritize the entanglement of religion and economy and corroborate Pope's findings a decade before his study was undertaken. As the novels accurately depict, Gastonia's established ministers preached an anti-union gospel, whereas independent, Appalachian preachers who were unattached to any institutional church supported the strike. In Lumpkin's *To Make My Bread*, preachers Warren, Warmsley, Turnipseed, and Simpkins defend the mill. In *Call Home the Heart*, Rev. James Mullen represents those who "shout against" the union "from their pulpits" (Dargan 290). There, Ella reminds Ishma to "remember who pays his salary. 'Taint us mill folks" (Dargan 315). In *Strike!*, Vorse portrays ministers who attempt to convince workers to quit the strike (Vorse 127). Similarly, in *The Shadow Before*, Rev. White encourages strikers to return to work and to accept a 5 percent wage cut (Rollins 182). Likewise, Page's *Gathering Storm* features preachers who go from home to home in the mill village, pleading with workers to end the strike, claiming that their actions violate Christ's ethics (*Storm* 225). In the same novel, 100 millhands are excommunicated from a company church for their union activism (*Storm* 362). In Anderson's *Beyond Desire*, we read of a church that was financed by the local mill, which pays "half of the salary of the regular preacher" (Anderson 18–19). When two workers are shot and killed by deputy sheriffs, the clergyman proclaims from the pulpit that "No Christian minister should perform the burial ceremony for them. They should be buried like dead mules" (Anderson 127–8).

In keeping with the facts, the novels also feature a small number of itinerant preachers "from the hills" who support the union, such as Howard Kingsley and Oscar Williams in *Strike!* (Vorse 21, 86, 211). In the novel, Williams is among the few area ministers who lead a church that is not "on mill ground" or beholden to "mill owners' money" (Vorse 232). Lumpkin aptly conveys the predicament of the ministry when she writes of a preacher "that has taken up for the union so he's been run out of his church by the mill" (364). On April 29, 1929, the Baltimore *Sun* reports on a church service at the strikers' tent colony led by a lay preacher, H. J. Crabtree. In his sermon, Crabtree espouses a proletarian Christology: "God's a poor man's God. Jesus Christ, Himself, was born in an old ox-barn in Bethlehem. He was kicked about, speared about and finally nailed on a cross.

And for what? For sin. It's sin that's causing this trouble. Sin of the rich man" (qtd. in Pope 277). Anderson incorporates this kind of proletarian Christology into *Beyond Desire*, where we read, "The preachers in the town of Birchfield were against the strikers. They were crying out against the new leaders the strikers had found" (303). However, one organizer entreats strikers to recall "how the Christ, the preachers were always talking about, had stood by the poor and lowly. He had stood by people in trouble, by people who were oppressed as the workers were. [She] had said that the attitude of the preacher was a betrayal not only of the workers but even of their own Christ" (Anderson 303). Elsewhere in the book, Ethel reads a Christ novel, *The Brook Kerith*[11] (1916), in which Jesus looks "far into the future" and is ashamed to find "commercialized churches, churches, like industry, controlled by money, churches turning away from the lowly, turning their backs on labor" (Anderson 115). Prior to the strike, as churches in Gastonia remained indifferent to the increasing misery of textile workers, their control over millhands diminished, which allowed union organizers to step in and take their place as the primary source of communal cohesion and leadership. Company preachers' efforts to break the strike made their complicity with the mills unmistakable, and further alienated workers from the established denominations in Gastonia. Page illustrates this in *Gathering Storm* where one striker remarks, "I've been a church-goin' man all my life. But after what Parsons Brown 'n Antell done to break this strike, I doan believe I'll ever set foot inside a mill church again" (*Storm* 226). The Gastonia novels not only document how mainline religious institutions were transformed by the development of the textile industry but also reflect how economic relations influenced Appalachian religious folkways operative outside the church.

Appalachian Religious Culture: Spirit, Grace, and Humility beyond the Church

"Piedmont" means foot of the mountain. This is indicative of the cultural milieu of the North Carolina piedmont in the early twentieth century. It was a liminal space between the Appalachian Mountains to the west and the coastal plains to the east. It was here, amid the region's textile boom, that scores of mountaineers migrated to find work, bringing with them their unique religious culture. By the early nineteenth century, the form of Christianity practiced in Appalachia

---

[11] Moore, George. *The Brook Kerith: A Syrian Story.* New York: Macmillan Company, 1916.

was a fully developed tradition that was separate and distinct from mainline Protestantism.[12] The fundamental theological differences between mountain religion and the dominant Protestant culture include the former's decentralized and nonhierarchical church polity and, in terms of doctrine, its basis on unconventional conceptions of spirit, grace, and humility.

G. C. Waldrep explains that "the defining characteristic of mountain religious life... was its emphasis on autonomous, nonhierarchical congregations" that were independent from national denominational institutions[13] (117). Appalachian Christians valued local control and self-determination, and therefore fiercely resisted the encroachment of institutional "bureaucracy and formalism" from both the North and the South (Callahan 28). In Appalachia, "church services were irregular and the majority of people were not church members" (Callahan 30). Irregular services led by lay preachers, periodic baptisms, funerals, and camp meetings were community-building affairs that families often traveled long distances to attend.

Perhaps most importantly, mountain religious culture is characterized by a deep and "pervasive sacramentalism" (Callahan 35). That is, in the folk belief of the region, the mundane, material world of humanity is intertwined with divine spirit. Residents believe that the boundary between the "natural and supernatural [is] often blurred" and therefore the Holy Spirit can act and be experienced in human society (Callahan 35). Because of this belief in the "synergic relation" between the spiritual and social worlds, "religion was never confined solely to the churches in Appalachia," where the sacred was inseparable from everyday life (Callahan 30). This aspect of Appalachian theology requires us to look beyond churches and organized religion to recognize how religion functioned in the daily lives of Gastonia millhands. Scholars of the region report that "people read God's plan and the invisible world through the everyday" (Callahan 36). While conducting fieldwork for her thesis, *Southern Cotton Mills and Labor* (1929), Myra Page found evidence consistent with that of later historians and social scientists. She writes, "Superstitious beliefs are commonly accepted, about god's interference in a most minute way, in human affairs, either to incite or prevent some act, or to reward or punish some individual's or group's conduct. Accidents, coincidences, illness and happenings in nature are frequently interpreted as 'signs from heaven' " (*Cotton Mills* 48). As one

---

[12] See McCauley, Deborah Vansau. *Appalachian Mountain Religion: A History*. Urbana: University of Illinois Press, 1995, 13; Callahan Jr., Richard J. *Work and Faith in the Kentucky Coal Fields: Subject to Dust*. Bloomington: Indiana UP, 2009, 21.

[13] See also McCauley 13, 38.

character in Lumpkin's novel put it, "You never can tell what the Lord will send" (Lumpkin 27). The sacramentalism of mountain religious culture led adherents to interpret the sacred through the lens of the secular, making them particularly susceptible to forms of apotheosis. For example, in *Beyond Desire*, Anderson remarks that, when "industrialism in its ugliest form" came to the South, "all that mixed up in the people with religion" (106).

Scotch-Irish Presbyterians' Calvinist theology significantly influenced the religious culture of southern Appalachia, as is evinced by their soteriology. The doctrine of salvation most commonly espoused in the region occupies a middle path between the traditional Calvinist concept of predestination, which holds that God alone elects those who will receive salvation, and the Arminian position that humans are in control of their redemption.[14] Appalachian Christianity, broadly construed, contends that only God by His grace can offer salvation to humans, who have the free will to accept or reject it. This emphasizes election by grace, obtained by the sanctification of the Holy Spirit. Here, human agency has a role but is not the initiator or ultimate authority. Whereas Arminians saw salvation as a matter of "human initiative and God's cooperation," mountain religious culture saw it as the result of "God's initiative and human cooperation" (McCauley 14). While this may appear to be a subtle theological nuance, Deborah Vansau McCauley explains that this gave rise to "two very different theological traditions—one centered on grace and the Holy Spirit, one centered on free will and rational decision," and that this "translated into two very different sets of religious values and worldviews" (14). This is a crucial distinction that Pope fails to acknowledge when he lumps the Gastonia millhands—scores of whom hail from the mountains—into mainline Arminian denominations.

One more doctrine that sets Appalachian religion apart from other forms of post-disestablishment Protestantism is its emphasis on fatalistic humility. Adherents firmly believe that the world is ordered according to God's design. To bemoan misfortune or oppose the social status quo, even in the face of great suffering, is regarded as a sinful defiance of God. In her fieldwork, Page found that mill village preachers encourage the "acceptance of things as they are as right and inevitable and part of god's will" (*Cotton Mills* 48). Such a doctrine, as we have seen, can lead to the naturalization of economic inequality. In *To Make My Bread*, Lumpkin represents this aspect of Appalachian theology in a manner that reflects the political quietism it mandates. We read, " 'Hit's funny,' Ora said, 'how some have such fine, pretty things and others not'... [Emma:] 'Hit's the

---

[14] See Callahan, 27, and McCauley, 14.

way the Lord made things to be... I have to remember whatever happens is the Lord's will.' [Ora:] 'There's got to be pore as well as rich to make up the world' " (Lumpkin 227). The residual Calvinism of mountain religion likely explains its tendency toward fatalism. However, the Appalachian "theodicy of disprivilege"—in Weber's terminology—was challenged as workers sought to reinterpret the sacred through the lens of industrial society.

In the context of life in the mill village system and work in the textile industry, the Appalachian doctrine of humility began to pose a theological problem. How were believers to reconcile the poverty, suffering, and injustice they endured with the image of a loving and omnipotent God? How could their faith make sense of the perennial problem of evil when faced with the new social ills caused by industrial capitalism? The Gastonia novelists suggest that three interrelated modes of apotheosis and a new concept of salvation were developed to quell workers' growing frustration: (1) the sanctification of suffering, (2) a soteriology of divine exchange, and (3) the transvaluation of life and death.

To justify the suffering and injustice they experienced in the textile industry, the Appalachian working-class formed a theodicy fit for the machine age. The sacramentalism of mountain religious culture caused workers to interpret their new social conditions and the hardships they encountered as being part of a divine plan they were unable to fully understand. As in much older models of theodicy, millhands held that this is the best of all possible worlds and that, while the good must suffer evil, they can take solace in the knowledge that this seeming injustice is part of a grand, divine design that humanity is too finite to comprehend. According to this view, if you submit to pain with humility and faith, you will be granted salvation. To resist or fail to be docile, on the other hand, is regarded as sinful or blasphemous. In *Gathering Storm*, Myra Page accurately represents this aspect of migrant workers' religious culture. The family matriarch explains that their misery is "all part of God's Plan, 'n if you trusted Him it'd all come out right some day... The thing, Parson Brown said, was to have faith" (*Storm* 47). Similarly, elsewhere we read, " 'Ma, why is it, mill folks has it so hard? Does God plan it thisaway, or what?' 'Everything's God's Will, Marge. It's hard, but we'll understand it bettah by 'n by. Parson Brown saws we gotta bear our cross in patience, 'n re-sign ourselves to God's mysterious Plan' " (*Storm* 37). Moreover, it is thought to be "wicked" to doubt or oppose this plan (*Storm* 47). The theodicy of the millhands is an ideal example of apotheosis. Here, a subordinate class transforms the suffering they incur amid new social conditions and forms of work into the basis and proof of their salvation, and, more broadly, interpret their systemic exploitation as part of a divine drama from which they will ultimately emerge victorious.

In order to further justify the pain and privation they suffer, millhands exalt their defining traits and social conditions, turning them into the qualities of righteousness. As Pope put it, "they transmute poverty into a symptom of Grace" (137). Excluded from the more affluent community, they "affirm separation from the world," "because they have no jewelry to wear, they make refusal to wear jewelry... a religious requirement" (Pope 137). In penury, they sanctify simplicity. In *Call Home the Heart*, the champagne socialist Derry Unthank mocks the sanctification of suffering as a means of coping with systemic exploitation. He remarks, "we had accepted sorrow and given it beauty. We made songs for shadows and suffering. Over ugliness and defeat, we threw the sheen of art, the pale holiness of resignation. We guarded our griefs jealously. We hugged them as from God. We went about our jails and almshouses with the shining stolidity of virtue" (Dargan 326). Dargan contends that the privileged class utilizes the Appalachian doctrines of grace and humility to turn quietism and docility into prerequisites of redemption. In a moving speech, Jed proclaims,

> You couldn't fool us without [religion]. You take a man an' lash his back an' tell him not to worry about his onery red blood runnin' inter the ash-pan, so long as he keeps his spirchal life-blood goin' good. You tell him to believe in God an' his justice —whack! whack!—an' go to church an' drop his pore little squeezed out dimes inter the plate—whack! whack!—what's a slaves back fer anyhow?—whack! whack!—what's his tongue fer? Pray! pray! whack! whack!
>
> (Dargan 367)

Another element of working-class theodicy in the region was the development of a soteriology of divine exchange. This economy of redemption was predicated on a compensational theory which held that the poor and righteous who suffer injustice in this world will be rewarded in the afterlife, while the rich and wicked will be punished. Workers adapt their response to the problem of evil, in the context of textile industrialism, through the apotheosis of finance or commerce. Here, God incurs a debt to the humble that is to be repaid after death when the divine ledger is balanced. According to this sacramental view, endurance amid suffering is a sign of grace and piety. In her fieldwork, Myra Page found that company ministers preached "meek endurance of this world's hardships with faith in the reward hereafter in a heaven of peace and glory" (*Cotton Mills* 48). In Page's novel on the Loray Mill, a striker, confident in the righteousness of the poor, takes solace in the belief that "the Lawd'll sure punish the mill men for their wickedness" (*Storm* 295). Similarly, Lumpkin depicts the theodicy of migrant mountaineers, writing, "It seemed that the Lord took pleasure in shearing his poor sheep and fattening the rich ones. Maybe he did it on purpose so that in heaven the sheared ones would enjoy their riches more, and in hell the rich would burn better for their fatness" (59). Later in the same novel, Rev. Warmsley delivers a sermon in which he glorifies the spiritual wealth of the millhands, proclaiming that this, in the eyes of God, is superior to the material wealth of the mill owners. With ecclesiastical authority, he promises that the piety and suffering of the workers will be compensated with "eternal salvation and heavenly reward" in the hereafter (Lumpkin 268-269, Callahan 23). However, apotheosis is not limited to the disempowered but is humanity's primary mode of religious ideation. As a result, the affluent also adhere to a concept of salvation that is modeled on commercial exchange. In Anderson's *Beyond Desire*, Ethel reflects that, among the privileged class,

> there had been a kind of deal made with God. "All right, we'll give you this one day of the week. We'll go to church. We'll put up enough money to keep the churches going. In return for that you give us Heaven when we get through with this life here, this life of running this cotton mill, or this store, or this law office... Or being sheriff or deputy sheriff or being in the real-estate business. You give us Heaven when we get through with this and we'll hold up our end."
> (Anderson 113)

Appalachian millhands adapted their fatalistic doctrine of humility to the new conditions created by the textile boom by further emphasizing the otherworldly aspect of their faith. This was a move Pope called "the transvaluation of life," that is, a theology that negates the value of earthly existence and affirms the supremacy of the afterlife (88). This functioned as a coping mechanism for the working-class and rationalized why the unjust thrived while the just suffered. Pope found that this could "take the form of reassurance or of escape, or both. By affirmation of values denied in the economic world, the church provides comfort and ultimate assurance; in its religious services it often affords escape temporarily from the economic and social situation in which workaday life must be spent" (89). Page offers a poignant depiction of the way theology was reshaped to accommodate the needs of the newly proletarianized southern workers:

> Desperately, Marge turned to religion for peace and understanding. Ma found solace in it... With summer came the revivals. Every night for a week, meetings

were held in the company church and all turned out to hear the visiting preacher, who exhorted old and young to turn away from sin and the ways of this world, and fix their eyes and thoughts on the next... he waxed eloquent over the joys of 'the land whar all is res' "n peace"... He pictured Jesus, arms open, waiting to rescue them. His audience was swayed, lifted up to the heights and plunged to the depths, swept completely off their feet. Forgotten for a few hours was the mill drudgery and their devastating poverty and ignorance, as the revivalist's voice rose and fell, sounding on their ears like poetry or a rushing waterfall.

(*Storm* 103–4)

The emotional fervor of the revival service is, of course, calculated to "induce the high emotional crisis of 'being saved'—saved to a personal security that transcends the troubles of the world" (Pope 91). To be saved, to attain salvation, workers must "turn away from... the ways of this world" and become resigned to injustice. Lumpkin writes of a hymn that aptly reflects a theology that negates life and its social ills: they sing, "I'm but a stranger here... Heaven is my home. Earth is a desert drear. Heaven is my home"[15] (279).

However, as their living and working conditions deteriorated, millhands began to challenge the doctrine of humility, arguing that theodicy had been seized upon and promoted by mill preachers to encourage docility and acquiescence among the workforce. This is a clear indication that new economic conditions introduced by industrialization and the paternalistic mill village system caused theodical aspects of mountain religious culture to be adapted by adversaries in class struggle and mobilized in service to their political priorities. For mill owners, theodicy was a means of social control, for millhands, a source of consolation, and for labor activists, it was an ideological foil. The Gastonia novelists who focused on the experience of Appalachian migrants were familiar with this phenomenon and documented its role in the region's class conflict. Myra Page found that "religion as it was practiced by the mill workers appeared to be a handicap. Believing deeply that they were going to go to somewhere better... made it easier for mill workers to put up with terrible conditions in the present" (Baker 113). Workers were encouraged to believe that humility, in the form of indifference to social suffering, was a prerequisite of salvation. Page reports common refrains among millhands such as: "We mustn't concern ourselves with earthly things. It is all in God's hands... my thoughts are on the world to come" (*Cotton Mills* 50). Particularly the younger generation of Appalachian migrants began to ask "why the preachers... keep their eyes

---

[15] Taylor, Thomas Rawson. "I'm But a Stranger Here" (1836).

on death, and not on life" (Lumpkin 325). Emerging activists argued that Christianity was too otherworldly, whereas the labor movement allowed people to practice their religious values and attain salvation here and now. While formerly millhands had been taught to think, "What is there to do, except wait and hope for heaven?" many began to ask, "What has [this] life got for me and mine?" (Lumpkin 276). Lumpkin draws a direct line of causation from workers' rejection of mill theology to the organization of the Loray Mill strike. Millhand and organizer John Stevens announces,

> You speak of preachers who talk of death. I want to tell you now about the people who speak of life: and who are killed for speaking so. No wonder preachers speak of death to us poor, for if they spoke of life as these others have done, they would be punished by the rich. [...] The rich will never give [freedom] to us. We must take it for ourselves... And so we won't do anything about our misery, they keep us in the darkness of ignorance and talk about death, to keep our eyes on death and heaven, so we won't think too much about life. We are taught that to struggle is a sin. But it ain't a sin, John. People must learn that. We must work in a strike.
> (Lumpkin 326, 328)

In contrast to the doctrine of humility and the transvaluation of life, which promotes a compensatory and otherworldly model of salvation, Gastonia labor activists espouse a gospel of immanent salvation that rejects theodicy and all theological justifications for economic injustice. It is worth recalling that in his "On the History of Early Christianity," where he draws lines of commonality between Christianity and the worker's movement, Engels notes that their difference hinges on this question of salvation. He writes,

> The history of early Christianity has notable points of resemblance with the modern working-class movement. Like the latter, Christianity was originally a movement of oppressed people: it first appeared as the religion of slaves and emancipated slaves, of poor people deprived of all rights, of peoples subjugated or dispersed by Rome. Both Christianity and the workers' socialism preach forthcoming salvation from bondage and misery; Christianity places this salvation in a life beyond, after death, in heaven; socialism places it in this world, in a transformation of society. Both are persecuted and baited, their adherents are despised and made the objects of exclusive laws, the former as enemies of the human race, the latter as enemies of the state, enemies of religion, the family, social order.

Each of the shared elements Engels describes here is taken up in their turn by the Gastonia novelists.

Union as Church, Strike as Revival

Humanity's innate form of religious ideation coupled with the sacramentalism of mountain culture caused Gastonia's millhands to apotheosize every aspect of the new southern industrial economy, including their embattled social position. They had invested their migration with religious import and fetishized the mills when they arrived. It should come as no surprise, then, that when economic conflict in the region reached a point of crisis, workers interpreted it according to the religious poetics of their culture. Millhands adapted their religious concepts and practices in response to their new economic conditions and needs; as a result, the Loray Mill strike took the form of a revival,[16] the union was regarded as a church, the affirmation of anti-capitalism was conflated with salvation, and labor leaders were revered as martyrs and messianic figures.[17]

The strikers' religious interpretation of class conflict is a prominent feature of all the Gastonia novels and is consistent with the facts of the event. In his memoir, Fred Beal recalls, "these simple mountain-folk... made something of a spiritual revival of the strike" (*Proletarian* 156). Mary Heaton Vorse's rendering of Beal in *Strike!* similarly complains, "You know, Roger, these folks... think a Union is like a church. It's kinda like salvation. You belong to the Union, and somehow or other, you're saved. They have a mystical feeling about the Union" (109). Sylvia Jenkins Cook concurs, writing that "The strikers see the union not as a rational means of organizing but as something mystical, more akin to religion, a power that exists independently of them" (*Tobacco* 95). What these authors understood to be mysticism was the strikers' Appalachian sacramentalism recalibrated according to their new socioeconomic environment. Their theological outlook predisposed them to conflate the sacred and the secular, and therefore what outsiders considered a purely economic dispute Appalachian Christians saw as a metaphysical "test of faith" that would have eternal repercussions (Dargan 334). The Gastonia case offers an ideal example of how apotheosis works. Here, workers deify the union, transforming a system composed of numerous

---

[16] On "revolutions as religious revivals" see Tiryakian, Edward A. "From Durkheim to Managua: Revolutions as Religious Revivals," in *Durkheimian Sociology: Cultural Studies*, ed. Jeffrey C. Alexander. Cambridge: Cambridge UP, 1988.

[17] As Kenelm Burridge notes, "An awakening of religious activity is a frequent characteristic of periods of social unrest. The weakening or disruption of the old social order may... give rise to religious movements that strive to sanction social and political aspirations. Communities that feel themselves oppressed anticipate the emergence of a hero who will restore their prosperity and prestige. And when the people are imbued with religious fervor the expected hero will be regarded as a Messiah. Phenomena of this kind are well known in history, and are not unknown at the present day" (433).

individuals into a single supernatural entity "that exists independently of them" and has the power to confer or deny salvation.

From the start, the Loray Mill strike was invested with the qualities of a revival. Frequent strike meetings were held in an open air space and conducted in the manner of a camp meeting. Speeches delivered on the grounds—where workers also held church services during the strike—were "religious in tone" (Pope 274). After strikers were evicted from their mill-owned homes, they built a tent colony on the grounds, furthering workers' inclination to see the strike as a religious affair. Anderson depicts the sanctification of the strike when Red Oliver arrives at the grounds and immediately recognizes its resemblance to a revival. He writes,

> The camp into which Red had come reminded him of something... There was a little open place with shacks... There were a few tents. It was like places Red had seen before. In the South... there were such places set up sometimes in a field at the edge of town or in the country at the edge of a pine forest. The places were called camp meetings and people came there to worship. They got religion there. [...] Poor people of the South, religious enthusiasts, Methodists and Baptists for the most part, gathered in such places. They were poor whites from nearby farms. They had put up little tents and shacks as in the camp of strikers to which Red had now come. Such a religious meeting, in the South, among poor whites, was carried on sometimes for weeks or even months. People came and went... They dressed in their best clothes... There was preaching going on day and night. There were long prayers said. There was singing... People suddenly got religion.
> (Anderson 251–2)

While Anderson indicates the strike's infusion with a southern form of revivalism, Lumpkin further portrays its roots in mountain religious culture. She writes that, on the picket line, "The women were dressed in the best they had, and the men looked as if they had prepared for church... There was a feeling like that of an outdoor church meeting in the mountains, for people were talking as neighbors do who have not seen each other in a long while" (Lumpkin 338).

In addition to possessing the formal characteristics of a revival that distinguish it as a ritualized social practice, the Loray Mill strike was also a catalyst of spiritual awakening that revived workers' religious belief. For example, in *Call Home the Heart*, Ella happily reports that the "new union" has "got me back to the faith" (Dargan 221). Speeches given at strike meetings were modeled on revival sermons that were calculated to induce conversion through the manipulation of emotion. In *Strike!*, we read that "Brother Williams, the bearded preacher from the hills... spoke now in the language of their emotions. He unleashed the emotions which had been gathering and gathering in that large audience" (Vorse 233). Earlier in the novel, the Appalachian preacher opens a strike meeting with a prayer:

> *Oh*, how these people have suffered, Lord!
> *Oh*, Lord, hear them in their struggle!...
> *Oh*, the Lord sent the children of Israel out of bondage!
> *Oh*, the Lord softened Pharaoh's heart!
> *Oh*, ain't Basil Schenk's heart goin' to be softened?...
>
> He went on with this chant, staccato, exciting, until the meeting swayed in unison with his cry; until there was a low sigh of "Oh," throughout the audience. The old women stood with their eyes tightly closed. The young men and young women watched him intently. The prayer had knit them together and focused their emotion into a flame.
>
> (Vorse 52)

The phenomenon of apotheosis causes a bidirectional "slippage between political and religious feeling" (Gray 318). Here, strikers projected the qualities and goals of revival Christianity onto their political protest. As a result, one of the principal aims of the strike was to induce conversion. Because they conflated Christianity and anti-capitalism, obtaining salvation and joining the labor movement were regarded as synonymous. As Vorse's Beal put it, "You belong to the Union, and... you're saved." In *Strike!*, for example, we read that Jolas, a lay preacher "much respected in the in the mill village," could "preach Union as well as anyone. He had a compelling gay way in telling his experiences. It was he who started the experience meetings, 'How I came to be a Union man,' modeled on the 'How I came to be saved meetings' " (Vorse 135). In Gastonia, and in the movement nationwide, labor activists used the revivalist practice of testifying about one's conversion experience in order to incite the conversion of others. As we have seen, this tactic was not limited to the South. Anderson contributed his own testimonial to the *New Masses*' "How I Came to Communism" series in 1932.[18] Jolas's account began, "Brothers and sisters! I heard a voice asayin' to me, 'jine the Union!' " (Vorse 135). We might expect a response of "Praise the Lord!" for, though Vorse's is a fictional rendering, this "was a characteristic exclamation of approval from workers at strike meetings" in Gastonia (Pope 263).

---

[18] *New Masses* 8.3 (1932): 7–10.

Mountain religious culture teaches that life is an ongoing "drama of sin and salvation, culminating in the radical transformation of the conversion experience" (Callahan 23). The structure of this journey to salvation is marked by "an increasing intensification of troubles until they became unbearable, compelling a change"; when the burden of sin is at its zenith, the grace of the Holy Spirit initiates "a sudden reversal" or conversion and the supplicant is "saved" (Callahan 164). Due to their sacramentalism, Appalachians read "social history as divine drama" (Callahan 36). Therefore, Gastonia's millhands interpreted their working life as being part of this "drama of salvation" (Callahan 23). Religious feeling in the region is characterized by a "fluctuating rhythm" where the pious endurance of suffering is "punctuated by startling moments of release" or "sudden moments of emotional violence" (Gray 314, 316). This corroborates Durkheim's contention that there is "no people for whom the great solemn rituals of the cult are not more or less periodic... The religious life of the Australian," for example, "alternates between phases of utter slackness and hyper excitement, and social life shifts according to the same rhythm" (164). Further, Durkheim finds that "it is in these effervescent social settings"—in these "startling moments of release" and "emotional violence"—"and from this very effervescence" that religious ideas are born (Durkheim 164).

When mill churches deprived workers of the emotional release afforded by enthusiastic forms of revivalism, millhands redirected their desire for "ritualized catharsis" into class politics (Gray 316). Organizers' failure to establish labor unions in the South, both prior and subsequent to the Loray Mill strike, is largely attributable to this structure of religious feeling in the region. Northern organizers were baffled by the inconsistency of strike enthusiasm in the South and couldn't understand "how mountain folk could make such alternately quiescent and rebellious workers" (Gray 317). However, this is explicable when we recognize that Appalachian millhands infused their work life and anti-capitalist activism with the characteristics of their religion. As a result of this conflation, strikes became "the cathartic rituals" of "suffering and release" that the working-class had formerly performed in revivals (Gray 314). Callahan explains that "revivalism taught that the drama of salvation was often episodic"; therefore, "periodic revivals alone were sufficient for most people. They did not join a church. They returned to their daily lives not without religion but without feeling the need for sustained organizational worship. When another revival took place, they likely took part" (Callahan 23, 163). Similarly, southern workers' interest in union activity was temporary but recurrent. Failing to recognize this process of conflation and the practice of irregular worship in the mountains, Pope mistakes low church membership among Gastonia's millhands as evidence of a lack of religious conviction. Instead, we must see that "union participation followed the pattern of revivals" (Callahan 163). To reformulate Callahan's observation, periodic strikes alone were sufficient for southern workers. They did not need to join a union. They returned to their daily lives not without anti-capitalist sentiment but without feeling the need for sustained union membership. When another strike took place, they would likely take part. Unionism in the South, therefore, was invested with the episodic structure of the drama of salvation.

Labor activists in Gastonia and the partisan authors who wrote about the strike claimed that unionism is a religion. Certainly, this was anathema to the orthodox atheism of the Communist Party. However, this position was commonplace in America in the early decades of the twentieth century. From a Durkheimian standpoint, professions of belief or unbelief, as well as the existence of a faith-based institution, are irrelevant to whether unionism meets the criteria to warrant its recognition as a religion.

The Gastonia novelists offer an accurate representation of local organizers' and strikers' contention that unionism is a religion. However, activists did not attempt to portray unionism as a new faith, but rather sought to prove its consistency with Christianity. Vorse writes that strikers in Gastonia "were dedicated to Unionism. For them it was a religion" (145). Similarly, Anderson's Red Oliver wonders, "This communism—is that the answer? Could it be made a kind of religion? The religion the Western world had given itself to wouldn't do. It had got, in some queer way, corrupt—no good now. Even the preachers knew it" (315). Here, Anderson introduces a common view among American leftists, namely, that Christianity in its modern form is inadequate, whereas organized anti-capitalism—in the form of trade unionism, socialism, or communism, depending on the advocate—is a return to, or revival of the authentic form of Christianity that has been corrupted by capitalism.[19] G. C. Waldrep found that southern "textile unionists identified their movement with what they saw as true Christianity" and therefore sought "to merge the principles of Christianity and unionism" (121, 122). He writes, "To unionists, church and union stood for the same thing: the dignity and redemption of human beings" (Waldrep 119). Along the same lines, Cook argues that Gastonia activists worked to "assimilate the

---

[19] Engels acknowledges that this motif in revolutionary movements' appeal to Christianity has recurred for millennia. He writes, "These risings, like all mass movements... were bound to wear the mask of religion and appeared as the restoration of early Christianity from spreading degeneration... But behind the religious exaltation there was every time a very tangible worldly interest."

salvation offered by the National Textile Workers Union to the only system they knew that offered hope of a better world" (63). In *The Shadow Before*, Rollins uses the labor organizer and former Sunday school teacher, Marvin, to make this claim. Like Anderson's Red Oliver, he does not relinquish Christianity in favor of the labor movement but instead takes up the latter because he believes it to be more dedicated to Christian ideals than the church. Marvin quotes from the beatitudes in Matthew 5 to show that Christianity and the labor movement are not only compatible, but that they are identical. We read,

> Blessed are they which do hunger and thirst after righteousness: for they shall be filled. Blessed are they which are persecuted for righteousness' sake: for their's is the kingdom of heaven. Ye are the light of the world. Let your light so shine before men that they may see your good works, and glorify your Father which is in heaven.
>
> (Rollins 174)

Similarly, in Lumpkin's *To Make My Bread*, John Stevens quotes James 5:1-6 in their entirety to articulate the workers' gospel. It reads, in part, "Go to now, ye rich, weep and howl for your miseries that are coming upon you. Your riches are corrupted" (Lumpkin 325). While Rollins demonstrates the unity of Christian and unionist philosophy, Lumpkin appeals to scripture to prove that the Bible endorses, and therefore sanctifies, revolutionary direct action. In her empirical research, Page found that "mill workers quoted scripture to prove god's approval of unionism" (*Cotton Mills* 50). Through the "melding of Christianity with unionism," workers maintain that both share the same ethics, that those norms are of divine origin, and that conformity to them will result in redemption (Hall 16n31). This bidirectional "melding," which works to collapse the sacred and the secular, functions to sacralize the priorities and personnel of the labor movement. Thus, the labor organizer, union, and anti-capitalist crusade are endowed with the same divine legitimation and metaphysical authority assigned to the evangelist, church, and revival.

It is significant, as well, that the organizers of the Loray Mill strike and most of the Gastonia novelists were raised in devoutly religious families. Their religious upbringing led them to see commonalities in the ethics of Christianity, Judaism, and anti-capitalism. Page explains, "Many of us in the movement came from a religious background that, for all its faults and rigidities, had a certain energy and poetry that caught hold of us" (Baker 113-114). Beal had been a Sunday school teacher and wrote that he was drawn to communism because he saw it as "an idealistic faith" ("Martyr" 45). One of the four principal organizers, Vera Buch Weisbord, recalled that, in her Scotch Presbyterian family, "religion was a fundamental part of life" (7). Another member of the core group, Amy Schechter, was the daughter of the president of the Jewish Theological Seminary of America, Dr. Solomon Schechter. Grace Lumpkin's radicalism was rooted in Christianity, as was her later repudiation of communism.[20] In the "First-Person Biography of Myra Page," we read,

> The church was an important part of my growing up... My religious values were deeply ingrained. I was taught the importance of assuming public and social responsibility for myself and for my neighbors, friends, and society. I learned that one should feel concern not only for one's own child but also for all children. For years I taught Sunday school.
>
> (Baker 23)

Like Anderson's Red and Rollins's Marvin, Page explains that she "lost faith in the church as an organized institution because the churches weren't practicing what they preached... I still believed in the ideals and the vision of brotherhood and peace given in the New Testament" (Baker 38). Though the organizers of the Loray Mill strike and the novelists who documented it had lost faith in institutional religion, they believed that the ethics of the labor movement were consistent with Judeo-Christian ethics. This position is evinced in the Gastonia novels, which both bear witness and contribute to the glorification of the strike leaders.

Strikers in Gastonia revered union organizers as prophetic or messianic figures who were instruments of God's will. In *Strike!*, young workers address Deane (Beal) with the "earnest simplicity of worship [...] as though he were God" (Vorse 4, 12). Vorse writes, "Fer appeared... as a Messiah to the workers" (32). In *Call Home the Heart*, Ishma defends the organizers against accusations of atheism inveighed in the local press. We read,

> "No, they were not outsiders, any more than Jesus was an outsider in Galilee, or Paul on Mars hill."
> "But folks say they don't believe the Bible."
> "Well, there is one part of it they believe anyway; the part that says that one man shall not sow and another reap, one man shall not work and another eat up the harvest; the rich shall not add house to house and acre to acre, while the workers

---

[20] See Lumpkin, Grace. *Full Circle*. Boston: Western Islands, 1962.

are without roof or land. [...] They are worthy of trust as deep as the people of old gave to Isaiah with his words of fire."

(Dargan 277–8, 284)

In Page's *Gathering Storm*, workers appeal to a familiar biblical idiom when describing labor organizers and the salvation the union represents. Page writes,

> "the good Lawd... sent Moses to lead His people from the land of bondage, 'n I believe He sent George n' Mister Tom here to deliver us from bondage."
> "No, Uncle John. It was the Union who sent us," Tom corrected.
> The old man looked down at him. "Maybe, son, that's what you think. But I feels the Lawd's hand in it... thar's a Great Day comin' bye 'n bye, a day of deliverance from mill slavery, when all will live like freed men."

(282)

By venerating strike leaders and praising the righteousness of their purpose, millhands fortified the bonds of the community and gave transcendent meaning to their shared suffering.

Trade unionism was perceived as a religion because it served the functions of religion. Durkheim argued that religion consists of the concepts and practices that unify a community, regulate behavior, and provide meaning and purpose in the face of suffering. It is composed of the ideas and actions that produce social cohesion, control, and order. Durkheim famously wrote that "society is the soul of religion"; that is, religion is the expression of the norms that hold a community together (191). Unionism and the labor movement broadly construed performed these functions for the workers in Gastonia, as well as for organizers and writers from the region and beyond. Vorse writes, "They were all absorbed in something bigger than they were—something that brought them all together and merged them in something outside of themselves. I reckon this is the solidarity that they's always talking about, thought Mamie Lewes" (27). Workers who migrated to mill villages from the hills felt acutely the loss of their tightly knit mountain communities. Segregated and alienated from the surrounding townspeople, millhands embraced the shared beliefs and rituals that distinguished their community. Religion was instrumental in creating and periodically reviving social cohesion in mill villages. Hall and her team write that revivals "enriched and sustained" village communities (*Family* 178). In particular, "the emotional fervor of a revival" produced a sense of "communal solidarity" that fortified "the bonds of mutual respect and obligation that linked them to one another"

(*Family* 178). Revivals "also dramatized the social and psychological distance between mill owners and many of their employees" (*Family* 178). The fact that "the millhands' faith was not that of the owners" strengthened ties between members of the village community (*Family* 178). Durkheim writes that "A religion is a unified system of beliefs and practices... which unite into one single moral community called a Church, all those who adhere to them" (129). As industrial development advanced in the South, and the years of Depression following the First World War created a fully proletarianized working-class, millhands found their principal means of social cohesion in class solidarity and the shared values of unionism. For example, in *Strike!* we read, "Now they were all together... They were no longer separated people. They were... banded together in a great cause. No longer individuals, mean, frightened, stunted. They had all been released and felt full of one common generous aim" (Vorse 168). Class solidarity produced social cohesion among the millhands, their proletarian salvation ethic constituted the shared behavioral norms that afforded social control, and the ultimate *telos* of the labor movement—whether revolutionary or reformist—gave them purpose and meaning. From a Durkheimian perspective, then, unionism was not *like* a religion, it was a religion.

Two religious concepts borrowed from Christianity were particularly useful to the labor movement, namely, conversion and martyrdom. These ideas were critically important to the maintenance and growth of the movement, and were seized upon by writers representing the Loray Mill strike, who employed them as central tropes in their respective novels. Activists and artists utilized the power of these concepts to unify their community and to galvanize their dedication to a shared purpose. All of the Gastonia novels feature the conversion trope that is so prevalent in proletarian fiction. The rebirth of consciousness that characters undergo in this motif is modeled on the idiom of revival conversion. In labor fiction, converts—to trade unionism, progressive socialism, or revolutionary communism—"get saved" or attain salvation through the acquisition of class-consciousness, which characters experience as a kind of awakening or revelation that causes them to be "born again." This takes the form of either a protracted or instantaneous experience. In Anderson, Dargan, and Vorse's novels, we find the former; in Page, Lumpkin, and Rollins's, the latter. As in the revival context, conversion is prompted by an acute personal crisis. In the case of Gastonia millhands, converts to the labor movement experience a crisis of faith in traditional, institutional Christianity as well as a profound sense of alienation—a lack of belonging, community, and purpose. This new faith and its church—the union, the party, or the labor movement broadly—meet their needs in a manner that is not only consistent with their formerly held ideals but appears to be a superior implementation of those beliefs. That is, the movement provokes a revival of their religion. By foregrounding conversion, the authors of the Gastonia novels mobilize the evangelical idiom for their political purposes even when a novel does not overtly thematize religion. In this way, even those authors who are suspicious of organized religion—Dargan, Page, and Vorse—implicitly attest to the compatibility of Christianity and the labor movement.

Conversion to unionism as it is depicted in the Gastonia novels is not such that characters adopt a secular political ethos in place of their formerly held religious convictions. Instead, it is portrayed as a revival of characters' religious ideals through their adaptation to modern industrial culture. Their alienation and spiritual malaise are alleviated by adherence to a new salvation ethic, one that gives them a renewed sense of purpose and community. For example, in Myra Page's *Gathering Storm*, we read that "through his reading, arguments with Jake and other wobblies, and his fresh experiences, a new world began to emerge before Tom's eyes... and he discovered a new purpose in living" (84). Tom Crenshaw explains to his sister Marge that this experience of rebirth has caused him to "feel different, like new. I got something to live by, now" (*Storm* 141). When she undergoes her own conversion at the beginning of the strike, we read that "Marge felt a new life rising in herself, in those around her, uniting them in one tremendous mass" (*Storm* 285). In Rollins's *The Shadow Before*, the conversion of the Baptist Sunday school teacher-turned-labor organizer, Marvin, is described in much the same way. Rollins writes,

> And then, after talking with Joe Gainor, overnight it seemed, he saw the incongruity of his heaven, lifeless finite goal, against the living fluidity of mankind. What had a dead tale of the desert... to do with the living struggling mass?... The misery and drabness around him, which he had sensed as individual misfortunes, he now saw consciously as a whole; and seeing it as a whole, he found the substitute for his old Brotherhood of Man: *class consciousness!*"
>
> (175–6)

Here, a standard implication in labor fiction is explicitly stated, namely, that conversion is synonymous with class-consciousness. As in the revival context, the unconverted, in a state of acute crisis, experiences an awakening that allows them to acknowledge and repudiate false-consciousness, or sin, and to see the world anew. They reject the theodical focus on salvation in the afterlife and commit themselves to a new covenant, to a new doctrine of redemption that privileges struggle on behalf of the poor in order to attain salvation in this life. Converts are born again into "a new life" with "a new purpose in living" and find that this ethos repairs the alienation of the community, affording them a means of social cohesion that unites "them in one tremendous mass."

By beginning *Beyond Desire* with a conversion story, Sherwood Anderson signals that his protagonist's own religious awakening will be the thematic foundation of the novel. When Red Oliver receives a letter from Neil Bradley, he is surprised to find his old friend writing about God; he thought Neil was a nonbeliever. However, Neil has written with news of his engagement to a "revolutionist" and Red gathers that "he must have got" this newfound concern with religion "from his woman" (Anderson 3). Neil explains that, before meeting his fiancé, he was consumed by spiritual malaise and an absence of existential meaning and purpose. He writes, "You remember the empty feeling we had when we were in school together ... I had it all the time I was in college and after I came home ... I guess ... that all of us younger men and women ... have it now" (Anderson 3). He goes on to argue that traditional Christianity has become alienated from God and is incapable of meeting the needs of modern Americans.

> "We can't hear His voice or feel Him in the land," he said. He thought perhaps the earlier men and women in America had something he and Red had missed. They had "God," whatever that had meant to them. The early New Englanders ... must have thought they had God really. If they had, what they had, it had come down to Neil and Red in some way pretty much weakened and washed out. Neil thought that. Religion, he said, was now an old gown, grown thin and with all the colors washed out of it. People still wore the old gown but it did not warm them any more.
>
> (Anderson 3)

The faith of America's "younger men and women" had become "weakened and washed out" by an obsolete theology. Revolutionism, Anderson suggests, revives religion with a new image of God that offers meaning, purpose, and consolation to those living in an industrialized society. The subsequent narrative is an account of Red's gradual conversion to communism, which he likens to religious salvation. His awakening is fraught and incremental but culminates in his decision "to come to the communist camp" that always reminds him "of his mother getting religion in the little church at the edge of the mill village" (Anderson 255).

Dargan's Ishma Waycaster eventually "coverts to Communism," but this process is so gradual that it extends over two novels, *Call Home the Heart* (1932) and its sequel, *A Stone Came Rolling* (1935) (Hapke 166). Borrowing from the dramatic structure of both the *bildungsroman* and revival traditions, Ishma's sociological education is achieved slowly and in stages, over the course of an ideological odyssey that leads from the Appalachian mountains to a mill village, to the employ of a wealthy mill owner and his family,[21] ultimately to union evangelism, and her return to the mountains. Her time among the Grant family brings Ishma to the "edge of revelation," but it is the strike that finally elicits her conversion (Dargan 257). When she becomes a union organizer, Ishma envisions her role as a kind of evangelist or itinerant preacher. "She would go to a mill-town where the workers had never heard that they could be free, that the world could be theirs; and she would teach them and stay with them until they held her vision. Then she would go to another town… and another… and another" (Dargan 424). Laurie J. C. Cella has ably shown that Dargan proposes a feminist alternative to the "masculine ideologies at stake" within the "standard proletarian conversion narrative" (Cella 39, 40). Similarly, Kathy Cantley Ackerman contends that Dargan contributes to a form of feminist literature that is characterized by a woman's "quest for spiritual awakening" which culminates in existential "wholeness" through the attainment of "social consciousness" (Ackerman 118, 119).

Strike!'s Roger Hewlett also experiences a progressive conversion by attaining class-consciousness but, unlike Red Oliver and Ishma Waycaster, he is a middle-class northerner. He had come to the strike as an ostensibly objective observer, there to cover the event for a New England paper. Much as Ishma's conversion was propelled by her experience with the privileged life of the Grants, Roger is awakened from false-consciousness by being immersed in the life of the millhands. Roger functions as a proxy for middle-class readers who, Vorse suggests, would recognize the justice of labor's cause if they could only experience workers' lives. Vorse shows that "what Roger Hewlett feels, any reader might feel also" (Reilly 506). Like the testimonials that are an essential feature of revivals, Vorse's account of Roger's salvation is an evangelical tactic meant to elicit the conversion of middle-class readers.[22]

Martyrdom was another prominent trope in the theological poetics of the Gastonia novels as well as in the dramaturgy of the strike. The exaltation of the martyr is a mode of apotheosis that makes earthly causalities of class war

---

[21] Dargan uses a common device found in proletarian fiction, where a contrived scenario—often a job—gives a character occasion to see how the other half lives, allowing the author to juxtapose the classes and their respective traits and forms of life. This experience spurs the character's loss of false-consciousness and is calculated to have the same affect on readers.

[22] Similarly, Suzanne Sowinska describes Myra Page as "a missionary hoping for converts" (127).

into combatants in a transcendent holy conflict. Workers and labor activists sanctified their conditions and practices by characterizing them as the emulation of divinity. Alongside poverty, evangelism, and persecution, they interpreted martyrdom as the ultimate imitation of Christ. Atheist northern communists and southern believers alike identified unionism with early Christianity and regarded labor activists as akin to the disciples of the ancient church. In this context, death and imprisonment amid the battle against capitalism were considered Christ-like acts of self-sacrifice.

The importance and ubiquity of this motif in the Gastonia novels supports Ackerman's contention that "the formula of the strike novel requires a martyr" (150). In Vorse's *Strike!*, impending martyrdom is foreshadowed in the opening pages of the novel. Ferdinand Deane—Vorse's true to life rendering of Fred Beal—arrives in Gastonia with the fatalistic expectation that he will die there. He remarks, "This is a hell of a place. They're going to pop off one of their guns one of these days... and they'll get me" (Vorse 7). Deane is sullen but resigned to his fate. When Deane is ultimately murdered, we read, "He always knew... he knew he was going to go" (Vorse 223). Deane did not accept his impending martyrdom out of pride or a foolhardy hope for fame, but because he believed that dutiful self-sacrifice would eventually lead to the salvation of the working-class. Vorse writes, "Being killed with him was part of the day's work. You got killed if you had to. [...] This was the price you paid for unionism" (223, 230). Other, more zealous organizers welcome the opportunity to sacrifice themselves. Irma Rankin, who Vorse modeled on the communist organizer Vera Buch Weisbord, states, "'I think there's a fair chance of any organizer that comes from the North, getting either lynched or shot—or a long jail sentence.' There was a certain undercurrent of exultation in her voice. She was the kind that expect martyrdom and are a little disappointed if they don't get it" (Vorse 9). Like so many others in the movement, Vorse recognized the political utility of apotheosis, but she quietly lamented its dishonesty. After Deane is murdered, we read, "the enormous arc of events had lifted Ferdinand Deane into the place of a great hero. And he had not been a hero... The memory of him was already being obliterated... They would... idealize him and, therefore wipe out and create in his place an unreal hero, a composite of all virtues which he had not possessed" (Vorse 235). As Beal himself would write years later, this is "how Communist saints are made" ("Martyr" 33). Martyrdom is an apotheotic process that transforms flawed, finite, and earthly people into saints who function as "the personification of collective beliefs" (Urgo 70). The martyr had little to do with the real person and instead served as a mechanism of anthropotheism that allowed workers to equate their own traits and economic commitments with the divine. Anderson's view of the martyr, however, was more optimistic.

Sitting alone in a field, moments before he is murdered by the strikebreaker Ned Sawyer, Red Oliver recalls the agony of Jesus in the garden of Gethsemane prior to his crucifixion. Like Jesus, Red is hesitant to sacrifice himself[23]—though his spirit is willing, his flesh is weak. The scene clearly prompts readers to see Red as a Christ figure who willingly gives his life in an effort to secure the salvation of humanity. Red reflects,

> Suppose... you were a man in America who really wanted God—suppose, you wanted to try really to be a Christian—a God man. How could you do that? All society would be against you. Even the church wouldn't stand that—it couldn't. Just the same there must have been—once—when the world was younger—when men were more naïve—there must have been godly men, willing and ready enough to die for God. They might even have wanted to.
>
> (Anderson 319)

Unlike Vorse and Page's uneasy relationship with Christianity, Anderson unambiguously identifies unionism with the early church and equates labor activists with those Christians who were willing to die for the cause. He contends that those fighting on behalf of labor are truly "godly" whereas the institutional church in modern America professes beliefs that are antithetical to authentic Christianity.

In *To Make My Bread*, Lumpkin suggests that martyrdom is not only something to be revered, but will be a necessary and ongoing requirement to achieve the goals of the working-class. The novel's Bonnie McClure, who is modeled on the murdered Gastonia balladeer Ella May Wiggins, is gunned down at the close of the novel. At her funeral, her brother John explains that the red band he wears on his sleeve "stands for blood that has been shed, and that will be shed before we reach that which we are fighting for... This is just the beginning" (Lumpkin 383-4). Voicing a widely held view, Lumpkin argues that self-sacrifice is an essential aspect of salvation history. The ultimate redemption of the nation may be deferred but martyrdom is a necessary step along the way. Similarly, Rollins argues that by "sacrificing together" strikers are contributing to "the progression

---

[23] There is some critical disagreement about Red Oliver's intentions. One group of critics argues that Red's martyrdom is accidental. See, for example, Laura Hapke (174). The other group, with whom I agree, read Red's actions as his choice to "sacrifice himself in [an] attempt at martyrdom" (Urgo 80). See also Walter Rideout's introduction to *Beyond Desire* (xi).

of mankind, of the cosmos" (228). At Ella May's actual funeral, a eulogizing striker regarded her death as a Christ-like sacrifice, stating that "She died for us and the union" (qtd. in Pope 294). The labor press immediately canonized Wiggins alongside the likes of Sacco and Vanzetti, and in the decades since her murder, she has been invariably remembered as the martyr of Gastonia. Hapke calls her murder a "crucifixion" and writes that both the strikers and the Gastonia novelists "sanctified" Ella May Wiggins; Schreibersdorf recounts how she came to be "revered," "immortalized," and accorded the "iconic status" of a martyr[24] (Hapke 165, 180; Schreibersdorf 318n5, 307).

It is crucial to recognize that martyrdom was not merely a literary device or a matter of high-flown, figurative language used by the Gastonia novelists. Martyrdom was also a key feature of communist ideology at the time of the Loray Mill strike. In 1937, after his disillusionment with communism, Beal wrote his essay "I Was a Communist Martyr," for *The American Mercury*, in which he explained that the martyr was a "central figure" in the Communist Party's "carefully stage-managed" public relations machine ("Martyr" 32). He details a process in which a continual procession of martyrs are presented as "human symbols of revolutionary sacrifice" in a large-scale spectacle that included rallies, speaking tours, and endless coverage in the labor press ("Martyr" 45). Utilizing the same tactics as revivalists, "emotion-movers" in the party put on "a maudlin exhibition" and with "tear-squeezing," "dripping sentimentality," used the martyrs and their stories to manipulate their audience ("Martyr" 32). For example, in an article in the *Daily Worker*, the jailed strikers and organizers who were still on trial were referred to as the "Gastonia martyrs." In her memoir, Vera Buch Weisbord—who Vorse described as the quintessential party zealot—recalls that those imprisoned deeply resented this characterization. "Did they consider us as good as dead? What kind of augury was this for the defense that would soon have to be made?" (Weisbord 235). Clearly, as with Vorse's Deane, the party decided that the activists on trial would be more useful as sanctified personifications of communist beliefs.[25]

---

[24] See also Hapke 153, 163, and Salmond 34, 50, 131.
[25] It must be noted, however, that just as the martyrdom of Ella May Wiggins and the jailed strikers allowed for the apotheosis of labor's traits and economic commitments, the death of Chief Aderholt served the same function for those who sided with the textile industry and with capitalism more broadly.

Rituals of Expulsion: Litigating the Sacred and the Profane

The integral role played by apotheosis in the labor conflict of the Depression-era South is made evident in the trials that followed the collapse of the Loray Mill strike. Because each class in the conflict sanctified the economic model that best served their interests, both unionists and capitalists believed they were taking part in a holy crusade to defend righteousness and authentic Christianity against evil. As a consequence of conflating capitalism and Christianity, the propertied class interpreted union activism not as a protest against modes and relations of industrial production, but as an assault upon the sacred.

The campaign to turn public opinion against the strikers on the basis of religion, specifically through the charge of atheism, began long before the trials. On the second day of the strike, mill management distributed handbills and circulars warning citizens, "Our Religion, Our Morals, Our Common Decency, our Government and the very foundations of Modern Civilization, all that we are now and all that we plan for our children IS IN DANGER. Communism will destroy the efforts of Christians of 2000 years" (qtd. in Garrison 216). In a full-page ad in the *Gastonia Gazette*, mill interests claimed union members have "no religion" and are "a menace to all that we hold most sacred" (qtd. in Pope 254, 286). The paper published increasingly provocative denunciations calculated to incite mob violence against the union from the moment the strike began. One of its staff writes, "How our good mill people can be led by these people... who defy God, flout religion, denounce our government and who are working for social equality among white and black is a mystery" (qtd. in Salmond 36). Charges of atheism and the public sanctioning of anti-union violence were not limited to the local paper. The Charlotte *News* declared that the strike leaders were "undermining all morality, all religion... everyone knows that they deserve to be shot at sunrise" (qtd. in Garrison 226). By 1929, capitalism had become the source of social cohesion in America; therefore, it had become the nation's dominant religion. To criticize or reject capitalism, then, was to "defy God" and threaten American society.

The Gastonia novels accurately convey the centrality of apotheosis on both sides of the labor conflict. Though Beal "appeared as...a Messiah to the workers," the jury believed that he "and his companions were a form of anti-Christ" (Vorse 32, 208). Given the politics of anthropotheism, "he was all these things" (Vorse 32). In Vorse's account, the propertied class not only accuse labor activists of atheism but regard them as "demons" with "hoofs and a tail" and contend that "unionism in any form is the work of the devil" (21, 18, 12). In *Beyond Desire*, the respectable stance is that unionists "ought to be wiped out, every one of them. They are against God. They are against America. [...] They are against religion" (Anderson 347, 352). In Dargan's novel, the comfortable people consider the union to be a "godless crew" (330). Similarly, in *The Shadow Before*, unionism is equated with "godlessness" (Rollins 130). In that novel, the mill superintendent, Thayer, considers himself a "Crusader" who has been called upon to defeat "infidels" who "preach" the "doctrine" of labor[26] (Rollins 375). However, because unionists conflated anti-capitalism and Christianity, they viewed themselves in much the same light. As Waldrep explains, from the perspective of Christian labor activists, "an individual's refusal to join the union could be understood as a rejection of the Almighty" (120). To criticize or reject unionism, then, was to "defy God." The apotheotic process, intensified and brought into sharp focus during a period of paradigmatic change, caused combatants in this labor conflict to believe they fought to defend the sacred against the encroachment of the profane.

The show trials of the Gastonia unionists clearly exemplify the ordering and integrative functions of ritual sacrifice described by Durkheim and Girard in their respective theories of the sacred. The distinction between the sacred and the profane provides fundamental structure to the social order and is the means by which a group imposes norms and values on its members. While union members saw those on trial as embodiments of the sacred—the sanctified "personification of collective beliefs"—capitalists viewed them as embodiments of the profane—"a menace to all that we hold most sacred." Therefore, the strikers simultaneously functioned as symbols of the sacred and the profane. Yet, their ritualized exclusion from society ultimately served the ends of both sides of the class war by reinforcing the fundamental distinction that sustained the norms and values of each group, thereby annealing their identity and solidarity. That is, the scapegoating of the strikers validated the perceived righteousness of each class, further uniting their ranks.

The collective act of sacrifice is a performance of devotion to the sacred that is intended to reproduce social order and strengthen the mutual bonds of the populace. Girard posits that, in times of crisis, a community chooses a victim to be the subject of ritual sacrifice. The people believe that the chosen scapegoat is the source of chaos disrupting the community and that sacrificing them will restore order. Sacrifice, then, is an act of collective victimization that is thought

---

[26] For anti-union terrorism as a "holy crusade," see also Vorse 189.

to reestablish peace and order in a community.[27] Girard writes that "unanimous violence" or "generative violence" creates social stability (Girard 250, 253). He writes, "the surrogate victim dies so that the entire community... can be reborn in a new or renewed cultural order" (Girard 255). The sensational and highly publicized trial of the Gastonia strikers functioned as a ritual sacrifice—in this case, a ritual of expulsion rather than a blood sacrifice, despite the efforts of the lynch mobs—an act of violence committed by a dominant social group with the intention of reestablishing peace and order. North Carolinians' ceremonial expulsion of sixteen Gastonia activists was a communal act of victimization that served to reinforce the cohesion of the capitalists and to further solidify the identity of their group.

The entanglement of religion and economics in Gastonia was made apparent by both parties' choice of trial counsel and by the prosecution's overriding strategy. For example, Major A. L. Bulwinkle was lead counsel for the Loray Mill and a member of the Lutheran church's Board of Deacons (Salmond 12). Prior to the trial, Bulwinkle had orchestrated violent acts of vigilantism against the strikers and later defended the killers of Ella May Wiggins (Salmond 38, 12). The prosecution team also included Clyde R. Hoey, brother-in-law of North Carolina governor and mill owner, Max Gardner (Garrison 216). The defense was led by Tom P. Jimison, a Methodist preacher–turned-lawyer who had left the ministry in 1924, as he put it, "because of constant conflict between me and the authorities of my church on economic and social questions" (qtd. in Salmond 29). After the trials, Jimison vowed to return to preaching but took up journalism instead. Adopting the oft-deployed subjunctive, he criticized moral hypocrisy in his *Charlotte News* column, claiming that the city's citizens would crucify Christ again, "right in front of the First Presbyterian Church if he ever dared to show up here" (qtd. in Salmond 176). In her journal, Vorse described the former preacher as "a spiritual adventurer" who knew "how to use people's emotions like stops in an organ" (qtd. in Garrison 226).

During the trial, when two union organizers, Amy Schecter and Edith Saunders Miller, were cross-examined about their religious beliefs, they readily admitted to being atheists, in keeping with the orthodox communist position at the time. Jimison objected to this line of questioning but Judge Harding overruled him. Citing an anachronistic, eighteenth-century "Statute of Oaths" which stipulated that one "must believe in divine punishment after death to

---

[27] Ernst Cassirer writes, "Particularly in times of distress, when the community is endangered and its existence seems threatened, this renewal of its primordial physical-religious power is necessary. But the true accent of the sacral act is on performance by the community as a *whole*" (227).

qualify as a witness," prosecutors argued that, under North Carolina law, the testimony of an atheist is illegitimate (Pope 298n377). The prosecution held that, if a witness does not believe in God, then their oath is meaningless and their testimony untrustworthy. Or, as Vorse put it in *Strike!*, they argued "that a person who did not believe in God could not tell the truth" (208). From this point forward, the religious beliefs of the unionists became the central issue of the murder trial. For this reason, a chorus of dissenters, including journalists and members of the ACLU, joined the defense in likening the proceedings to a heresy trial.[28] Moreover, it was not merely figurative to describe the case in these terms. At one point, prosecutors sought to include religious heresy among the crimes charged against the strikers (Pope 297). Ultimately, the activists were not on trial for murder, but for violating the dominant concept of the sacred.

Arthur Roach, a member of the so-called Committee of One Hundred who fired on strikers that fateful night, testified that his actions were justified by the unionists' alleged atheism: "We don't need any Russians in North Carolina that don't believe in God" (qtd. in Salmond 140). In an outraged telegram to Governor Gardner, Jimison decried the false justification for anti-union mob violence. He blamed "the organized Babbittry of Gaston County" where strikers "have been branded opponents of God… because they have asked for a living wage" (qtd. in Salmond 42). The prosecution's case against the strikers was predicated on the apotheotic exaltation of mill interests and on the necessary counterpart to such an idealization, the assertion that union members were the very embodiment of evil. The prosecution's John Carpenter described the killed chief of police, Orville Aderholt, as a "stainless Christ-like chap" and the local police as "God-fearing… Christian gentlemen" (qtd. in Salmond 147, qtd. in Pope 303). By contrast, he described the workers as "coming from hell"; they were "fiends incarnate, stripped of their hoofs and horns, bearing guns instead of pitchforks… They came… to sink damnable fangs into the heart and lifeblood of my community… creeping like the hellish serpent into the Garden of Eden" (qtd. in Pope 303–4).

However, supporters of the textile industry were not the only ones to indict their opponents on charges of heresy; for the Christian unionists in Gastonia, it was the mill loyalists who were atheists. For both adversaries, apotheotic self-sanctification and the concomitant reduction of their enemies to purveyors of evil served to justify collective violence in the effort to secure the dominance of their economic system. Arthur Roach believed that unionists' alleged atheism

---

[28] See Pope 302; Salmond 87, 94, 142–3, 151.

justified his act of sacrificial violence. While the organizers of the Loray Mill strike persistently emphasized the necessity of maintaining a non-violent strike, and though the facts of that deadly night remain obscure, it is clear that American revolutionary communists in the early decades of the twentieth century consistently employed modes of apotheosis to justify the use of force to dismantle capitalist society. This maneuver was not reserved for rationalizing the harm of enemies alone; in their exaltation of martyrdom, they appealed to apotheosis to justify violence against their own, in the name of defending the sacred against the profane.

Modes of apotheosis undoubtedly served to unify emerging classes in the new industrial economy of the South and to codify the behavioral norms necessary for each group to maintain order and collectively pursue shared objectives. However, the primary function of apotheosis was to lend ultimate, transcendent legitimation (in the sense of *legitimatus*, to make legal) to their respective economic systems and the norms that ensured the reproduction of those systems. In a period of intense cultural conflict, social solidarity, order, and purpose are necessary but insufficient outcomes of religious practice. Combatants in early-twentieth-century class struggle used apotheosis to obtain theological justification for direct, and often violent, action. As the case of the Loray Mill strike makes abundantly clear, religion played a vital role in machine age class antagonism. Gastonia provides us with a "remarkable laboratory" in which to investigate how alterations in America's material conditions caused fundamental changes in Protestant institutions, doctrines, and practices, and sheds light on the way these changes continue to shape American culture.

7

"The Blackness of God": Race and Religion in the Literature of the Harlem Renaissance

The ivory gods,
And the ebony gods,
And the gods of diamond-jade,
Are only silly puppet gods
That the people themselves
Have made.

—from "Gods" (1924) by Langston Hughes[1]

Race is not secular. The sacred is one of the main components in the engineering of race as a concept and technology of social domination. I use the term technology in this context because technology is the application—or misapplication—of science to achieve practical objectives. The alleged truth of race is contingent on appeals to science—as has been widely acknowledged—*and to the metaphysical*. However, as I have shown in previous chapters, apotheosis—the means of producing the sacred—mediates both systems of domination and liberation. If we look to the way race struggle was mediated by religious symbols in works of literature in the 1920s and 1930s, we can readily observe how the sacred was used by vying groups as a mechanism of oppression and resistance. Black modernists, including atheists and the newly doubtful, who recognized how religion had been used to justify and empower resource colonialism and the slave trade, self-consciously developed new religious symbols, by way of apotheosis, to legitimate and mobilize Black liberation. To counteract this, some white writers appropriated those symbols, foremost among them the figure of the Black God, to reproduce existent relations of domination and exploitation.

---

[1] *The Messenger* (March 1924): p. 94.

The Cry for Salvation

W. E. B. Du Bois's *Darkwater* (1920) begins and ends with an impassioned plea for salvation. In the volume's first poem, "The Litany of Atlanta," a collective narrator who speaks for all Black people cries, "*Great God, deliver us!... Kyrie Eleison!... We beseech Thee to hear us, good Lord!*" (18, 19). The book's final poem, "A Hymn of the Peoples," repeats their entreaty: "we cry: / Save us... Help us, O human God" (212). Similarly, in "Feet o' Jesus" (1926), Langston Hughes implores, "Jesus... Please reach out your hand" (78). Jean Toomer, the consummate image-maker, ends *Cane* (1923) with an iconic religious symbol that embodies the collective call for redemption expressed by Harlem Renaissance writers. At the close of "Kabnis," Carrie kneels at the feet of Father John and "her lips murmur, 'Jesus, come.' Light streaks through the iron-barred cellar window" and holds them "within its soft circle" (158). Though the barred window is a figure of bondage, the light that shines on the prophet of the Black Christ is a portent of salvation to come.

In his *Economy and Society*, Max Weber explains that the "need for salvation is an expression of some distress" and further that "social or economic oppression" is the most common "source of salvation beliefs" (107). "Salvation religion," he writes, is more important "for politically and economically disprivileged social groups, in contrast to privileged groups" (106). That is, a greater focus on the concept of salvation will be found in the religion of oppressed social groups, and that focus will intensify in proportion to the suffering a group is made to endure. He continues, "under the pressure of typical and ever-recurrent distress, the religiosity of a 'redeemer' evolved" (273). "The lower the social class" and the more acute the distress the group experiences, "the more radical are the forms assumed by the need for a savior" (102). Theologies that feature a messianic savior figure originate with poor and oppressed social groups. However, apotheosis requires a *logos*; an account of the sacred must be given symbolically. Therefore, the desire for a redeemer and the salvation they promise has been, from antiquity to the twentieth century, expressed in works of literature. For example, Weber writes that among "the Israelites, the title of 'savior' (Moshuach) was originally attached to saviors from political distress" and "transmitted by hero sagas (Gideon, Jephthah)" (273). In these savior myths, "suffering became the most important topic"; more specifically, "the suffering of a people's community, rather than the suffering of an individual, became the object of hope for religious salvation" (273). Christianity is a "pariah faith," a religious form developed by a systematically excluded and persecuted social group which foregrounds the concept of salvation and a savior figure (Weber 228).

Like those suffering from oppression in antiquity, Black Protestants in the 1920s vehemently appealed to Christianity's savior god and his promise of salvation. However, in response to their cry for salvation, Black people were confronted with God's silence, a silence collectively represented in the literature of the Harlem Renaissance. In "The Litany of Atlanta," Du Bois writes, "*Keep not Thou silent, O God!*" (19). "O silent God... *Hear us*... our faces dark with doubt" (17). In "The Prayers of God" he laments, "The earth is mad... And Thou art dumb" (191). Countee Cullen echoes Du Bois's growing doubt in the pointedly titled "Pagan Prayer" (1925), "Our Father, God; our Brother, Christ, / Or are we bastard kin, / That to our plaints your / ears are closed / Your doors barred from within?" (17). These writers represented a collective dissatisfaction with the traditional theodicical responses to the suffering of Black people. They grappled with the problem of evil in the context of a culture of white supremacy, asking,

> Is this Thy Justice, O Father, that... the innocent be crucified for the guilt of the untouched guilty? [...] We raise our shackled hands and charge Thee, God, by the bones of our stolen fathers, by the tears of our dead mothers, by the very blood of Thy crucified Christ: what meaneth this? Tell us the plan; give us the sign!
>
> (Du Bois 17, 19)

Black Americans increasingly reasoned that a God who would remain silent in the face of slavery, lynching, and the manifold injustices they suffered must be a white, racist God. Du Bois writes, "Thy silence is white terror to our hearts" (19). In "Seventh Street," Toomer reflects that a Black God could not abide the bloodshed that plagued the D. C. ghetto, writing, "A Nigger God! He would duck his head in shame and call for the Judgment Day" (53). Generally speaking, a god who does not reflect the group and is allied with its oppression must necessarily be rejected and replaced with a god that mirrors the group and underwrites its liberation. In the literature of the Harlem Renaissance, the silence of the white God is a figure of the growing inadequacy of this religious symbol for Black Protestants. In response to this failure to reflect the people and their needs, the group had to create a new God, a new Jesus, and a new theology.

Death of the white God

The literature of the Harlem Renaissance stages the cultural death of the white God and the birth of a Black God in his place. The New Negro's modern cosmopolitanism and outspoken suspicion of their elders' religion give the impression of a shift toward the secular when in fact the Renaissance was a period of heightened religious innovation that produced new forms of the sacred. This process was certainly marked by a kind of religious skepticism, most famously exemplified by Hughes's "Goodbye Christ" (1932), but what has been widely mistaken for atheism[2] was a necessary stage in the creation of a new, primary religious symbol, a new God, or, in Durkheim's terminology, a new collective representation.

Voicing a shared sentiment, Du Bois asks, "Wherefore do we pray? Is not the God of the Fathers dead?" (17). Similarly, in "Blue Meridian" (1936), Toomer's poem about the rise of a new God for a new America, he writes, "The old gods, led by an inverted Christ, / A shaved Moses… And a moulting dollar, / Withdrew into the distance and died" (*Poems* 51). The death of the white God—that is, Black Protestants' waning faith in a God that they increasingly recognized as complicit in their suffering—and the apotheotic creation of a new God that accurately reflect the group is an uneven cultural process that does not happen overnight. Black writers of the 1920s and 1930s expressed the concerns of their peers by examining how the white God participated in their oppression, actively, through colonialism, and passively, by remaining silent amid their cries for salvation.

Just as southern Appalachian millhands were rejecting the theodicy promulgated by their oppressors, Black Christians in the North began to express a similar critique. Countee Cullen's "The Black Christ" (1929), for example, features an emblematic generational conflict in which two sons refuse to accept their mother's appeal to theodicy to cope with racism and the culture of lynching. She tries to cultivate humble docility in them by retelling the savior myth of Moses and his liberation of the enslaved Jews, a familiar tale for all Black readers, one that urges the acceptance of suffering in the present in exchange for salvation to come. Cullen writes, "The seed / They planted in her children's breasts / Of hatred toward these men like beasts / She weeded out with legends how / Once there had been somewhere as now / A people harried, low in the dust; / But such had been their utter trust / In Heaven and its field of stars / That they had broken down their bars, / And walked across a parted sea / Praising His name who set them free" (167–8). Black Americans and the working-class were all too familiar with this manner of justifying evils, big and small, by apotheosizing inequality and imagining it as part of an indiscernible divine plan. But this is not solely a modern American phenomenon. Weber explains that salvation-based religion

---

[2] For an excellent, rigorous examination of "Goodbye Christ" and its context, see "Concerning 'Goodbye Christ,'" in *Langston's Salvation: American Religion and the Bard of Harlem*, ed. Wallace D. Best. New York: New York University Press, 2017, 108–51.

is "the most widely diffused form of mass religion all over the world" and that "a theodicy of disprivilege, in some form, is a component of every salvation religion which draws its adherents primarily from the disprivileged classes" (108, 113). As the sons in Cullen's poem grow older, they become dissatisfied with their mother's theodicical explanation for God's silence: "We had no scales upon our eyes; / God, if He was, kept to His skies, / And left us to our enemies" (168). Speaking for a generation of Black Christians, the narrator asks his mother, "But Christ who conquered Death and Hell / What has He done for you who spent / A bleeding life for His content? / Or is the white Christ, too distraught / By these dark sins His Father wrought?" (189). Here, Cullen links the passive complicity of the white God—by remaining silent—with his active participation in colonialism, slavery, and the ongoing suffering of Black people. In "Conversion," Toomer evokes the role of Christianity in slavery when he writes that African captives were forced to submit to "a white-faced sardonic god" (35). Elsewhere in *Cane*, Father John proclaims that white Americans' greatest misdeed was to use Christianity, or more specifically apotheosis, as an instrument of oppression. We read, "Th sin whats fixed... upon white folks...—f tellin Jesus—lies. O th sin th white folks 'mitted when they made th Bible lie" (157).

Similarly, in "The Prayers of God," Du Bois argues that apotheosis was weaponized by colonizers and used to justify the exploitation of the global south. In the poem, written in the voice of a white speaker in conversation with God, we read,

> War? Not so; not war—
> Dominion, Lord, and over black, not white;
> Black, brown, and fawn,
> And not Thy Chosen Brood, O God,
> We murdered.
> To build Thy Kingdom,
> To drape our wives and little ones,
> And set their souls a-glitter—
> For this we killed these lesser breeds
> And civilized their dead,
> Raping red rubber, diamonds, cocoa, gold!
>
> (193)

Du Bois shows that apotheosis was integral to the invention of race. That is, European colonizers apotheosize the idea whiteness, forming an image of God and the sacred by projecting their traits into the heavens. As a colonial classifier, the concept of race presupposed that European colonizers were the earthly mirror-images of God and that this justified their "dominion" over people who possessed traits different from those deemed sacred. Du Bois argues that colonizers use apotheosis to create an image of God modeled on themselves and then appeal to the whiteness of God to legitimate imperialism, slavery, capitalist exploitation, and white supremacy.[3]

Birth of the Black God

A social group's relation to itself is mediated by its symbols of the sacred. In the early twentieth century, many Black Americans became increasingly alienated from the God of Christianity, who they perceived as a participant in their past and ongoing oppression. If God were to remain meaningful for Black people, this foremost religious symbol had to become a more precise reflection of the group. The vital question of the moment, then, was "not whether blacks believe in God, but whose God?" (Cone 61).[4] Du Bois conveyed communal fears when he wrote, "Surely Thou, too, art not white, O Lord, a pale and bloodless, heartless thing!" (19). Though Black theology would not be formalized until the 1960s,[5]

---

[3] In his incisive new book, *Bonhoeffer's Black Jesus: Harlem Renaissance Theology and an Ethic of Resistance* (Baylor 2014), Reggie L. Williams shows that Dietrich Bonhoeffer had a conversion experience during the year he spent in Harlem at the height of the Renaissance. Williams argues that Bonhoeffer's encounter with the religion of the Black Christ made him aware of the phenomenon of apotheosis for the first time and its integral role in forms of social-political domination such as colonialism and imperialism. The literature and theology of the Black Jesus, Williams contends, was the catalyst of Bonhoeffer's later activism and self-sacrifice in opposition to Nazism.

[4] While our subject here is how Black Americans in the northeast who were disaffected by mainstream Christianity created a new theology—that is, a new image of God—a second and equally important epicenter of Black Christian innovation in the early twentieth century was located on the West Coast, in Los Angeles. The Black members of the burgeoning Pentecostal movement were also creating new symbols of the sacred, but their focus was on the Holy Spirit and its presence among collected worshippers. In this case, the symbols were practices, behaviors, and events that served as vehicles for a new concept of salvation. Pentecostal Christians introduced a second stage to salvation that they believed occurred after one's "New Birth" experience—baptism in the Holy Spirit—which is evidenced by glossolalia, overwhelming enthusiasm, and feelings of ecstasy. The most significant event in the origin of Pentecostalism was the Azusa Street revival, led by William J. Seymour, that began on April 9, 1906. Accounts of its duration vary, but the revival is said to have continued unabated for nine years. The Azusa Street revival was a quintessential example of effervescence, a significant moment in the history of desegregation, and an event that continues to shape much of contemporary American Protestantism. It certainly warrants a rigorous analysis using the tools of the Durkheimian paradigm, however, that is beyond the scope of this chapter. See Alexander, Estrelda Y. *Black Fire: One Hundred Years of African American Pentecostalism.* Downer's Grove: IVP Academic, 2011; Hollenweger, Walter J. *The Pentecostals: The Charismatic Movement in the Churches.* Minneapolis: Augsburg, 1972; Hollenweger, Walter J. *Pentecostalism: Origins and Developments Worldwide.* Peabody: Hendrickson, 1997; MacRobert, Iain. *The Black Roots and White Racism of Early Pentecostalism in the USA.* London: Palgrave Macmillan, 1988; Robeck, Jr., Cecil M. *The Azusa Street Mission and Revival: The Birth of the Global Pentecostal Movement.* Nashville: Thomas Nelson, 2006; Yong, Amos and Estrelda Y. Alexander, eds. *Afro-Pentecostalism: Black Pentecostal and Charismatic Christianity in History and Culture.* New York: NYU Press, 2011.

[5] See Cone, James H. and Gayraud S. Wilmore, eds. *Black Theology: A Documentary History, Volume 1, 1966–1979.* 2nd Ed., Revised, New York: Orbis Books, 1993.

it originated in this period. James Cone, one of the founders of Black theology, would later write, "Either God is identified with the oppressed to the point that their experience becomes God's experience, or God is the God of racism" (Cone 67). In Toomer's words, the people were "waiting for a new God" so artists began "to spiritualize experience," that is, the experience of Black communities (48, 52). As Caroline Goeser has ably shown, "Harlem Renaissance illustrators in the 1920s and early 1930s... explored Judeo-Christian subjects in their work. Some challenged white religious tradition by highlighting the contribution of those described in biblical and early Christian texts as African or black-skinned" (207). Others who were "more daring," such as Aaron Douglas,[6] "colored biblical figures black who had been conventionally represented as white... In this body of art, artists often crossed racial barriers in creating a new iconography" (Goeser 207). Together, Harlem Renaissance writers and other cultural producers of the era created a new collective representation of the sacred in the form of the Black God. As is true for all social groups, creating its own symbol of the sacred—through apotheosis—is beneficial for the group by affording it identity, solidarity, understanding, and power. That is, it legitimates the identity of the group, strengthens internal social integration, and generates feelings of empowerment that often motivate collective action.

Cullen's "Heritage" (1925) is a poem that is self-consciously about apotheosis and illustrates that the blackness of God is not merely skin deep but entails a negation of the traits of the oppressor god. Cullen considers the art of anthropotheism in the African religions his people have been forcibly alienated from, "Quaint, outlandish heathen gods / Black men fashion out of rods, / Clay, and brittle bits of stone, / In a likeness like their own" (30-31). Then, as though in dialog with Toomer's "Conversion" and Du Bois's "The Prayers of God," he writes, "My conversion came high-priced; / I belong to Jesus Christ, / Preacher of humility; / Heathen gods are naught to me" (31). As in Toomer's poem, Cullen's reference to conversion—which seems to imply choice in a free religious market—is an ironic allusion to the violent imposition of slavers' ideology. Like the colonizer's Jesus, his religion of docility, Cullen suggests, is a reflection of the interests of white people, which include the continued subordination of Black Americans. Recognizing this, the narrator expresses a growing estrangement from the white God and longs for a Black God, who would embody values antithetical to those of the hegemonic group. "Father, Son, and Holy Ghost, / So I make an idle boast; / Jesus of the twice-turned cheek, / Lamb of God, although I

---

[6] See also Powell, Damon A. "The Crucifixion: Black American Religious Aesthetics and the Painting of Aaron Douglas," *Black Theology* 12.2 (2014): 161–85.

Figure 7.1 In a 1925 letter to Langston Hughes, Douglas wrote, "Let's also make gods. Black gods. Disconcertingly black" (qtd. in Goeser 220). *The Crucifixion*. "Illustrations" by Aaron Douglas, copyright © 1927 by Penguin Random House LLC, copyright renewed © 1955 by Grace Nail Johnson; from *God's Trombones* by James Weldon Johnson. Used by permission of Viking Books, an imprint of Penguin Publishing Group, a division of Penguin Random House LLC. All rights reserved. James Weldon Johnson Memorial Collection in the Yale Collection of American Literature, Beinecke Rare Book and Manuscript Library.

speak / With my mouth thus, in my heart / Do I play a double part. / Ever at Thy glowing altar / Must my heart grow sick and falter, / Wishing He I served were black" (31). The subsequent lines in the poem call to mind Weber's finding that the suffering of the savior figure and its relation to the suffering of a community of systemically excluded people is central to the theological poetics of salvation religion. "Thinking then it [the Black God] would not lack / Precedent of pain to guide it, / Let who would or might deride it; / Surely then this flesh would know / Yours had borne a kindred woe" (31). This conveyed the growing feeling among many Black Christians that the suffering of a white Jesus, who remained silent and indifferent, was not a reflection of their own pain. The poem concludes with a promise to create a Black God and an accompanying religious ethos that would contradict the values of white Christianity. "Lord, I fashion dark gods, too, / Daring even to give You / Dark despairing features where, / Crowned with dark rebellious hair, / Patience wavers just so much as / Mortal grief compels, while touches / Quick and hot, of anger rise / To smitten cheek and weary eyes. / Lord, forgive me if my need / Sometimes shapes a human creed" (31).

Du Bois fashions a dark God in many of the poems in *Darkwater*. In "The Call," God is imagined as a heavenly monarch who has called on his only true servant, a poor Black woman, to do battle on his behalf. We read, "Whereat the King cried: 'O maid, made Man, thou shalt be Bride of God.' And yet… the woman shrank at the thunder in her ears, and whispered: 'Dear God, I am black!' The King spake not, but swept the veiling of his face aside and lifted up the light of his countenance upon her and lo! it was black" (126). The poem's titular call to arms is echoed elsewhere in the book. Like "The Call," "Children of the Moon" features a God who wears a veil that conceals a "blazing blackness" (149). This poem is about achieving "freedom and… salvation" by looking at the face of God and seeing that it is Black. God the Father intones to his children, "I am Freedom—/Who sees my face is free / He and his" (149). Here, Du Bois contends that salvation requires the recognition of God's blackness. Like "The Call," there is a direct militancy in the poem, as when God commands his followers to "fight face foremost, force a way, / Unloose, unfetter, and unbind; / Be men and free!" (148). Just as Cullen casts aside "Jesus of the twice-turned cheek," Du Bios rejects a God who would command passive progressivism. In this poem, salvation— to become unfettered and free—requires that Black people "fight" and "force a way." Similarly, in "The Litany of Atlanta" Du Bois defends active resistance: "*Vengeance is Mine; I will repay saith the Lord!* Thy Will, O Lord, be done!" (19). Cone later explains, "the oppressed must define their being by negating everything oppressors affirm" (61). If the white God is the "preacher of humility," if he is the docile "Lamb" of the "theodicy of disprivilege," then the Black God must be rebellious, angry, and ready to fight. Cone writes, "oppressed humanity is free to revolutionize society, assured that acts of liberation are the work of God" (80). For oppressed and oppressor alike, God serves as a legitimating projection. "I am black because God is black!," Cone writes, "God… is the ground of my blackness (being), the point of reference for meaning and purpose in the universe" (80). "The blackness of God… is the heart of black theology" (Cone 67). It is in this way that God, as an outcome of apotheosis, serves as a "transcendental anchorage for ethics" (Weber 90). Cullen recognized in "The Prayers of God" that Europeans imagined a pale-skinned imperial God to justify the slave trade and to position themselves as the essentially superior, "Chosen" people. Similarly, in all theologies of the oppressed, God is figured as a champion of the disprivileged who looks favorably on oppositional action and shares the traits of the subaltern group, who are also believed to be his chosen people. More generally, this seeming contradiction—two monotheistic gods whose traits and imperatives are diametrically opposed, who simultaneously exist within the same religion, in the same nation—exemplifies how apotheosis functions as a means of legitimation, solidarity, and empowerment among social groups in conflict, and how those functions are mediated by the concept of salvation.

In addition to reimagining Christianity's God the Father as part of an emerging Black theology, Harlem Renaissance writers recreated the symbol of the Son. As Weber explains, a messianic savior figure is central to the salvation religions of systematically oppressed social groups all over the world. In the context of Jim Crow America and widespread racist violence, as evinced by the recent Red Summer and the frequency of lynching, it seemed Black Christians' need for a savior had never been greater. As Cullen put it, "my need... shapes a human creed," and the collective desire for liberation among Black Christians did indeed reshape the existent creed (31).

In "The Second Coming," Du Bois imagines the nativity of the Black savior. In his modern version of the story, the three wise men are reconceived as a white bishop from the North, a Black cleric from the south, and a visiting Japanese priest. They are called to the bedside of Lucy, who has just given birth to the Black Christ. Lucy is passing, which causes the white priest to be shocked when bends "over the baby. *It was black!*" (83). In place of the virginal Mary, Du Bois creates a holy mother who is both the offspring and victim of rape by the same white man, a governor. The southern priest explains, "She's not really white; I know Lucy—you see, her mother worked for the governor" (83). In this poem, Du Bois creates a symbol of the sacred that incorporates multiple facets of Black exploitation. Here, the social exclusion central to the nativity story, in the context of Black Americans' experience, is a consequence of God's blackness. This, among other examples of the literature of the Black Christ, shows that the blackness of God is not a superficial alteration of the white, European version of Jesus, but rather constitutes the creation of an entirely new God, one that, through apotheosis, is the incarnation of Black suffering. By depicting a "Dark Madonna" who gives birth to a biracial messiah who is the outcome of white rape, Du Bois turns the collective sexual trauma of slavery and colonialism into the sacred attributes of God (Cullen 7). Further, in this rendition of the Second Coming, the arrival of a Black savior is the harbinger of Black revolution. The southern governor laments, "They're leaving by the hundreds and those who stay are getting impudent! They seem to be expecting something... The crowd is growing strangely on the streets... I never saw so many people here—I fear violence" (83). This exemplifies how the figure of the Black Christ is a collective representation of the salvation hopes of a pariah people.

In Jean Toomer's "Box Seat," the coming of the Black Christ is foretold by one of *Cane*'s many prophets, others being characters like Barlo and Father John. In this case, the prophet is a mentally ill young man who follows a woman he is courting to the theater. Over the course of the vignette, the man has a series of visions that he interprets to be portents of impending salvation. We read, "I am Dan Moore. I was born in a canefield. The hands of Jesus touched me. I am come to a sick world to heal it" (*Cane* 75). Like other characters in this literature, Dan sees modern America as a "sick" society where people cry out for salvation, and he believes he has the answer to that call. In his first vision, Dan imagines the Second Coming:

> Dan goes to the wall and places his ear against it. A passing street car and something vibrant from the earth sends a rumble to him. That rumble comes from the earth's deep core. It is the mutter of powerful underground races. Dan has a picture of all the people rushing to put their ears against walls, to listen to it. The next world-savior is coming up that way. Coming up... the new-world Christ.
>
> (76)

Contrary to the celestial, ascendant white messiah, the "new-world Christ" will arise from underground, "from the earth's deep core." Later, he repeats, "a new-world Christ is coming up" (83). In his second vision, Dan imagines himself to be a heroic prophet, fit for the machine age. He predicts, "I am going to reach up and grab the girders of this building and pull them down. The crash will be a signal. Hid by the smoke and dust Dan Moore will arise. In his right hand will be a dynamo. In his left, a god's face that will flash white light from ebony" (*Cane* 87). Here Toomer creates an icon of the modernist Black messiah—dynamo in one hand, symbol of America, industry, the new world, the future—and a fetish in the other, symbol of Africa, tradition, history. In his third prophecy, Dan has a vision of Jesus in the beaten and bloody face of the dwarf boxer—a person whose difference and public suffering are entertainment for others. We read,

> Words form in the eyes of the dwarf:

> Do not shrink. Do not be afraid of me.
> *Jesus*
> See how my eyes look at you.
> *the Son of God*
> I too was made in His image.
>
> (88–89)

Toomer's use of specular imagery here is crucial. Harlem Renaissance writers often return to this formulation, which emphasizes God's blackness and Black humanity's mirroring of that blackness, in works of literature that reinterpret biblical figures. But again, this is not a matter of outward image alone. In a reverie, Dan, who "don't fit in," cries out, "JESUS WAS ONCE A LEPER!" (78, 89). In what may first appear to be the raving of a fictional madman, we find further proof that the Black Christ is the apotheosis of the embodied suffering and pariah status of Black people in modern America.

The Lynching of the Black God

In addition to the nativity, Du Bois gives an account of the crucifixion of the Black Christ, as the suffering of the Black God and his sacrifice by white racists are integral to the meaning and power of the specular symbol. "Jesus Christ in Texas," originally published as "Jesus Christ in Georgia" in 1911, is a short story that depicts the return of Jesus set in the modern American South, his interaction with local townspeople, and his ultimate fate. Like Lucy, his "dark madonna," Du Bois's Black God can pass so the white townsfolk initially fail to recognize his blackness in the dim twilight. When they realize their mistake, they forsake him. The whites' failure to recognize the blackness of God is significant, as it is a mark of their sin. As in all liberation theologies, Black theology's doctrine of salvation (soteriology) entails a particular doctrine of sin (hamartiology). This view holds that salvation is linked to the liberation of oppressed social groups, and that sin is linked to anything and anyone complicit in their oppression. As in "The Second Coming," the story features a biracial Christ whose mortal father is a white rapist. We read, "the man was a mulatto... his face was olive, even yellow" (97). In this literature, the Black Christ incarnates the sexual violence of slavery and its aftermath. In his face, the story's white colonel sees a reflection, not of himself, but of the victim of his oppression: "had he seen those eyes before? He remembered them long years ago. The soft, tear-filled eyes of a brown girl" (97). The white minister fails to recognize Jesus as well: "I think I have met you?" he asks (99). To which Christ replies, "I never knew you" (99). White people cannot recognize this God because he does not reflect them; he is not a collective representation of white people. By contrast, the Black servants are immediately awestruck and humble themselves in his presence. As Claude McKay would later put it in his sonnet, "The Negro's Tragedy" (1945), "Only a thorn-crowned Negro and no white / Can penetrate into the Negro's ken" (50). For Christianity to be meaningful for modern Black Americans, its foremost symbol of the sacred had to be a precise reflection of them, and the experience that most circumscribed the lives of modern Black Americans was suffering. Therefore, their God could not be dark-skinned alone, but "thorn-crowned" if he were to be recognized by them. Contrary to the ostensibly pious white people, Du Bois's Black convict recognizes Jesus, "Why, you are a nigger, too" (100). Later, when the convict is lynched, his murder takes the form of a crucifixion: "He stretched his arms out like a cross, looking upward" (103). In the ecstatic melee, the lynch mob burns the cabin of a nearby Black family. Du Bois writes that beyond the tableau of the murder, the prisoner's lynching is mirrored by the crucifixion of the Black Christ: "behind the roped and swaying form below hung quivering and burning a great crimson cross... There, heaven-tall, earth-wide, hung the stranger on the crimson cross, riven and bloodstained, with thorn-crowned head and pierced hands" (104). Then, the story ends with a promise of salvation to victims of racist violence: Jesus's "calm dark eyes, all sorrowful, were fastened on the writhing, twisting body of the thief, and a voice came out of the winds of the night, saying: 'This day thou shalt be with me in Paradise!'" (104).

Figure 7.2 Charles Cullen's frontispiece for *The Black Christ & Other Poems* (1929).

In Langston Hughes's similarly titled "Christ in Alabama" (1931), the traits and narrative of the Black Christ replicate those represented in *Darkwater*. Hughes writes,

> Christ is a nigger,
> Beaten and black...
> Mary is His mother:
> Mammy of the South...
> God is His father:
> White Master above...
> Most holy bastard
> Of the bleeding mouth,
> Nigger Christ
> On the cross
> Of the South.
>
> (143)

The Black Christ is the apotheosis of modern Black Americans as a group, and as such, is a symbol that makes sacred the attributes and experiences that characterize their status as a pariah people. By way of this process, multigenerational suffering is sanctified; all Black Americans are collectively represented by the symbol of this "most holy bastard" and collectively sacrificed on the figurative "cross of the South."

Though the Harlem Renaissance authors were reimagining ancient figures and stories, the literature of the Black Christ was focused on the immediate social and political needs of Black people. The sacrifice of the white Jesus was a remote and increasingly alien symbol for modern Black Christians, whereas the unjust murder of innocent Black people and the sanctification of the victims of racist violence was a daily reality for them. The proximity and intensity of this conflict fueled the religious awakening in Harlem that produced a new formation of the sacred in the figure of the lynched Black Christ. As is illustrated in Cullen's "Christ Recrucified" (1922), the function of this new image of Jesus is to identify God with the victims of racist violence and oppression. Cullen writes,

> The South is crucifying Christ again...
> Christ's awful wrong is that he's dark of hue...
> But lest the sameness of the cross should tire,
> They kill him now with famished tongues of fire.
>
> (238)

Again, this is not the God sacrificed in antiquity, "they kill him now." Similarly, in Du Bois's "The Prayers of God," the speaker of the poem, a white colonist and slaver, boasts to a God he presumes is white that, "in Thy name" he lynched a Black man, only to learn that what he did "to the least of these," he did to God. "*Thou? / Thee? / I lynched Thee?... That black and riven thing—it was Thee?*" (193). In these lines, we find another element of Black theology—as well as liberation theology—namely, the idea that a human's relation to God is mediated by their relation to others, the poor and oppressed in particular, a doctrine based on the parable of the Sheep and Goats in the Gospel of Matthew, also known as the Judgement of Nations. According to this view, every act of racist violence is an act committed against God. By identifying God with the oppressed in this way, Black people as a group are made sacred while their white oppressors are associated with the biblical group who God "cursed, into the eternal fire which is prepared for the devil" (Matthew 25:41). By identifying themselves with God through the symbol of the lynched Christ, Black Americans strengthened internal bonds of solidarity, encouraged collective resistance to their oppressors, and contributed significantly to the cultural work of imagining a "New Negro." More generally, this demonstrates how apotheosis reproduces social integration, manages conflict with other groups, and mediates a group's conception of itself.

Eric Sundquist claims that, "by the time Countee Cullen wrote his long narrative poem 'The Black Christ' in 1929, the concept of a black messiah, as his flaccid poem proves, had nearly been drained of literary effectiveness" (593). However, rather than being a feeble retread of a tired motif, Cullen's poem is the apex of the literature of the Black Christ. The value of this symbol and its repeated appearance in these works is not a matter of "literary effectiveness" but of social power and the full force of the apotheosis of modern Black Americans was still nascent in 1929. It would further flower into Black theology, the liberation theologies of other people of color, the Black Arts and Black Power movements, and the civil rights movement. Rigorously describing this development is beyond the scope of this chapter,[7] but if we look to Cullen's "The Black Christ," we find that each stage of the apotheotic process collectively represented in the literature is superbly conveyed in a single work.

Cullen begins in an epic register to say that the poem is ultimately about recognizing a lineage that originates with the biblical Jesus and extends to Black

---

[7] For a book-length analysis of the ways that the image of Jesus "has been used to justify the worst atrocities of white supremacy as well as inspire the most heroic of civil rights crusades," see Blum, Edward J. and Paul Harvey. *The Color of Christ: The Son of God and the Saga of Race in America*. Chapel Hill: The University of North Carolina Press, 2012, 7.

Americans and to all oppressed people around the world. He writes that it is about,

> How Calvary in Palestine,
> Extending down to me and mine,
> Was but the first leaf in a line
> Of trees on which a Man should swing
> World without end, in suffering
> For all men's healing, let me sing.
>
> (162)

There will be more to say about the function of this claim when Cullen returns to it in the denouement. The poem is narrated by one of two brothers and relates their progressive loss of faith in the face of racism and the constant threat of murder, despite the reassurances of their mother, who believes in the traditional theodicy of disprivilege that Cullen's generation wishes to reject. Indeed, the brothers embody Cullen's generation, whose belief in God wavered as he remained silent amid America's culture of white supremacy and Black Christians' cry for salvation. The narrator asks, "We cry for angels; yet wherefore"? (163). God's silence, that is, his seeming inability or unwillingness to intervene to remedy Black suffering, suggested his complicity. We read, "A man was lynched last night… Maybe God thinks such things are right. / Maybe God never thinks at all—/ Of us" (168).

Eventually, the narrator's brother, Jim, loses faith in a God who either is a participant in racist oppression or remains remote and indifferent to it. He concludes, "Likely there ain't no God at all" (169). However, the cultural death of the white God precedes or coincides with the birth of the Black God. Cullen writes,

> Rebellion barked now like a gun;
> Like a split dam, this faith in one
> Who in my sight had never done
> One extraordinary thing
> That I should praise his name, or sing
> His bounty and his grace…
> I have done with deities…
> God is a toy; put Him away.

The subsequent lines, reminiscent of his poem "Heritage" (1925), are crucial as Cullen acknowledges the social nature of apotheosis and the value of using it to craft a God that reflects contemporary Black people. He writes,

> God is a toy; put Him away.
> Or make you one of wood or stone
> That you can call your very own...
> Who does not... promise you fine things aloft
> While back and belly here go bare...
> Better an idol shaped of clay
> Near you, than one so far away...
> Better my God should be
> This moving, breathing, frame of me,
> Strong hands and feet, live heart and eyes;
> And when these cease, say then God dies.
>
> (173–4)

Cullen then goes on to do precisely that, to "make" a God that modern Black Americans "can call [their] very own," who is "near" rather than silent and remote, who looks like them, and who ultimately sanctifies the victims of oppression by making their suffering sacred through his sacrifice.

The poem culminates when Jim is lynched for daring to actively resist racism. Jim's murder causes the narrator to lose the last vestige of his faith, but it is soon reborn anew when Jim is resurrected as "Christ Himself" (194). Though the brother's commitment to Christianity is reawakened, it is to a religion and godhead transformed. Here, a Black American—synecdoche of all victims of oppression—is so conflated with God that they become one. The sacrifice and resurrection of the Black Christ is a revelation that causes the narrator to interpret Christianity in a new way, one that will become the basis of liberation theologies in the decades to come. He reflects, "O lovely Head to dust brought low / More times than we can ever know... There is no hood of pain I wear / That has not rested on His hair / Making Him first initiate / Beneath its harsh and hairy weight" (192, 193). As the poem's invocation promised, the apotheosis of Black Americans in the figure of the lynched Black God identifies them, and all oppressed social groups, with divinity. Certainly, Jesus had long been the god of the poor and excluded, but it is the modern liberation theologies of the Americas, produced by Black and Latin Americans, that employed apotheosis to formulate an anti-colonial, anti-racist theology born of the suffering of oppressed people of color. A fundamental aspect of modern Christian liberation theologies is an apotheotic reading of Matthew 25 that interprets God as a divine reflection of the oppressed and regards the socially and economically marginalized as God's chosen. The sacrifice of the incarnate savior god, who is thought to be the ideal embodiment of the oppressed, functions to make them and their suffering sacred. We recall that it is necessarily through symbolic media, in this case a poem, that collective representations of the sacred—such as the figure of the Black Christ—do the work of legitimating the value of a social group, formalizing their identity, and sanctioning the actions they take in conflict with opposing groups.

In their landmark treatise on sacrifice and the sacred, Henri Hubert and Marcel Mauss report that "the theme of the sacrifice of the god" is prevalent in religious traditions around the world (82). They explain that, in sacrifice, there is "a sort of mythological doubling of the divine being and the victim" (85). "Sacrifice, of itself, effects an exultation of the victims, which renders them directly divine. There are numerous legends in which these apotheoses are related," such as the stories of Heracles, Attis, and Toci (79). They continue, "the sacrificial apotheosis is none other than the rebirth of the victim... The victim is invested with the highest degree of sanctity—a sanctity organized and personified in the sacrifice" (80). The rigorous account of Durkheim's students at times belies the ambiguity of sacrifice. When we think of sacrifice only as an inherently religious, planned ritual act, we forget that a sacrifice is not necessarily regarded as such by all participants. For example, from the perspective of Jesus's executioners, they carried out a legal, state-endorsed death sentence, not a sacrifice. Similarly, lynch mobs claim that their acts are extrajudicial executions. In diverse cases, from that of ancient Christians to the modern American designers of the Black messiah, we find that it is the subsequent cult formed by victims' fellow group members and targets of the same collective violence at the hands of a hegemonic group that transforms an unjust death into a sacred act of deification. Hubert and Mauss further explain that sacrificial apotheosis comes to fruition through literature and mythology broadly construed. They write, "Sacrifice has furnished the elements of divine symbolism. But it is the imagination of the creators of myths which has perfected the elaboration of the sacrifice of the God" (81). In a process they call "progressive divination" the victim of a sacrifice is elevated to a god through repeated literary and symbolic iterations (81). As in examples drawn from antiquity, it is by means of the modern literature of the Black Christ that victims of lynching are made sacred and transformed into incarnations of God. In these works, the Harlem Renaissance authors convert the all too familiar aspects of lynching into "the elements of divine symbolism."

Hubert and Mauss found that, in religions that feature a sacrificed god, "the death of the god is often by suicide" (84). This typically takes the form of immolation or hanging. They write, "Herakles on Oeta, Melkart at Tyre, the god Sandes or Sandon at Tarsus, Dido at Carthage—all burnt themselves to death... Greek mythology has goddesses who bore the name of Απαγχομενη, the 'hanged' goddesses: such were Artemis, Hecate, and Helen. At Athens the hanged goddess was Erigone… At Delphi she was called Charila" (84). Similarly, Frazer refers to numerous examples of the hanged god in Greek and Scandinavian religious traditions (837–838). In addition to those who commit suicide by hanging, there are various examples of mortal victims of murder by hanging who are subsequently worshipped, such as the cult of Helen in Rhodes. In "The Black Christ," Jim exemplifies both the deified victim and the suicide god. Jim knows what the outcome of his resistance will be, and, in this sense, it is an act of self-sacrifice on behalf of all oppressed Black Americans. As in diverse religious traditions that feature a sacrificed god, Jim is killed by hanging and by fire. These "elements of divine symbolism" are iconically represented in Charles Cullen's illustration, where the figure of the lynched Black Christ is surrounded by stylized flames and a column of smoke.

As Hubert and Mauss point out, the sanctity with which the sacrificial victim is invested is predicated on the victim's suffering, it is "organized and personified in the sacrifice." Turning back to Weber's findings, we recall that historically religions that feature a redeemer or savior figure, and the salvation they invariably promise, are the expressions of economically and politically oppressed social groups. Again, he writes that it is "the suffering of a people's community, rather than the suffering of an individual" that is "the object of hope for religious salvation" (273). In the figure of the lynched Black Christ, modern Black Americans created a symbol that embodied their collective suffering and transformed it into a sacred demand for the liberation of the oppressed. This was certainly not a figure "flaccid" and "drained" of power as Sundquist would have it, and it was not merely a literary trope; rather, it was a powerful medium of social consciousness formation that was critical to the political trajectory of Black America for the next half-century. The immense significance of the Black Christ and the Black God more generally demonstrates that apotheosis was central to the development of modern American culture.

The Racial Politics of Apotheosis: Moses, Ham, and the Old Testament

In the preface to *God's Trombones: Seven Negro Sermons in Verse* (1927), James Weldon Johnson describes the social importance of antebellum Black preachers and their methods. He writes that the "old-time" Black preacher "was an important figure, and at bottom a vital factor. It was through him that the people of diverse languages and customs who were brought here from diverse parts of

Africa and thrown into slavery were given their first sense of unity and solidarity. He was the first shepherd of this bewildered flock" (2). Johnson explains that these preachers produced social integration and feelings of solidarity among the diverse people of the African diaspora through apotheosis, that is, by adapting the symbols, stories, and figures of the Old Testament to reflect the attributes and experience of the group, putting them all on common sacred ground. Further contextualizing how this process occurred, Johnson writes that the antebellum preachers "were the first of the slaves to learn to read, and their reading was confined to the Bible, and specifically to the more dramatic passages of the Old Testament" (3). However, Johnson is quick to emphasize that the Black preacher and his apotheotic methods are as influential in modernity as in the years of slavery. "This power of the old-time preacher... is still a vital force [in 1927]; in fact, it is still the greatest single influence among the colored people of the United States. The Negro today is, perhaps, the most priest-governed group in the country" (2). Four years earlier, Toomer devoted the final moments of *Cane* (1923) to just such a revered "old-time" preacher. With the same messianic overtones as "Box Seat," Toomer describes the prophetic Father John as "a mute John the Baptist of a new religion—or a tongue-tied shadow of an old" (142). We learn that he was a "slave boy whom some Christian mistress taught to read the Bible. Black man who saw Jesus in the ricefields, and began preaching to his people. Moses- and Christ-words" (*Cane* 142). With a better understanding of apotheosis, we can see why a preacher with origins "back there in th'sixties" would appear to be, at once, the minister of "a new religion" and the "shadow of an old"; they were indeed both of these things (*Cane* 153, 142). Armed with a limited set of religious symbols received from their slavers, antebellum Black preachers developed a form of Christianity that was populated by a small pantheon of biblical characters and set pieces drawn primarily from the Old Testament that were returned to again and again. Most importantly, they recreated these biblical figures in their own image and adapted their stories to reflect the concerns and interests of Black people. As Johnson explains, apotheosis had been a cornerstone of the Black Church since the era of slavery, and now, amid the awakening of the Harlem Renaissance, Black modernists were offering representations of Old Testament symbols to strengthen social solidarity, empower Black people, and encourage political engagement.

Second only to Jesus Christ, Moses was a central figure in the history of Black Christianity. Like other luminaries in their small pantheon, Moses was often represented as Black, one modernist example being Zora Neale Hurston's *Moses, Man of the Mountain* (1939). Indeed, examinations of the immense cultural significance of Moses in Black history could fill a library. Most recently, in *Excavating Exodus: Biblical Typology and Racial Solidarity in African American Literature* (2021), J. Laurence Cohen offers an excellent, rigorous analysis of the diverse ways Moses has been reinterpreted and deployed as a cultural symbol to achieve a range of social and political aims over the last two centuries. While presenting an adequately thorough account of the Black Moses is not possible here, we should briefly turn to one Harlem Renaissance work that featured Moses's Black wife and son, May Miller's play, "Graven Images" (1929).

The premise of the play is based on a piece of scripture that serves as its epigraph: "And Miriam and Aaron spake against Moses because of the Ethiopian woman he had married" (Numbers 12:1). The one-act play takes place during the Exodus and features a group of Israelite children playing together. When Aaron's son, Ithamar, finds the golden bull the adults have cast aside, he suggests they "play worship" and each make an offering in turn (336). When Eliezer, Moses and Zipporah's son, arrives, he mocks their game and suggests they worship him instead:

> I shall make a far better idol than this. Look, this idol is gold. (*he strips his tunic off to the waist*) Am I not gold? Come feel your idol. It is cold but I am warm. Warm gold. And see! see! You worship this thing that does not so much as nod his thanks. It's still, but I move, I move.
>
> (338)

Just as Cullen had expressed the collective need to reject a silent and alien God that does not resemble its adherents, writing, "Better my God should be / This moving, breathing, frame of me," Miller voices the same desire among modern Black Christians that their God not be a figuratively cold and indifferent thing, but a living God that assures its worshippers, "I move, I move" (174, 338). In Eliezer, Miller creates a messianic figure that fuses the Black Moses and the Black Christ. When Miriam, Moses and Aaron's sister, sees the children at play and asks about the game, they explain, "we worship a child whom God hath created in his own image" (338). Previously, Miriam—who embodies racism in the play—argued that Eliezer and his brother "are no true children of Israel" because Zipporah is Black (337). Now, enraged, she exclaims, "In his own image, indeed! Pray did Father Moses tell you God was an Ethiop?... This child is no image of God Jehovah. He is Black like his mother" (338). Eliezer prophetically warns that "God will punish anyone who says I am not" made in the image of God and shortly thereafter Miriam is stricken with leprosy (340). Eliezer's playmate, who had doubted the blackness of God, seeing Miriam's fate, is afraid and agrees to "play worship" with Eliezer, who makes him recite, "I worship a child whom God hath created in his own image" (341). In a negation of the received narrative associated with the white church, where the Israelites are punished for worshiping a golden idol in Moses's absence, here, an Israelite is punished for refusing to worship a golden-complected biracial child who is said to resemble God, as a son resembles his father, again while Moses is absent. As Craig Prentiss writes, "Graven Images" "poignantly reflects the manner in which biblical narratives can be appropriated in the construction of a positive social identity—one in which 'blackness' reflects the image of God" (151). By way of this specular mechanism of social reproduction and empowerment, blackness is made sacred. As was common in Black adaptations of Moses, Miller is also trying to establish a direct line of descent from Moses to modern Black Americans, similar to the lineage Cullen and others sought to establish in their Christology.

Zora Neale Hurston's play "The First One" (1927) also uses a story about the son of a major Old Testament figure to sanctify blackness. The play reimagines the story of Noah and the so-called Curse of Ham related in Genesis. In the biblical account, Noah becomes drunk and passes out naked in his tent. Noah's son Ham sees this and tells his brothers who avert their eyes and cover their father. When Noah wakes, he punishes Ham by condemning his son Canaan to a life of servitude. Historically, American advocates appropriated this passage to justify slavery. In their adaptation, Canaan was dropped from the story and Ham—the biblical patriarch of Africa—became the target of Noah's curse. Just as they had employed apotheosis to imagine themselves as God's chosen replicas, white supremacists used the same means to argue that Ham and his Black descendants are slaves ontologically, essentially and by nature, those chosen by God to serve white people. Frederick Douglass had famously attempted to dismantle this myth in the opening pages of *Narrative of the Life of Frederick Douglass, an American Slave* (1845) by referring to the scores of biracial children of slavers who remained in servitude. He writes,

> a very different-looking class of people are springing up at the south, and are now held in slavery, from those originally brought to this country from Africa; and if their increase do no other good, it will do away the force of the argument, that God cursed Ham, and therefore American slavery is right. If the lineal descendants of Ham are alone to be scripturally enslaved, it is certain that slavery at the south must soon become unscriptural; for thousands are ushered into the world, annually, who, like myself, owe their existence to white fathers, and those fathers most frequently their own masters.

In Hurston's anti-capitalist reappropriation of the story, Ham is converted from a villainous figure to a heroic embodiment of freedom whose brothers' greed for more vineyards and land lead them to betray him, and subsequently to Noah's curse. As in racist representations, in Hurston's play Noah turns Ham's skin black—an act that does not occur in the Bible. She writes, "He shall be accursed. His skin shall be black!... He and his seed forever. He shall serve his brothers and they shall rule over him" (331). Though Hurston writes of the seeming "curse of thy Blackness," she, and numerous others working in a tradition that stretched back to the early nineteenth century, used Ham as a religious symbol that could unite the diverse peoples of the African diaspora (333). Craig R. Prentiss explains,

> while the narrative [of Ham] served their oppressors, African Americans themselves recoded the tale as one of potential uplift. The phrase "children of Ham" became a shorthand for slaves and their descendants, connecting them to great African civilizations of the past... In the hands of African Americans, being aligned with the "children of Ham" provided fertile ground for cultivating pride rather than suffering derision. Having traced their lineage to Ham, African Americans used the Ethiopianist prophecy of Psalm 68:31 to... undermine the stigma associated with their once shunned patriarch and recognize themselves as participants in a divinely ordained destiny.
>
> (153)

By remolding the plastic symbols of the Old Testament, Black artists and clergy—antebellum and modern—collectively represented a lineage that made Black Americans members of God's chosen family. By making blackness sacred, the people become more tightly integrated and empowered to combat antagonistic groups. The cultural history of Ham is a superb example of apotheosis. Just as the symbol of Jesus was used by both the leisure and working-classes to legitimate antithetical interests, to increase group cohesion, and to codify a shared group identity, Ham was used by both oppressor and oppressed groups, by both white supremacists and Black Americans to serve the same social functions. Moreover, as we have seen, ongoing group conflict is mediated by religious symbols and processes of apotheosis. When Black modernists joined the tradition—going back to the "old-time" preacher—of turning biblical figures into heroes of Black liberation, reactionary white writers of the 1920s responded by hijacking images of a Black God and an Old Testament populated by Black people to create competing narratives and reinforce systematic racial oppression in the United States.

Plantation Modernism on Broadway

As I have stated previously, religion is a vital matrix of social dynamics and a principal medium through which vying groups struggle for power and perpetuation. In the preceding sections of this chapter, we saw that apotheosis was used to legitimate Black liberation in the 1920s and 1930s. In what follows, we will see that it was used to legitimate white supremacism as well. At the same time that Harlem Renaissance artists and ministers were creating symbols that represented a new form of the sacred in the figure of the Black God, reactionary white writers were appropriating the practice of Black apotheosis for antithetical ends, namely, to reproduce the existent conditions of Black oppression. In a series of related texts released from 1926 to 1936—including short stories, novels, a Pulitzer Prize–winning play, and a Hollywood film—Roark Bradford and Marc Connelly used the specular mechanism of apotheosis to create false reflections of Black Americans in an effort to reproduce the economy of plantation feudalism.

In the preface to *God's Trombones* (1927), Johnson explains that Black Christianity in America is distinguished by religious symbols that are truly collective representations in that they are the product of an oral tradition with no single author. He writes, "I remember hearing in my boyhood sermons... that passed with only slight modifications from preacher to preacher, and from locality to locality" (1). This tradition consisted of "stereotyped" sermons on a small number of figures and narratives drawn from the Old Testament that preachers would continually return to, such as the stories of the Creation and Eden, Noah and the Flood, and Moses and the Exodus that Johnson replicates in *God's Trombones* (1). Most importantly, the foundation of this tradition was the symbol of "a personal and anthropomorphic God" (Johnson 4). In 1926, a journalist from New Orleans began publishing a series of stories in the *New York Times* that represented the tradition of Black apotheosis described by Johnson, but written from the perspective of a white southern patrician. The author, Roark Bradford, was a regular contributor to popular publications like *Harper's*, *Collier's*, and the *Saturday Evening Post*. In 1927, his story "Child of God" won the O. Henry Award and in 1928, Harper and Brothers published the *Times* series as *Ol' Man Adam an' His Chillun, Being the Tales They Tell about the Time When the Lord Walked the Earth Like a Natural Man*. The book's ostensible conceit is to retell the stories of the Old Testament from a modern Black American's point of view by putting them in a contemporary setting and by making all the humans in the stories Black.

In the foreword to *Ol' Man Adam an' His Chillun*—originally published separately as "Notes on the Negro" in the November 1927 issue of *Forum*—Bradford explains why he considers himself an authority on Black culture:

> All my life I have been puzzled by something in the Negro people. I believe I know them pretty well. I was born on a plantation that was worked by them; I was nursed by one as an infant and I played with one when I was growing up. I have watched them at work in the fields, in the levee camps, and on the river. I have watched them at home, in church, at their picnics and their funerals. I know their songs and dances, and their trials and triumphs. I know pretty well what to expect of them in any given set of circumstances.
>
> (ix)

Bradford goes on to describe the pseudo-sociological "study of the black race" he has developed on the basis of this purported knowledge (x). Bradford contends that "the black race" is "divided it into three general groups: The 'nigger,' the 'colored person,' and the Negro" (x). He continues, "The Negro, in my classification... realizes that his people could not possibly have acquired in two hundred years the same particular brand of civilization that the white people built up in thousands of years" (x). The "colored person," typically "of mixed blood," is bitter because "he can't be white" and is "ashamed of being black" (xi). Remarkably, he argues that it is this group who "incite race riots and lynchings" (xi). Lastly, Bradford comes to the group whose religious culture he claims to represent in the book. The award-winning author so celebrated in New York City writes,

> The nigger interests me more than the rest. He has not learned many of the finer points of our white civilization, such as intolerance... hate... [and] money as the basis of all values. In fact, the nigger hasn't learned very much about anything [...] He is... entirely irresponsible... He has the intuition of a child... He will lie about anything, if a lie seems more appropriate than the truth... He is... a shiftless ne're-do-well who is the bugaboo of our ideals. He... has neither object nor aim, and isn't the kind of a fellow who will ever be President or a leading citizen.
>
> (xiii)

Crucially, to legitimate this colonial myth about the absence of Black culture, Bradford appeals to apotheosis. He argues that "black people brought to America... nothing in the way of civilization" and, "having no particular religion, took the white man's religion... and adapted it, applying his own photographic imagination and his simple reasoning to it as he did" (xv–xvi).

Because the figure of a Black Christ who suffers with oppressed people is a potent symbol of liberation, Bradford claims that "one hears very little about the New Testament" in Black Christianity (xviii). Making a claim we have seen refuted again and again in the literature of the Black Christ, Bradford writes, "the story of the Crucifixion, with the central character suffering death upon the Cross, seems to be all wrong; it doesn't appeal to his imagination" (xviii). In the closing of his apologia, Bradford adopts a tone of plantation nostalgia and makes it clear that his fantasies of Black religion serve conservative interests, writing, "the unfortunate part of it seems to be that something is being destroyed about [Black people] that cannot be replaced" (xxiii).

While I hesitate to amplify Bradford's words by repeating them here, with a few exceptions, contemporary critical analyses of *The Green Pastures* fail to adequately acknowledge the details of Connelly's source material. Critics past and present argue that Connelly's adaptation is "radically different" from the overtly racist *Ol' Man Adam an' His Chillun*; however, ample evidence shows that Connelly took pains to remain consistent with Bradford (Daniel 22). For example, forty years after the cultural phenomenon of *The Green Pastures*, he explained, "I tried to echo Brad [Roark Bradford] as much as I could, so I used a lot of lines straight out of his book" (*Voices* 74).

Bradford's stories are narrated by an "old-time" preacher and written in a version of Black vernacular, as is Connelly's stage adaptation, though its use in literature had been explicitly rejected by Black artists by the 1920s, the only noteworthy exception being Hurston. In his preface to *God's Trombones*, Johnson writes, "*traditional* Negro dialect as a form for Aframerican poets is absolutely dead" (6). He explains that no literature "is being written in dialect by the colored poets of today" because it is a far too "limited instrument. Indeed, it is an instrument with but two complete stops, pathos and humor" (5). Johnson voices the consensus among Black writers of the time that the use of dialect in literature is an inadequate means of creating accurate representations of Black society. Further, that the use of dialect is steeped in political significance, as it suggests that Black people are essentially limited to the dehumanized tragic-comic caricatures deployed during slavery and its cultural aftermath. Johnson writes,

> The Negro poet in the United States... needs now an instrument of greater range than the dialect; that is, if he is to do more than sound the small notes of sentimentality... the colored poet in the United States needs to... find a form that will express the racial spirit by symbols from within rather than symbols from without... He needs a form that is freer and larger than dialect, but which will still hold the racial flavor; a form expressing the imagery, the

idioms, the peculiar turns of thought and the distinctive humor and pathos, too, of the Negro, but which will also be capable of voicing the deepest and highest emotions and aspirations.

(6)

Here, Johnson precisely describes the extensive corpus of literature, theater, and visual art created by the artists of the Harlem Renaissance who crafted symbols of a Black God that expressed "the imagery, the idioms" and the social-political aims of modern Black Americans. Modern Black Christians who were more politically oppositional than their predecessors transformed received religious "symbols from without," through the mechanism of apotheosis, into "symbols from within." Believers and professed atheists alike labored to produce new symbols of the sacred, motivated by the need to instill a greater sense of self-worth among Black people, to strengthen social bonds among a migrant and diasporic population, and enliven their will to actively combat oppression. The works of Bradford and Connelly, by contrast, are reactionary countermeasures to the literature of the Black God that express a collective effort to reproduce racist social formations in America and to accomplish aims diametrically opposed to those of the Harlem artists. The immense popularity of Bradford and Connelly's work in the 1920s and 1930s means that they must not be regarded as the collaborative vision of two individuals alone, but, rather, as collective representations. Bradford and Connelly's choice to employ a contrived form of southern Black vernacular is calculated to conjure nostalgic fantasies of plantation society and the desire to re-establish an ostensibly vanishing white supremacist culture.

Like *God's Trombones*, Bradford's *Ol' Man Adam an' His Chillun* begins with a Black preacher's account of the Creation. In stark contrast to Johnson's, however, Bradford's version is a sanitized apotheosis of the dawn of slavery in America, where God and the angels' relation to humanity mirrors that between white plantation owners and Black slaves, and, later, field hands and sharecroppers. Bradford envisions the Garden of Eden as God's original plantation. Upon seeing God's creation, the preacher tells his audience, Gabriel said, "Now looky what you done done, Lawd... somebody got to go work dat land, 'cause you know good as me dat de land ain't gonter work hitself" (4). God and the angels were "mighty busy" so God created Adam to work the land, and then Eve, to impose domestic responsibilities on Adam so he would be a more docile and dependable worker (4). When Adam tells God that he "ain't got no family," "de Lawd" replies, "I got to change dat. I ain't gonter have none of deseyar single mens workin' on my farm. They runs around wid de women all night and come de next day they's too sleepy to work" (5). Bradford goes on to portray the expulsion of Adam and Eve from the Garden as the eviction of a sharecropper:

> De Lawd... got mad, 'cause he didn't aim to have nobody on his place which stole his apples. So he bailed old Adam's trover and leveled on his crop and mule, and put Adam and Eve off'n de place. And de next news anybody yared of old Adam, he was down on de levee tryin' to git a job at six bits a day.
>
> (8)

When Bradford writes that God "bailed old Adam's trover and leveled on his crop and mule," he means that God repossessed the mule he had leased to Adam, his tenant farmer, and the crops Adam had been working to pay the debts he owed to God, the landowner. Bradford further embellishes Adam's dismal fate—leaving him poor and unemployed—to turn the Bible's story of the Fall into a cautionary tale for southern Black workers who would dare challenge their white bosses.

Bradford makes the whiteness of his God clear, both in A. B. Walker's original illustrations for the book, which depict God as a white southern squire, and in his mockery of Nicodemus in the book's final chapter. American evangelical Christians derive the concept of being "born again" that is so fundamental to their doctrine of salvation from Jesus's conversation with Nicodemus in the Gospel of John. As Daniel Burke has noted, to Black Americans "after the Civil War, [Nicodemus] was a model of rebirth as they sought to cast off their old identity as slaves" ("Mystery"). With this sacred symbol of Black liberation in mind, Bradford transforms Nicodemus into "Nigger Deemus," and when God invites him to join his disciples, he replies, "Lawd, you knows I ain't got no business goin' round de wilderness wid you and all dem white folks. I know my place" (260–1). In his rendering of the Old Testament patriarchs, Bradford continues to represent God's relationship to humanity as that of a white landowner to Black tenant farmers. God promises Abraham that Isaac's "grandchilluns is gonter work all dis land I been givin' you" (51). The version of Christianity that Bradford presents in *Ol' Man Adam an' His Chillun* is the apotheosis of white supremacist plantation feudalism and its practice of multigenerational exploitation. The underlying aim of Bradford's book—as well as Connelly's subsequent stage and screen adaptations, which would offer the American public more palatable and sanitized versions of the original—was to counteract the liberation of Black Americans and demand that they return to their ostensibly God-ordained "place" of social subordination.

As the title of his book suggests, one of Bradford's primary methods is to essentialize white supremacists' cultural infantilization of Black people by means of apotheosis. He attempts to sacralize racist paternalism by portraying God as a heavenly white father and the Israelites as his earthly Black children. We read, "de Hebrew chilluns was de Lawd's chilluns, but they was jest chilluns. And chilluns ain't steady" (174). In this version of salvation history, the "Hebrew chilluns" continually fail to "march wid de Lawd" (183). Generation after generation, they revert to "devilment" and end up on a "chain-gang" (175). As Bradford makes clear in his Foreword, the book is a coded argument about the superiority of "white civilization"—figured as God—and the inferiority of Black civilization—figured as the Old Testament Israelites. Bradford's argument is not exactly subtle: like the biblical Jews, modern Black Americans are all "sinful scound'els," and, like God, white Americans should not expect them to change for centuries, but must rather take them firmly in hand as an authoritative father does an incorrigible child (175). His God explains, "I ain't blamin' my chilluns... De chilluns is young and ain't got no better sense" (175). We recall that social conflict is mediated by religious symbols formed through apotheosis. Here, Bradford attempts to legitimate and advance the interests of his group by reforming dominant religious symbols to make them mirror the social formation he wants to reproduce. Once we unlock this simple apotheotic code, we see that the book's epigraph is a kind of white supremacist motto: "Well, they was some mighty men in them days and times. And the Lord was beyond them all." By reimagining God as the essentially superior white overseer of his inveterately criminal Black workers, Bradford attempts to both essentialize racial inequality and justify the criminalization of Black bodies. In his adaptations, Connelly magnifies this aspect of Bradford's book to argue that the natural viciousness of Black people requires that white Americans continue to dominate them.

Bradford undoubtedly recognized the political power of apotheosis, but it was Marc Connelly who self-consciously leveraged its capacity to excite social feeling into making a Broadway hit starring the Black God. In both his stage (1930) and screen (1936) adaptations of Bradford's book—now renamed *The Green Pastures* after one of its chapters—Connelly begins by making a prefatory statement to the audience in which he attempts to describe this specular phenomenon and its cultural significance. Like Bradford, Connelly adopts the knowing posture of an expert social scientist. However, though he had traveled widely in Europe and the Mediterranean, Connelly had never even been to the South before briefly visiting Bradford in 1929. In the "Author's Note" that appeared in the playbill and published play, Connelly explains,

> "The Green Pastures" is an attempt to present certain aspects of a living religion in the terms of its believers. The religion is that of thousands of Negroes in the deep South. With terrific spiritual hunger and the greatest humility these

untutored black Christians—many of whom cannot even read the book which is the treasure of the faith—have adapted the contents of the Bible to the consistencies of their everyday lives.

(xv)

Though Connelly never shied from attributing his source material, he sanitizes its overt white supremacy to make it more palatable to a national, multiracial audience while remaining politically in lockstep with Bradford. His underlying position is evident here, where he suggests that Black people are largely illiterate and uneducated, though the literacy rate among Black Americans was comparable to whites in 1930 (Margo 7). He continues, "Unburdened by the differences of more educated theologians they accept the Old Testament as a chronicle of wonders which happened to people like themselves… and of rules of conduct, true acceptance of which will lead them to a tangible, three-dimensional Heaven" (xv). In a promotional featurette, Connelly turns to apotheosis to describe the film as well: "*The Green Pastures* is a story of heaven and of earth as it might be imagined by very simple, devout people. And they look at heaven and they look at earth in terms of their own daily experience." The film begins with scrolling text, a "Foreword" that reads, "God appears in many forms to those who believe in Him. Thousands of Negroes in the Deep South visualize God and Heaven in terms of people and things they know in their everyday life. The Green Pastures is an attempt to portray that humble, reverent conception" (Connelly 1936).

In 1929, Connelly read Bradford's book and immediately obtained dramatic rights from Harper's. Within just a few months he had written a script and assembled an extravagant stage production. *The Green Pastures* opened on Broadway at the Mansfield Theatre in February 1930 to immediate critical acclaim. Brooks Atkinson of *The New York Times* called it "the divine comedy of the modern theater," and William Bolitho of the *New York World* proclaimed the musical drama "a masterpiece" (1, 6). It was performed at the Mansfield for sixteen months and garnered evermore praise along the way. Echoing the consensus among white critics and theatergoers, Alexander Walcott called *The Green Pastures* "the finest achievement of the American theater in the hundred years during which there has been one worth considering" (qtd. in Daniel 17). By May Connelly had won the Pulitzer, and in March of 1931 Richard Harrison, the actor who portrayed the play's Black God, was awarded the NAACP's prestigious Spingarn Medal, its highest honor. Other recent recipients of the award included James Weldon Johnson and W. E. B. Du Bois, who received the medal in 1920 and gave the keynote address at Harrison's ceremony. On the final night of its New York run, Roark Bradford attended a party celebrating the occasion alongside "major New York publishers, critics, and other celebrities, including Eleanor Roosevelt, Dorothy Parker, and Robert Benchley" (Daniels 107). After the enormous success of the 640 performances on Broadway, Connelly and company took the show on the road, mounting five consecutive national tours at the height of the Depression, from 1931 to 1935, crisscrossing the United States to bring *The Green Pastures* to 203 cities and towns in nearly every state. The effusive reception the play had received in New York continued in the wake of the tours, with the Chicago *Sunday Tribune*'s Fanny Butcher, for example, writing that it is "one of the great plays in the history of drama" (6). By the time the company returned to Broadway in February 1935, *Time* could accurately describe the play as a "United States institution" (qtd. in Daniel 109). Then, after playing the role of God in 1,657 consecutive performances on an intensely grueling schedule that included promotional duties off-stage, Richard Harrison collapsed in his dressing room and later died on March 14, 1935. Connelly did not attend either of Harrison's funerals, in Harlem or Chicago.

Though Du Bois had reviewed *The Green Pastures* favorably in *Crisis*, writing that it was "an extraordinarily appealing and beautiful play based on the folk religion of Negroes," Black audiences and critics were ambivalent about it (qtd. in Daniels 94). As Walter Daniels put it, "Surely, they were proud of the attention the drama and its cast were receiving throughout the nation, but they realized the play was basically a white man's creation and that he and his associates were reaping the major benefits from its success" (120). Few Black Americans could afford tickets to see the play, and those who could were consigned to segregated seating. They largely regarded it as "a white folks' enterprise" (Daniels 110). Ultimately, *The Green Pastures* was a "play about black folk, played by black actors to the accompaniment of black music sung by black singers—all performed primarily for the delectation of white audiences" (Daniels 83).

As the play's cultural impact intensified, the tours came to be popularly regarded as a kind of traveling revival that was awakening the faith of modern Americans and serving as a catalyst of conversion. For example, Whitney Bolton writes in the *New York Telegram* that Harrison's portrayal of God "has awakened more humans to the frailties of their souls than a host of thundering from the pulpits" (8). Similarly, theologian Charles T. Holman wrote that Harrison "viewed his task as a genuine religious ministry. And so it was" (452). As Holman indicates, Harrison believed the play and his role in it were agents of redemption. When a reporter asked him whether he knew of "actual concrete cases of people who have been helped, religiously, by the play?" Harrison replied, "Indeed, we do. Many and many of them" (Knowles 7). Harrison attributed the success of the play to Americans' increased desire for salvation amid modernity and economic depression. He explained,

> In these days of sinking sand, I believe the human heart wants something (or somebody) to hang on to. Even the educated. Even the cultured. Even the agnostic. The secret of the appeal of our play is that it makes vivid a superior power—even hearts who don't know it want something to convert them, to convert them from the way things are going.
>
> (Knowles 7)

The timing of the play's appearance—just four months after the stock market crash of 1929—the collective, shared nature of the experience, its extravagant pageantry, and its ritualization over the course of the Depression were all key factors of *The Green Pastures*' cultural effect. Bradford, whose name appeared alongside Connelly's in the playbill and film, followed 1928's *Ol' Man Adam an' His Chillun* with two novels that used the same gimmick—*This Side of Jordan* (1929) and *Ol' King David and the Philistine Boys* (1930)—but neither sold well. Though Connelly had some prior success, nothing he ever did after *The Green Pastures* approached its acclaim. It was the effervescence triggered by *The Green Pastures* event that made it such a phenomenon. As we have seen, in times of economic hardship, people of all classes look to religion for social and psychological stabilization, but the way religion serves that need differs among groups in asymmetrical relations of power. Harrison was right to regard the play as an agent of salvation and religious awakening. As a story that depicts the primitivism of Black religion, it reassured effete white audiences of their own salvation, secure in the belief that they had evolved to a far more advanced stage in the salvation history of humanity.

As Johnson explained in *God's Trombones*, by the 1920s Black writers had repudiated the use of dialect in literature because it was "an instrument with but two complete stops, pathos and humor" (5). Dialect was rightly associated with dehumanizing representations of Black people in post–Civil War plantation fiction that reduced them to two-dimensional, childlike, sentimental figures who never fail to bring forth "the tear and the smile" from white people (Daniels 165). Connelly's use of long-outmoded dialect[8] and the discourse of cultural immaturity that pervades reviews of the play show that it expresses a point of

---

[8] Weisenfeld writes, "Before he returned to New York [from his visit to Bradford in Louisiana], he tested the dialect in his work before groups of servants in the homes of various wealthy whites... and reported that their responses to the language were favorable" (Weisenfeld 58).

view that is consistent with Bradford's more overtly white supremacist argument. In the criticism, we see the same loaded terminology used again and again. For example, Jonathan Daniels writes in the *Saturday Review of Literature* that white people "pour into Mansfield... to laugh and cry together at the simple Negroes who in their simplicity understand their god" (941). Similarly, Bolitho writes that the play conveys "the secrets of that strange, poor people who make you cry when they sing and laugh when they talk," that is, to "laugh in a peculiar way—the way you laugh at a baby" (6). George C. Warren, a drama critic in San Francisco, congratulated the "highly civilized" Connelly for managing to represent the Bible stories "as the naive children of Africa understand them" (8). Stark Young, drama editor of the *New Republic*, writes that *The Green Pastures* reveals the religion Black Americans hold in "their warm, childish hearts," while Atkinson marvels at the "simplicity and warmth" of Richard Harrison and the "artless hopes of an ignorant people" (Daniel 103, "The Play" 16). Reviewers of the film regularly used infantilizing language as well. For instance, the *Motion Picture Review*'s notice said the film gave viewers "a deeper understanding of a simple, childlike race" and the *Commonweal*'s reviewer wrote that the film depicts the "childish intimacy with which the illiterate, primitive Negro imagines his relationship" with God (qtd. in Weisenfeld 82).

As its touring history and the reception of the "great white public on Broadway" and off make clear, *The Green Pastures* event should be regarded as a collective representation and collective experience that used a symbol of Black religion to legitimate and reproduce white social authority amid the economic collapse of the Depression (Broun 415). It conveyed a structure of feeling that allowed upper-class white Americans to imagine themselves as loving Black people while simultaneously reinforcing the legitimacy of inequality. The kind of sentimentality that suffused the popularity and critical reception of *The Green Pastures* was integral to the political aesthetic of plantation modernism. From the perspective of white audiences, the charm and beauty of *The Green Pastures* was predicated on seeing Black people as cultural children who are inferior by essence. The mass-infantilization of Black Americans experienced by over a thousand audiences nationwide reinforced the idea that Black civilization will evolve eventually but at present is subordinate to white cultural adulthood. *The Green Pastures* was a symbolically mediated mechanism that reproduced white Americans' imagined relationship to the real social conditions of modern America. The play reassured anxious white audiences that, just as a parent loves a child but does not regard them as a social-political equal, they could love Black people while also believing that that they are not yet fully human.

Rather than claiming outright that Black people are perpetually childlike, as Bradford does, Connelly attempts to conceal the infantilization of Black people in his addition to the frame story. As in Bradford's book, the conceit of the play involves sermons being delivered in dialect by an "old-time" preacher, but in this case, the preacher is telling Old Testament stories to a Sunday School class. What the audience then sees on the stage and the screen is a representation of how a child in the class "visualize[s] God and Heaven" in her imagination while listening to the preacher's stories. Like Bradford, Connelly presents himself as a gentleman sociologist who is conveying to the masses the religious culture of an entire people and what the frame story suggests is that, according to his pseudo-scientific findings, the sophistication of this "living religion" is on par with the fancies of a child.

Connelly's appropriation of the Black God was another key factor of *The Green Pastures'* cultural power, but this was a bridge too far for many white viewers. In a letter to the editor published in *The Nation* in May 1930, a Mary Burrill complained that "Those of us who are bound by ties of blood, who have lived in the South, and who therefore truly know the Negro, realize that when the Negro... visualizes God, he visualizes Him not as a kindly preacher of his own race but as an anemic-looking *white* gentleman with golden beard and flowing hair" (600). She insisted further that Black Christians believe that when they attain salvation and enter heaven "they will blossom out in all that this world holds dear—fair faces, golden hair" (600). Similarly, Nick Aaron Ford argued that Connelly

> has misrepresented the unlettered Negro's conception of the physical features of God. Because of religious indoctrination during slavery, the Negro cannot imagine a black God. In all of his testimony concerning his visions and dreams about God, he pictures God and the angels as white. He is sure that the color of his skin is only a sign of his mortality, and that when he dies and goes to Heaven he will be transformed into a white angel. If Mr. Connelly... would have sat at the feet of some of these "old Negro preachers" and sought the truth... he would have learned that... so far as unlettered Negros are concerned, only the devil is black. God, the angels, and all the heavenly creatures are as white as the drifting snow.
> (68–69)

These reactions underscore the link between forms of the sacred and race as a concept as well as a mechanism of oppression in American culture. As Cone put it, from the perspective of Black theology, "blackness [and] salvation... are synonyms... The question 'How can white persons become black?' is analogous to the Philippian jailer's question to Paul and Silas, 'What must I do to be saved?'"

(69). In this view, salvation is a becoming-Black. From the perspective of white supremacist theology, by contrast, salvation is a becoming-white. In the American context, the very idea of race has historically been predicated on the whiteness of God, which legitimates and authorizes the Anglo domination of people of color. Some white viewers of *The Green Pastures*, like these writers, feared that by countenancing a Black God and the notion that salvation is not a becoming-white, the play undermined their social position. The concept of racial superiority is contingent on the sacredness of whiteness, and they believed the play posed a threat to that. Further, their reaction exemplifies the apotheosis of Jim Crow America by racist white people who cannot imagine their kind Black nanny in hell but cannot abide by the idea of having to share heaven with Black people either.

Walter C. Daniel writes that *The Green Pastures* was able to remain lucrative during the height of the Depression because it offered "a balm sufficient for the longings of the times" (95). He is right but the question is, whose longings and for what? The play's enormous success among white audiences throughout the nation is a collective representation of a conservative desire to reinforce Black servitude. As a work of plantation modernism, *The Green Pastures* expresses nostalgia for diminishing relations of domination and functions to revive faith in the legitimacy and security of white affluence and power amid the social and economic upheavals of the Depression. Matters of race and class intersect here, as the play functions to allay the anxiety of upper-class urban white people amid the northern migration of working-class rural Black people and the rise of poverty nationwide.

In previous chapters, we have examined the theology of the working-class. This play provides an occasion to look more closely at the theology of the privileged class. Weber explains,

> classes with high social and economic privilege... assign to religion the primary function of legitimating their own life pattern and situation in the world. This universal phenomenon is rooted in certain basic psychological patterns. When a man who is happy compares his position with that of one who is unhappy, he is not content with the fact of his happiness, but desires something more, namely the right to this happiness, the consciousness that he has earned his good fortune, in contrast to the unfortunate one who must equally have earned his misfortune.
>
> (107)

In the history of American Protestantism, the need to justify economic inequality gave rise to the notion that poverty is a sin, an "earned... misfortune" that is reflective of vice, impiety, or laziness, whereas wealth is a sign of virtue, hard work, and salvation. "What the privileged classes require of religion," Weber writes, "is this psychological reassurance of legitimacy" (107). The hamartiology of high-profile white preachers at the turn of the century reinforced the ethos of capitalism by equating poverty with sin. For example, Henry Ward Beecher argued that "no man in this land suffers from poverty unless it be more than his fault—unless it be his *sin*" (qtd. in Fine 119). Similarly, celebrity evangelist D. L. Moody insisted that poverty is "the result of personal sin" and "of not being a converted Christian" (McLoughlin 254). Moody, who—was fond of quoting the saying, "rags are the emblems of the drunkard's child"—argued that the Depression was the result of widespread moral depravity, not a consequence of the economic system. He insisted, "I do not believe we would have these hard times if it had not been for sin" (qtd. in McLoughlin 254). Clerics bluntly proclaimed that "it is wrong to be poor" and that the wealth of the business class was a sign of virtue and the favor bestowed upon them by God (Fine 119). By making poverty and wealth a matter of moral integrity, the affluent class could deny their complicity in the suffering of the poor and take solace in the knowledge that their status was deserved. Affluent white Americans used *The Green Pastures*' representation of working-class Black religion and the Black God as a coping mechanism during the Depression. Just as the liberating Black Christ empowered the Black underclass, the Black God of plantation modernism empowered and reassured the white upper-class.

As Judith Weisenfeld observes about *The Green Pastures* film, after Adam and Eve are expelled from Eden, Connelly "locates sin in urban contexts, [leaving] the viewer with a strong message about the transformations in contemporary black life and the dangers these present to the nation" (79). *The Green Pastures* allayed white upper-class anxiety about Black migration into cities and the moral threat they believed was posed by an influx of the working-class by offering a fantasy about the containment of Black Americans in the Edenic green pastures of southern plantations, where they remain innocent, moral, and subordinate as opposed to free and sinful in the city. In his adaptations, Connelly downplays Bradford's plantation setting and expands on the theme of Black humanity's criminal nature. The bulk of the play consists of scenes of Black people practicing every form of urban vice, which is ostensibly meant to be a modernized imagining of the habitual sinfulness of humanity depicted in the Old Testament. However, by having an all-Black cast act out a litany of violence and immorality, Connelly sends the implicit message that free Black bodies are inherently transgressive and threatening. In the play, after centuries of failing to get his perpetually immoral "chillun of darkness" to obey the law, an exasperated God puts them in bondage, first in Egypt and then in Babylon, "to make you worthy of de breath I gave you" (156). God then imposes generations of servitude on the people "to cure" them of their inherent wickedness, and ultimately it is "through sufferin'" that they learn virtue (156, 167). Weber argued that the primary function of religion among the affluent class is to reassure them of the legitimacy of their power and comfort in the face of the suffering and disempowerment of the disprivileged classes. In the literature of the Black Christ and in Black theology in general, the unjust suffering of the oppressed is made sacred, but here, in the reactionary literature of white supremacy, it is the imposition of suffering and slavery as instruments of moralization that is made sacred. The former exemplifies the apotheosis of the oppressed, the latter, the apotheosis of the oppressor. While it is true that nineteenth-century Black preachers focused primarily on the Old Testament, Bradford and Connelly found figures like Abraham, Isaac, Jacob, and Noah more appealing than Jesus because they are docile and obedient servants of a paternalistic God; they are not liberators or politically oppositional figures who resist the status quo. By patterning humanity's relationship to God on antebellum master–slave relations, plantation modernists like Bradford and Connelly make Black servitude sacred and thereby reassure affluent white Americans that their position and ethos are legitimate.

The Green Pastures can be accurately described as a work of plantation modernism because the play was an aesthetic expression of "the plantation imaginary," while the theater company was a working post-emancipation plantation (Clukey and Wells 4). Connelly not only remade Bradford's story about southern plantation feudalism into something commercially palatable nationwide, but the production itself was a traveling spectacle that modeled the plantation in action on stage. The extravagant company of *The Green Pastures* featured an all-Black cast of nearly 100 characters and performers, more than had ever been employed in an American stage production. Though Connelly had cast a veritable who's who of Harlem's best actors, singers, and musicians, he and his partners told reporters they had been found in "kitchens and other out of the way places" around the city (qtd. in Daniels 74). In 1930 he told one paper that "there are only a few in this play who have ever been on the stage before" (qtd. in Weisenfeld 61). Those familiar with Black theater saw through Connelly's attempt to give the appearance of untutored folk authenticity. For example, John Williams, writer for the leading Black paper in Southern California, the *California Eagle*, writes that the cast is "oversupplied with dramatic and musical talent... It seems a pity that two voices such as are possessed by Marguarite Avery and Nell Hunter can be used only in the aggregate of 28 choir singers... there are actors and actresses in the cast who ordinarily might be headline features were circumstances more favorable" (4). Connelly turned *The Green Pastures* into a plantation enterprise by commodifying the Black God and exploiting the labor, the culture, and the bodies of this massive workforce of Black artists when they were at their most vulnerable. It is even plausible that Richard Harrison, the son of a slave, who collapsed in his dressing room while preparing to perform the role of the Black God for the 1,658th time, had been worked to death by trying to maintain his intensely grueling schedule for five years.

One of the most significant changes Connelly made in his adaptations of Bradford's book was the addition of spirituals, and by casting Hall Johnson and his choir to arrange and perform them, Connelly further reinforced the play's apparent authenticity. Explaining his work on spirituals, Hall Johnson writes, "we wanted to show how the American Negro slaves—in 250 years of constant practice, self-developed under pressure but equipped with their inborn sense of rhythm and drama (plus their new *religion*) created, propagated, and illuminated an art form that was, and still is *unique* in the world of music" (272). Black Americans had been made to perform "for the delectation" of white people since the time of slavery, but in this case, with the addition of Johnson's choir and the spirituals, Connelly exploited an exemplar of Black culture to legitimate a white supremacist fantasy of Black primitivism. Johnson later repudiated *The Green Pastures* as "a white-washed burlesque of the religious thought of the Negro" and said that he and the other cast members only participated because it afforded them an opportunity to perform on Broadway and in Hollywood (qtd. in Weisenfeld 86).

In order for *The Green Pastures* to function as a "reassurance of legitimacy," it was vital for Connelly to establish the authenticity of the religious symbols he claimed to faithfully reproduce (Weber 107). Bradford and Connelly's attempts to portray themselves as social scientists are likewise linked to this need to create the appearance of authenticity. Though it was a modest commercial success compared to the stage production, *The Green Pastures* (1936) was one of only six feature films in the Hollywood Studio era to feature an all-Black cast. Weisenfeld explains that *The Green Pastures* was the second film, after *Hallelujah* (1929),

> in a series of Hollywood's "all-colored-cast" films that rely on religion and would eventually... come to dominate white Americans' imaginings about black religion well into the twentieth century. In this regard [*The Green Pastures*]

proved a more resilient part of American popular culture than most other representations of African American religion, in part because it purported to be a self-representation.

(55)

Bradford and Connelly were able to make such an enormous social and political impact on America precisely because they appealed to apotheosis, to an image of the Black God that white audiences believed was an accurate reflection of Black religion. It was the professed authenticity of these religious images that allowed *The Green Pastures* "to secure a firm place in the American imagination" (Weisenfeld 87).

The literature of the Harlem Renaissance and the works of their reactionary opponents exemplify the process of apotheosis and its social effects. In the figure of the Black God, these works convey the specular structure of anthropotheism, and further, how the social-political power of groups is fostered through culture. Further still, this case shows how internal solidarity within groups and external conflict among groups is mediated by symbols of the sacred. Black modernist literature played a vital role in the fight for equality in interwar America and, as Weisenfeld suggests, representations of religion would continue to be integral to the struggle between Black liberationists and white supremacists "well into the twentieth century" (55). As we have seen, periods of paradigmatic economic change, such as the Market and Industrial revolutions, and periods of economic distress, such as the Depression, are also periods of religious awakening that are marked by an intensified focus on salvation. While his investigations yielded invaluable results, Weber's prediction about the disenchantment of modernity certainly did not come to pass, and that is because economy and the sacred are inextricably bound. Contrary to what he expected, modernity in America was a time of religious innovation and heightened salvation hopes, making it a particularly useful model of apotheosis. However, it is crucial to keep in mind that, though the relation of economy and religion becomes more visible during periods of effervescence and less apparent during profane time, the relation does not diminish as it is a universal aspect of human sociality.

Works Cited

Ackerman, Kathy Cantley. *The Heart of Revolution: The Radical Life and Novels of Olive Dargen*. Knoxville: The University of Tennessee Press, 2004.
Alcott, Louisa May. *Louisa May Alcott: Her Life, Letters, and Journals*. Edited by Ednah D. Cheney. Boston: Roberts Brothers, 1889.
Allitt, Patrick. "The American Christ." *American Heritage* 39.1 (1988): 128–41.
Althusser, Louis. *The Humanist Controversy and Other Writings*. Edited by François Matheron. Trans. G. M. Goshgarian. London: Verso, 2003.
Alves, Jaime Osterman. "She 'had such things to say!': Listening to 'deaf-mute' Catty in Elizabeth Stuart Phelps's *The Silent Partner*." *Saving the World: Girlhood and Evangelicalism in Nineteenth-Century Literature*, edited by Allison Giffen and Robin L. Cadwallader. New York: Routledge, 2017.
Anderson, Sherwood. *Beyond Desire*. New York: Liveright Publishing, 1961.
Applegate, Debby. "Henry Ward Beecher and the 'Great Middle Class': Mass-Marketed Intimacy and Middle-Class Identity." *The Middling Sorts: Explorations in the History of the American Middle Class*, edited by Burton J. Bledstein and Robert D. Johnston. New York: Routledge, 2001.
Arthur, Anthony. *Radical Innocent: Upton Sinclair*. New York: Random House, 2006.
Asad, Talal. *Formations of the Secular*. Stanford, CA: Stanford University Press, 2003.
Atkinson, Brooks. "The Play." *New York Times*, February 27, 1935, p. 16.
Atkinson, Brooks. "Sketch-book to Miracle Play." *New York Times*, June 8, 1930, sec. 9, p. 1.
Austin, Mary. *Christ in Italy: Being the Adventures of a Maverick among Masterpieces*. New York: Duffield & Company, 1912.
Baker, Christina Looper. *In a Generous Spirit: A First-Person Biography of Myra Page*. Urbana: University of Illinois Press, 1996.
Banta, Martha. *Taylored Lives: Narrative Productions in the Age of Taylor, Veblen, and Ford*. Chicago: University of Chicago Press, 1993.
Barth, Carl G. "Discussion." *Transactions of the American Society of Mechanical Engineers* 34 (1912): 1204.
Barton, Bruce. *The Man Nobody Knows: A Discovery of the Real Jesus*. Indianapolis: The Bobbs-Merrill Company, 1925.
Baym, Nina. *Woman's Fiction: A Guide to Novels by and About Women in America, 1820–1870*. 2nd ed. Urbana: University of Illinois Press, 1993.
Beal, Fred E. "I Was a Communist Martyr." *The American Mercury* 42 (1937): 32–45.
Beal, Fred E. *Proletarian Journey: New England, Gastonia, Moscow*. New York: Hillman-Curl, 1937.

Bell, Daniel. "The Engineers and the Price System." *Veblen's Century: A Collective Portrait*, edited by Irving Louis Horowitz. New Brunswick: Transaction Publishers, 2002.

Bennett, Mary Angela. *Elizabeth Stuart Phelps*. Philadelphia: University of Pennsylvania Press, 1939.

Bilhartz, Terry D. *Urban Religion and the Second Great Awakening: Church and Society in Early National Baltimore*. Rutherford: Fairleigh Dickinson UP, 1986.

Blum, Edward J. and Paul Harvey. *The Color of Christ: The Son of God and the Saga of Race in America*. Chapel Hill: The University of North Carolina Press, 2012.

Blumin, Stuart M. *The Emergence of the Middle Class: Social Experience in the American City, 1760–1900*. Cambridge: Cambridge UP, 1989.

Bolitho, William. "*The Green Pastures*." *New York World*, March 1, 1930, p. 6.

Bolton, Whitney. "The Stage Today." *New York Telegram*, February 28, 1935, p. 8.

Bradford, Roark. *Ol' Man Adam an' His Chillun, Being the Tales They Tell about the Time when the Lord Walked the Earth Like a Natural Man*. New York: Harper and Brothers, 1928.

Braley, Berton. "The Spirit of Management." *American Machinist* 40.1 (1914): 34.

Brodhead, Richard H. *Cultures of Letters: Scenes of Reading and Writing in Nineteenth-Century America*. Chicago: University of Chicago Press, 1993.

Broun, Heywood. "It Seems to Heywood Brown." *The Nation*, April 19, 1930, p. 415.

Budd, Louis J. "William Dean Howells' Debt to Tolstoy." *American Slavic and East European Review* 9.4 (1950): 292–301.

Burke, Daniel. "Nicodemus, The Mystery Man of Holy Week." *Religious News Service*, March 27, 2013. https://religionnews.com/2013/03/27/nicodemus-the-mystery-man-of-holy-week. Accessed April 14, 2021.

Burridge, Kenelm. *New Heaven, New Earth: A Study of Millenarian Activities*. Ann Arbor: University of Michigan Press, 1969.

Burrill, Mary. "*The Green Pastures*," letter to editor, *The Nation*, May 21, 1930, p. 600.

Butcher, Fanny. "The Armchair Dramatist." *Sunday Tribune*, September 6, 1931, p. 6.

Callahan, Raymond E. *Education and the Cult of Efficiency: A Study of the Social Forces That Have Shaped the Administration of the Public Schools*. Chicago: University of Chicago Press, 1964.

Callahan Jr., Richard J. *Work and Faith in the Kentucky Coal Fields: Subject to Dust*. Bloomington: Indiana UP, 2009.

Cassirer, Ernst. *The Philosophy of Symbolic Forms Volume II: Mythical Thought*. Trans. Ralph Manheim. New Haven: Yale UP, 1955.

Cella, Laurie J. C. "Radical Romance in the Piedmont: Olive Tilford Dargan's Gastonia Novels." *Southern Literary Journal* 39.2 (2007): 37–57.

Child, Lydia Maria. *Letters From New York*. London: Second Series, 1845.

Cioran, E. M. *A Short History of Decay*. Trans. Richard Howard. New York: Arcade Publishing, 2012.

Clement of Alexandria. *Miscellanies, Book VII*. Trans. Fenton John Anthony Hort and Joseph B. Mayor. New York: Garland, 1987.

Cone, James H. *A Black Theology of Liberation*. Maryknoll: Orbis, 2010.

Connelly, Marc. *The Green Pastures: A Fable*. New York: Holt, Rinehart, and Winston, 1958.

Connelly, Marc. *Voices Offstage: A Book of Memoirs*. New York: Holt, Rinehart, and Winston, 1968.

Cook, Sylvia Jenkins. *From Tobacco Road to Route 66: The Southern Poor White in Fiction*. Chapel Hill: The University of North Carolina Press, 1976.

Cook, Sylvia Jenkins. "Gastonia: The Literary Reverberations of the Strike." *The Southern Literary Journal* 7.1 (1974): 49–66.

Coolidge, Calvin. *Have Faith in Massachusetts: A Collection of Speeches and Messages*. Boston: Houghton Mifflin, 1919.

Coolidge, Calvin. "Speech Delivered to the *American Society of Newspaper Editors*." January 17, 1924. Washington, DC.

Cott, Nancy F. *The Bonds of Womanhood: "Women's Sphere" in New England, 1780–1835*. New Haven: Yale UP, 1977.

Crider, Gregory L. "William Dean Howells and the Gilded Age: Socialist in a Fur-lined Overcoat." *Ohio History* 88 (1979): 408–18.

Cullen, Countee. *Collected Poems*. Edited by Major Jackson. New York: Library of America, 2013.

Curd, Patricia, ed. *A Presocratics Reader: Selected Fragments and Testimonia*. 2nd ed. Trans. Richard D. McKirahan and Patricia Curd. Indianapolis: Hackett, 2011.

Daniel, Walter C. *De Lawd: Richard B. Harrison and The Green Pastures*. New York: Greenwood, 1986.

Daniel, Walter C. "'The Green Pastures': The Washington Performance." *Negro History Bulletin* 42.2 (1979): 42–3.

Daniels, Jonathan. "The Living God." *Saturday Review of Literature*, April 19, 1930, p. 941.

Dargan, Olive Tilford (Fielding Burke). *Call Home the Heart: A Novel of the Thirties*. New York: Feminist Press, 1983.

Davenport, Stewart. *Friends of the Unrighteous Mammon: Northern Christians and Market Capitalism 1815–1860*. Chicago: University of Chicago Press, 2008.

Davis, Charles Belmont. *The Adventures and Letters of Richard Harding Davis*. New York: Knopf, 1926.

Davis, Rebecca Harding. *Life in the Iron Mills and Other Stories*. Edited by Tillie Olsen. New York: Feminist Press, 1985.

Davis, Rebecca Harding. *Margret Howth: A Story of To-day*. New York: Feminist Press, 1990.

Debs, Eugene V. "Jesus, the Supreme Leader." *Labor and Freedom: The Voice and Pen of Eugene V. Debs*. St. Louis: Phil Wagner, 1916, 22–9.

Deloria, Jr., Vine. *God is Red: A Native View of Religion*. 2nd ed. Golden: North American Press, 1992.

Devinatz, Victor G. "The Needle Trades Workers Industrial Union: The Theory and Practice of Building a Red Industrial Union during Third Period Communism, 1928-1934." *Nature, Society, and Thought* 19.3 (2006): 261-94.

Dunne, William F. *Gastonia: Citadel of the Class Struggle in the New South*. New York: Workers Library, 1929.

Durkheim, Émile. *The Elementary Forms of Religious Life*. Trans. Carol Cosman. Oxford: Oxford UP, 2001.

Durkheim, Émile. *Professional Ethics and Civic Morals*. London: Routledge, 1957.

Earle, John R., Dean D. Knudsen, and Donald W. Shriver, Jr. *Spindles and Spires: A Restudy of Religion and Social Change in Gastonia*. Atlanta: John Knox Press, 1976.

Eliade, Mircea. *The Sacred and the Profane: The Nature of Religion*. Trans. Willard R. Trask. New York: Harper & Brothers, 1961.

Eller, Ronald D. *Miners, Millhands, and Mountaineers: Industrialization of the Appalachian South, 1880-1930*. Knoxville: The University of Tennessee Press, 1982.

Engels, Friedrich. "On the History of Early Christianity." *Marx & Engels Collected Works*. Volume 27. London: Lawrence & Wishart, 2010, 445-69.

Engels, Friedrich. "'On Morality' from *Anti-Dühring*." *The Marx-Engels Reader*. 2nd ed., edited by Robert C. Tucker. New York: W. W. Norton & Company, 1978.

Evans, Curtis J. "The Religious and Racial Meanings of The Green Pastures." *Religion and American Culture: A Journal of Interpretation* 18.1 (2008): 59-93.

Feuerbach, Ludwig. *The Essence of Christianity*. Mineola: Dover, 2008.

Fine, Sidney. *Laissez-Faire and the General Welfare State: A Study of Conflict in American Thought 1865-1901*. Ann Arbor: The University of Michigan Press, 1969.

Finke, Roger, and Rodney Stark. *The Churching of America, 1776-2005: Winners and Losers in Our Religious Economy*. New Brunswick: Rutgers UP, 2005.

Foner, Philip S., ed. *Jack London: American Rebel, A Collection of His Social Writings Together with an Extensive Study of the Man and His Times*. New York: The Citadel Press, 1947.

Ford, Henry. *My Philosophy of Industry*. New York: Coward-McCann, 1929.

Ford, Nick Aaron. "How Genuine Is *The Green Pastures*?" *The Phylon Quarterly* 20.1 (1959): 67-70.

Frazer, J. G. *The Golden Bough: A Study in Magic and Religion*. Auckland: Floating Press, 2009.

Fried, Richard M. *The Man Everybody Knew: Bruce Barton and the Making of Modern America*. Chicago: Ivan R. Dee, 2005.

Garrison, Dee. *Mary Heaton Vorse: The Life of an American Insurgent*. Philadelphia: Temple UP, 1989.

Geertz, Clifford. *The Interpretation of Cultures*. New York: Basic Books, 2017.

Gibson, Gloria J. "Historical Perspective: Film Music of *The Green Pastures* and *The Blood of Jesus*." *Black Camera* 2.1 (1987): 5-6.

Goeser, Caroline. *Picturing the New Negro: Harlem Renaissance Print Culture and Modern Black Identity*. Lawrence: University Press of Kansas, 2007.

Gottesman, Ronald. "Introduction." *The Jungle*. New York: Penguin, 1985.

Gray, Richard. *Southern Aberrations: Writers of the American South and the Problems of Regionalism*. Baton Rouge: Louisiana State UP, 2000.

The Green Pastures. Directed by Marc Connelly and William Keighley, Warner Brothers, 1936.

The Green Pastures Promotional Featurette. *IMDb*. https://www.imdb.com/video/vi1801979161?playlistId=tt0027700&ref_=tt_ov_vi.

Gutman, Herbert G. *Work, Culture, and Society in Industrializing America*. New York: Vintage Books, 1977.

Haber, Samuel. *Efficiency and Uplift: Scientific Management in the Progressive Era 1890–1920*. Chicago: University of Chicago Press, 1964.

Hall, Jacquelyn Dowd. "Women Writers, the 'Southern Front,' and the Dialectical Imagination." *The Journal of Southern History* 69.1 (2003): 3–38.

Hall, Jacquelyn Dowd, Robert Korstad, and James Leloudis. "Cotton Mill People: Work, Community, and Protest in the Textile South, 1880–1940." *The American Historical Review* 91.2 (1986): 245–86.

Hall, Jacquelyn Dowd, James Leloudis, Robert Korstad, Mary Murphy, Lu Ann Jones, and Christopher B. Daly. *Like a Family: The Making of a Southern Cotton Mill World*. Chapel Hill: The University of North Carolina Press, 1987.

Hapke, Laura. *Daughters of the Great Depression: Women, Work, and Fiction in the American 1930s*. Athens: University of Georgia Press, 1995.

Harde, Roxanne. "'A Startling Reform': Women and Christianity in the Work of Elizabeth Stuart Phelps." *Nineteenth-Century American Women Write Religion: Lived Theologies and Literature*, edited by Mary McCartin Wearn. Burlington: Ashgate, 2014.

Harris, Sharon M. *Rebecca Harding Davis and American Realism*. Philadelphia: University of Pennsylvania Press, 1991.

Harris, Sharon M. *Rebecca Harding Davis: A Life*. Morgantown: West Virginia UP, 2018.

Hatch, Nathan O. *The Democratization of American Christianity*. New Haven: Yale UP, 1989.

Holman, Charles T. "Richard Harrison Combined Humility with Dignity." *Christian Century*, April 3, 1945, p. 452.

Howe, Daniel Walker. "The Market Revolution and the Shaping of Identity in Whig-Jacksonian America." *The Market Revolution in America: Social, Political, and Religious Expressions, 1800–1880*, edited by Melvyn Stokes, and Stephen Conway. Charlottesville: University Press of Virginia, 1996.

Howells, William Dean. *Annie Kilburn*. In *Novels 1886–1888*. New York: The Library of America, 1989.

Howells, William Dean. "Are We a Plutocracy?" *North American Review* 158 (1894): 185–96.

Howells, William Dean. "Equality as the Basis of Good Society." *Century* 51 (November 1895): 63-7.
Howells, William Dean. *A Hazard of New Fortunes*. New York: Penguin Books, 2001.
Howells, William Dean. *Life in Letters of William Dean Howells Vol I*. Edited by Mildred Howells. Garden City: Doubleday, Doran & Company, 1928.
Howells, William Dean. "Lyof N. Tolstoi." *North American Review* 188 (1908): 851-2.
Howells, William Dean. *The Minister's Charge*. In *Novels 1886-1888*. New York: The Library of America, 1989.
Howells, William Dean. *My Literary Passions*. New York: Harper, 1895.
Howells, William Dean. *The Quality of Mercy*. New York: Harper and Brothers, 1892.
Howells, William Dean. *The Rise of Silas Lapham*. New York: Penguin Books, 1986.
Howells, William Dean. "A Traveller from Altruria." In *The Altrurian Romances*. Bloomington: Indiana University Press, 1968.
Howells, William Dean. *The World of Chance*. New York: Harper and Brothers, 1893.
Hubert, Henri and Marcel Mauss. *Sacrifice: Its Nature and Functions*. Trans. W. D. Halls. Chicago: University of Chicago Press, 1964.
Hughes, Langston. *The Collected Poems of Langston Hughes*. Edited by Arnold Rampersad and David Roessel. New York: Vintage, 1995.
Hughes, Robert. *American Visions: The Epic History of Art in America*. New York: Knopf, 1997.
Hunt, Edward Eyre, ed. *Scientific Management since Taylor: A Collection of Authoritative Papers*. New York: McGraw-Hill, 1924.
Hurston, Zora Neale. "The First One." *Black Theatre USA: Plays by African Americans, The Early Period 1847-1938*. Edited by James V. Hatch and Ted Shine. New York: The Free Press, 1996.
Jackson, Gregory S. "'What Would Jesus Do?': Practical Christianity, Social Gospel Realism, and the Homiletic Novel." *PMLA* 121.3 (2006): 641-61.
Jacob, Mary Jane. "The Rouge in 1927: Photographs and Paintings by Charles Sheeler." *The Rouge: Image of Industry in the Art of Charles Sheeler and Diego Rivera*. Detroit: Detroit Institute of Arts, 1978.
Johnson, Hall. "Notes on the Negro Spiritual." *Readings in Black American Music*, edited by Eileen Southern. New York: W. W. Norton & Company, 1971.
Johnson, James Weldon. *God's Trombones: Seven Negro Sermons in Verse*. New York: Penguin, 2008.
Johnson, Paul E. *A Shopkeeper's Millennium: Society and Revivals in Rochester, New York 1815-1837*. New York: Hill and Wang, 1978.
Johnston, Carolyn. *Jack London—An American Radical?* Westport: Greenwood Press, 1984.
Kanigel, Robert. *The One Best Way: Frederick Winslow Taylor and the Enigma of Efficiency*. New York: Penguin Books, 1997.
Kelly, Lori Duin. *The Life and Works of Elizabeth Stuart Phelps, Victorian Feminist Writer*. Troy: Whiston Publishing Company, 1983.

Kendall, Henry P. "Discussion." *Bulletin of the Taylor Society* 4 (April 1919): 18–19.

Kent, Robert T. "The Taylor Society Twenty Years Ago." *Bulletin of the Taylor Society* 17 (February 1932): 23–38.

Kessler, Carol Farley. *Elizabeth Stuart Phelps*. Boston: Twayne, 1982.

Kimball, Dexter. "Has Taylorism Survived?" *Bulletin of the Taylor Society* 27 (June 1927): 307–25.

Kirk, Clara and Rudolph. "Howells and the Church of the Carpenter." *The New England Quarterly* 32.2 (1959): 185–206.

Kirk, Clara and Rudolph. "William Dean Howells, George William Curtis, and the 'Haymarket Affair.'" *American Literature* 40.4 (1969): 487–98.

Knowles, R. E. "Kegs of Liquor for Noah Hit in Play, Says 'De Lawd.'" *Toronto Daily Mail*, March 20, 1933, p. 7.

Kozlov, Nicholas N. and Eric D. Weitz. "Reflections on the Origins of the 'Third Period': Bukharin, the Comintern, and the Political Economy of Weimar Germany." *Journal of Contemporary History* 24 (1989): 387–410.

Lacassin, Francis. "Upton Sinclair and Jack London: A Great Friendship... by Correspondence." *Jack London Newsletter* 9 (1976): 3.

Lang, Amy Schrager. "Class and the Strategies of Sympathy." *The Culture of Sentiment: Race, Gender, and Sentimentality in Nineteenth-Century America*, edited by Shirley Samuels. New York: Oxford UP, 1992.

Lang, Amy Schrager. "The Syntax of Class in Elizabeth Stuart Phelps's *The Silent Partner*." *Rethinking Class: Literary Studies and Social Formations*, edited by Wai Chee Dimock and Michael T. Gilmore. New York: Columbia UP, 1994.

Larson, John Lauritz. *The Market Revolution in America: Liberty, Ambition, and the Eclipse of the Common Good*. Cambridge: Cambridge UP, 2010.

Lasseter, Janice Milner. "The Censored and Uncensored Literary Lives of *Life in the Iron-Mills*." *Legacy* 20.1 & 2 (2003): 175–90.

Lazerow, Jama. *Religion and the Working Class in Antebellum America*. Washington: Smithsonian Institution Press, 1995.

Lears, T. J. Jackson and Richard Wightman Fox. *The Culture of Consumption: Critical Essays in American History 1880–1980*. New York: Pantheon Press, 1983.

Lenin, V. I. "The Taylor System—Man's Enslavement by the Machine." *Collected Works, Vol. 20, December 1913-August 1914*, trans. Bernard Isaacs and Joe Fineberg, edited by Julius Katzer. Moscow: Progress Publishers, 1977.

Lewis, Sinclair. *Babbitt*. New York: Random House, 2002.

Lewis, Sinclair. *Elmer Gantry*. New York: Signet Classics, 2007.

Lewis, Sinclair. *Main Street*. New York: Barnes and Noble Classics, 2003.

London, Jack. "Explanation of the Great Socialist Vote of 1904." *Jack London: American Rebel*, edited by Philip S. Foner, New York: The Citadel Press, 1947, 403–6.

London, Jack. "Introduction." *The Cry for Justice*, edited by Upton Sinclair, New York: Barricade Books, 1996, 9–11.

London, Jack. *The Iron Heel*. New York: Penguin Books, 2006.

London, Jack. *The Letters of Jack London*, vol. 1, edited by Earle Labor, Robert C. Leitz, and Irving Milo Shepard. Stanford: Stanford University Press, 1988.
London, Jack. "Revolution." *Jack London: American Rebel*, edited by Philip S. Foner, The Citadel Press, 1947, 488–504.
London, Jack. "Wanted: A New Law of Development." *Jack London: American Rebel*, edited by Philip S. Foner, New York: The Citadel Press, 1947, 431–45.
London, Jack. "What Communities Lose by the Competitive System." *Jack London: American Rebel*, edited by Philip S. Foner, New York: The Citadel Press, 1947, 419–30.
London, Jack. "What Life Means to Me." *No Mentor but Myself: Jack London on Writers and Writing*, edited by Dale E. Walker and Jeanne Campbell Reesman. Stanford, CA: Stanford Univ. Press, 1999.
London, Joan. *Jack London and His Times: An Unconventional Biography*. New York: Doubleday, 1939.
Lucic, Karen. *Charles Sheeler and the Cult of the Machine*. Cambridge: Harvard UP, 1991.
Lukács, Georg. *History and Class Consciousness. Studies in Marxist Dialectics*. Trans. Rodney Livingstone. Cambridge: The MIT Press, 1971.
Lumpkin, Grace. *To Make My Bread*. Urbana: University of Illinois Press, 1995.
Margo, Robert A. *Race and Schooling in the South, 1880–1950: An Economic History*. Chicago: University of Chicago Press, 1990.
Marx, Karl. *Marx on Religion*. Edited by John Raines. Philadelphia: Temple UP, 2002.
Marx, Karl and Frederick Engels. *The Marx-Engels Reader*, 2nd ed. Edited by Robert Tucker. New York: W. W. Norton & Company, 1978.
Mathews, Shailer. *Scientific Management in the Churches*. Chicago: University of Chicago Press, 1912.
Mauss, Marcel. *A General Theory of Magic*. London: Routledge, 2007.
Mauss, Marcel and Henri Beuchat. *Seasonal Variations of the Eskimo: A Study in Social Morphology*. Boston: Routledge & Kegan Paul, 1979.
Mazurek, Raymond A. "Rebecca Harding Davis, Tillie Olsen, and Working-Class Representation." *College Literature* 44.3 (2017): 436–54.
McCauley, Deborah Vansau. *Appalachian Mountain Religion: A History*. Urbana: University of Illinois Press, 1995.
McKanan, Dan. *Prophetic Encounters: Religion and the American Radical Tradition*. Boston: Beacon Press, 2011.
McKay, Claude. *Selected Poems of Claude McKay*. New York: Harcourt, Brace, and World, 1953.
McKinley, Michael. "Can the Technology behind Bitcoin be Used to Build a Belief System?" *America: The Jesuit Review*. June 14, 2018. https://www.americamagazine.org/politics-society/2019/06/14/can-technology-behind-bitcoin-be-used-build-belief-system. Accessed November 10, 2020.
McLoughlin, William G. *Modern Revivalism: Charles Grandison Finney to Billy Graham*. New York: Ronald Press Company, 1959.

McLoughlin, William G. *Revivals, Awakenings, and Reform: An Essay on Religion and Social Change in America, 1607–1977*. Chicago: The University of Chicago Press, 1978.

Merish, Lori. *Sentimental Materialism: Gender, Commodity Culture, and Nineteenth-Century American Literature*. Durham: Duke UP, 2000.

Miller, May. "Graven Images." *Black Theatre USA: Plays by African Americans, The Early Period 1847–1938*, edited by James V. Hatch and Ted Shine. New York: The Free Press, 1996.

Moody, Lisa. "The American 'Lives' of Jesus: The Malleable Figure of Christ as a Man of the People." *Christianity and Literature* 58.2 (2009): 157–84.

Moody, Lisa. *Religion and Realism in Late Nineteenth-Century American Literature*. 2009. PhD dissertation, Louisiana State University.

Moore, R. Laurence. "Religion, Secularization, and the Shaping of the Culture Industry in Antebellum America." *American Quarterly* 41.2 (1989): 216–42.

Murphy, Teresa Anne. *Ten Hours' Labor: Religion, Reform, and Gender in Early New England*. Ithaca: Cornell UP, 1992.

Nelson, Elizabeth White. *Market Sentiments: Middle-Class Market Culture in 19th Century America*. Washington, DC: Smithsonian Books, 2004.

Niebuhr, H. Richard. *The Social Sources of Denominationalism*. Cleveland: Meridian Books, 1967.

Nolan, Mary. *Visions of Modernity: American Business and the Modernization of Germany*. New York: Oxford UP, 1994.

Olsen, Tillie. *Silences*. New York: Delacorte, 1978.

Page, Myra (Dorothy Markey). *Gathering Storm: A Story of the Black Belt*. New York: International Publishers, 1932.

Page, Myra (Dorothy Markey). *Southern Cotton Mills and Labor*. New York: Workers Library Publishers, 1929.

Parrish, Timothy L. "Haymarket and *Hazard*: The Lonely Politics of William Dean Howells." *Journal of American Culture* 17.4 (1994): 23–32.

Pattison, Mary. *The Business of Home Management: The Principles of Domestic Engineering*. New York: Robert B. McBride, 1915.

Peabody, Francis Greenwood. *The Social Teachings of Jesus Christ*. Philadelphia: The Press of the University of Pennsylvania, 1924.

Pfaelzer, Jean. *Parlor Radical: Rebecca Harding Davis and the Origins of American Social Realism*. Pittsburgh: University of Pittsburgh Press, 1996.

Pfaelzer, Jean. "Rebecca Harding Davis (1831–1910)." *Legacy* 7.2 (1990): 39–45.

Phelps, Elizabeth Stuart. *The Silent Partner*. New York: Feminist Press, 1983.

Poovey, Mary. *Uneven Developments: The Ideological Work of Gender in Mid-Victorian England*. Chicago: University of Chicago Press, 1988.

Pope, Liston. *Millhands and Preachers: A Study of Gastonia*. New Haven: Yale UP, 1942.

Porter, Glenn. "Management." *A History of Technology*, vol. 6, edited by Trevor Williams. Oxford: Clarendon Press, 1978.

Porter, Katherine. "Flowering Judas." *Collected Stories and Other Writings*. New York: Library of America, 2008.

Prentiss, Craig R. *Staging Faith: Religion and African American Theater from the Harlem Renaissance to World War II*. New York: New York UP, 2014.

Privett, Ronna Coffey. *A Comprehensive Study of American Writer Elizabeth Stuart Phelps, 1844–1911: Art for Truth's Sake*. Lewiston: Edwin Mellon Press, 2003.

Prothero, Stephen. *American Jesus: How the Son of God Became a National Icon*. New York: Farrar, Straus and Giroux, 2003.

Rehn, Henry Joseph. *Scientific Management and the Cotton Textile Industry*. Chicago: The University of Chicago Libraries, 1934.

Reilly, John M. "Images of Gastonia: A Revolutionary Chapter in American Social Fiction." *The Georgia Review* 28.3 (1974): 498–517.

Renfroe, Alicia Micha. "A Story of To-Day. October 1861 Atlantic Monthly Comparative Text." *Rebecca Harding Davis: Complete Works*. https://rebeccahardingdaviscompleteworks.com/items/show/96. Accessed September 19, 2019.

Rideout, Walter B. *The Radical Novel in the United States: 1900–1954*. Cambridge: Harvard UP, 1956.

Rifkin, Jeremy. *Time Wars*. New York: Henry Holt, 1987.

Rollins, William. *The Shadow Before*. New York: Robert M. McBride and Company, 1934.

Rose, Jane Atteridge. *Rebecca Harding Davis*. New York: Twayne, 1993.

Rothenbuhler, Eric W. "The Liminal Fight: Mass Strikes as Ritual and Interpretation." *Durkheimian Sociology: Cultural Studies*, edited by Jeffrey C. Alexander. Cambridge: Cambridge UP, 1988.

Rourke, Constance. *Charles Sheeler: Artist in the American Tradition*. New York: Harcourt, Brace, and Co., 1938.

Royce, Josiah. "The Mechanical, the Historical, and the Statistical." *The Basic Writings of Josiah Royce*, vol. 2, edited by John McDermott. Chicago: The University of Chicago Press, 1969.

Ryan, Mary P. *Cradle of the Middle Class: The Family in Oneida County, New York, 1790–1865*. Cambridge: Cambridge UP, 1981.

Ryan, Mary P. *Womanhood in America: From Colonial Times to the Present*, 2nd ed. New York: New Viewpoints, 1979.

Salmond, John A. *Gastonia 1929: The Story of the Loray Mill Strike*. Chapel Hill: The University of North Carolina Press, 1995.

Sandstrom, Aleksandra. "5 facts about the Religious Makeup of the 116th Congress." *Pew Research Center*. January 3, 2019. https://www.pewresearch.org/fact-tank/2019/01/03/5-facts-about-the-religious-makeup-of-the-116th-congress Accessed May 8, 2021

Schantz, Mark S. *Piety in Providence: Class Dimensions of Religious Experience in Antebellum Rhode Island*. Ithaca: Cornell UP, 2000.

Schlesinger, Arthur M. *The Age of Roosevelt: The Crisis of the Old Order, 1919–1933*. Boston: Houghton Mifflin, 1957.

Schreibersdorf, Lisa. "Radical Mothers: Maternal Testimony and Metaphor in Four Novels of the Gastonia Strike." *JNT: Journal of Narrative Theory* 29.3 (1999): 303–22.

Scott, Donald. *From Office to Profession: The New England Ministry 1750–1850*. Philadelphia: University of Pennsylvania Press, 1978.

Sellers, Charles. *The Market Revolution: Jacksonian America, 1815–1846*. New York: Oxford UP, 1991.

Silet, Charles L. P. "Upton Sinclair to Jack London: A Literary Friendship." *Jack London Newsletter* 5 (1972): 49–76.

Sinclair, Upton. *The Autobiography of Upton Sinclair*. New York: Harcourt, Brace & World 1962.

Sinclair, Upton. *Hell: A Verse Drama and Photo-Play*. Pasadena: Upton Sinclair, 1923.

Sinclair, Upton. *The Jungle*. New York: Penguin Books, 2006.

Sinclair, Upton. *Mammonart: An Essay in Economic Interpretation*. Pasadena: Upton Sinclair, 1925.

Sinclair, Upton. *The Profits of Religion: An Essay in Economic Interpretation*. Pasadena: Upton Sinclair, 1918.

Sinclair, Upton. *Samuel the Seeker*. Racine: Upton Sinclair, 1910.

Sinclair, Upton. *They Call Me Carpenter*. Pasadena: Upton Sinclair, 1922.

Singer, Avery and Matt Liston. "Seven on Seven 10th Edition: Avery Singer and Matt Liston." *Rhizome*. May 19, 2018. https://vimeo.com/273914965. Accessed November 10,.2020.

Sowinska, Suzanne. "Writing across the Color Line: White Women Writers and the 'Negro Question' in the Gastonia Novels." *Radical Revisions: Rereading 1930s Culture*, edited by Bill Mullen and Sherry Lee Linkon. Urbana: University of Illinois Press, 1996.

Stella, Joseph. "The Brooklyn Bridge (a page of my life)." *Transition* 16.17 (1929): 87–8.

Stokes, Claudia. *The Alter at Home: Sentimental Literature and Nineteenth-Century American Religion*. Philadelphia: University of Pennsylvania Press, 2014.

Stokes, Claudia. "The Religious Novel." *The Oxford History of the Novel in English: Volume 6: The American Novel 1879–1940*, edited by Priscilla Wald and Michael A. Elliott. Oxford: Oxford UP, 2014, 168–83.

Stowe, Harriet Beecher. *The Minister's Wooing*. New York: Derby and Jackson, 1859.

Stowe, Harriet Beecher. *Uncle Tom's Cabin*, A Norton Critical Edition. 2nd ed., edited by Elizabeth Ammons. New York: Norton, 2010.

Suderman, Elmer F. "The Social-Gospel Novelists' Criticisms of American Society." *Midcontinent American Studies Journal* 7.1 (1966): 45–60.

Sundquist, Eric J. *To Wake the Nations: Race in the Making of American Literature*. Cambridge: Harvard UP, 1993.

Sutton, William R. *Journeymen for Jesus: Evangelical Artisans Confront Capitalism in Jacksonian Baltimore*. University Park: Pennsylvania State UP, 1998.
Tavernier-Courbin, Jacqueline. *Critical Essays on Jack London*. Boston: G.K. Hall & Co., 1983.
Taylor, Frederick W. "The Gospel of Efficiency: A New Science of Business Management." *American Magazine* 71 (1911): 563–81.
Taylor, Frederick W. "The Gospel of Efficiency II: The Principles of Scientific Management." *American Magazine* 71 (1911): 785–93.
Taylor, Frederick W. "The Gospel of Efficiency III: The Principles of Scientific Management." *American Magazine* 72 (1911): 101–13.
Taylor, Frederick W. and Upton Sinclair, "The Gospel of Efficiency: The Principles of Scientific Management: A Criticism by Upton Sinclair and an Answer by Frederick W. Taylor." *American Magazine* 72 (1911): 243–5.
Taylor, Frederick Winslow. *The Principles of Scientific Management*. New York: W. W. Norton & Company, 1947.
Taylor, Walter Fuller. "William Dean Howells and the Economic Novel." *American Literature* 4.2 (1932): 103–13.
Tompkins, Jane. *Sensational Designs: The Cultural Work of American fiction 1790–1860*. New York: Oxford UP, 1985.
Toomer, Jean. *Cane*. New York: Penguin, 2019.
Toomer, Jean. *The Collected Poems of Jean Toomer*. Edited by Robert B. Jones and Margery Toomer Latimer. Chapel Hill: The University of North Carolina Press, 1988.
Troeltsch, Ernst. *The Social Teaching of the Christian Churches*. London: George Allen & Unwin Ltd., 1950.
Urgo, Joseph R. "Proletarian Literature and Feminism: The Gastonia Novels and Feminist Protest." *Minnesota Review* 24 (1985): 64–84.
Veblen, Thorstein. *The Instinct of Workmanship and the State of the Industrial Arts*. New York: B. W. Huebsch, 1919.
Vorse, Mary Heaton. *Strike!* Urbana: University of Illinois Press, 1991.
Waldrep III, G. C. *Southern Workers and the Search for Community: Spartanburg County, South Carolina*. Urbana: University of Illinois Press, 2000.
Walker, Dale E. and Jeanne Campbell Reesman, eds. *No Mentor but Myself: Jack London on Writers and Writing*. Stanford, CA: Stanford UP, 1999.
Walsh, Harry. "Tolstoy and the Economic Novels of William Dean Howells." *Comparative Literature Studies* 14 (1977): 143–65.
Warren, George C. "Connelly Folk Pageant Opens Here." *San Francisco Chronicle*, March 17, 1932, p. 8.
Warren, Kenneth. *Black and White Strangers: Race and American Literary Realism*. Chicago: University of Chicago Press, 1993.
Watson, William L. "'These Mill-hands Are Gettin' Onbearable': The Logic of Class Formation in *Life in the Iron Mills* by Rebecca Harding Davis." *Women's Studies Quarterly* 26.1 & 2 (1998): 116–36.

Weber, Max. *From Max Weber: Essays in Sociology*. Trans. H. H. Gerth and C. Wright Mills. New York: Oxford University Press, 1958.

Weber, Max. *The Sociology of Religion*. Trans. Ephraim Fischoff. Boston: Beacon Press, 1993.

Weisbord, Vera Buch. *A Radical Life*. Bloomington: Indiana UP, 1977.

Weisenfeld, Judith. *Hollywood Be Thy Name: African American Religion in American Film 1929–1949*. Berkeley: University of California Press, 2007.

Welter, Barbara. "The Cult of True Womanhood: 1820–1860." *American Quarterly* 18.2 (1966): 151–74.

White, Elizabeth Alice. "Charitable Calculations: Fancywork, Charity, and the Culture of the Sentimental Market, 1830–1880." *The Middling Sorts: Explorations in the History of the American Middle Class*, edited by Burton J. Bledstein and Robert D. Johnston. New York: Routledge, 2001.

Wilentz, Sean. *Chants Democratic: New York City and the Rise of the American Working Class, 1788–1850*. New York: Oxford UP, 1984.

Williams, James. "Authorial Choice and Textual Meaning: The Sources of The Star Rover (Part Two)." *Jack London Newsletter* 21 (1988): 1–65.

Williams, Jay. *Author Under Sail: The Imagination of Jack London, 1893–1902*. Lincoln: University of Nebraska Press, 2014.

Williams, John. "Anent 'Green Pastures.'" *California Eagle*, July 15, 1932, p. 4.

Williams, Raymond. *Marxism and Literature*. Oxford: Oxford UP, 1978.

Winters, Donald E. *The Soul of the Wobblies: The I.W.W., Religion, and American Culture in the Progressive Era, 1905–1917*. Westport: Greenwood Press, 1985.

Yellin, Jean Fagan. "Afterword." *Margret Howth: A Story of To-day*. New York: Feminist Press, 1990.

Yezierska, Anzia. "America and I." *Children of Loneliness*. London: Cassell, 1923.

Index

America/Americans
  absolutization 33, 57
  acts of consumption 52
  antebellum 7, 25-6, 29-30, 37-8, 40-1, 43, 45-55, 61, 92
  belief-value system 37
  capitalist culture 90-1
  economic changes 30, 33, 91
  free-market capitalism 29
  literary realism 68
  Market Revolution 29-30
  pious behavior 60
  religious growth/life 18, 21, 37, 51-2, 77, 176, 186
  socialism 91
  society between 1815 and 1860 29-30
  working class before the Civil War 46
American Protestantism. *See also* Lewis, Sinclair; Taylor, Frederick Winslow
  apotheosis of standardization 158-64
  commercial culture 138-46, 151-4, 157-8
  commercialization of religion 153-8
  industrial rationalization 146-51
  justification of economic inequality 237-8
  Taylor's influence 137-64
Anderson, Sherwood 184, 187-9, 191, 196
  Beyond Desire 165, 169, 171, 174-5, 177, 180, 193, 199
  "How I Came to Communism" 185
anthropotheism 9-13, 26, 34, 151, 195-6, 198, 209, 241
  salvation politics 121-4
apotheosis 9-24, 30, 89, 95-6, 109, 112, 116-17, 207-9
  Arminianism 35
  Black suffering 212-14, 216-22, 225-7, 229-30, 232, 239, 241
  of capitalism 99-100, 109, 114, 121, 202-3
  and class formation/conflict 76-85, 104, 111, 135

  of commerce 152, 168
  cultural mechanism 34
  of domesticity 63
  Durkheim on 57
  of female piety 71
  forms of 32, 34, 47
  labor conflict 198
  literary representation 151-2
  of middle-class structure 64
  in modern America 24-7, 96-100
  ontological difference 100
  Protestantism aspect 48
  salvation history 122-4, 177-8, 185
  of socialism 121
  specular process 52
  of Taylorism 138, 143, 148-9, 158, 160-1, 164
  textile industry 168-71, 179-80
Arminianism 34-5, 109
  concept of salvation 145
Arminian soteriology 35, 41, 43, 49
Austin, Mary 116
  The Man Jesus 115

Barton, Bruce 26, 111, 121, 135, 152
  The Man Nobody Knows: A Discovery of the Real Jesus 118-20
Beecher, Henry Ward 114, 238
  Footsteps of the Master 115
  The Life of Jesus, the Christ 115
Black Christ 204, 206-7, 210-23, 226, 228-9, 232, 236, 238-9
Black Protestants 205-6
Black theology 208-9, 211-12, 214, 217, 236, 239
blockchain technology
  cryptoreligion 2
  use of commerce 1
Bradford, Roark 230-1, 233, 235-6, 238-41
  "Author's Note" 231
  Ol' Man Adam an' His Chillun, Being the Tales They Tell about the Time

When the Lord Walked the Earth Like a Natural Man 226–9, 234
Braley, Berton, "The Spirit of Management" 147
Bushnell, Horace, *On Christian Nurture* 67

Callahan, Raymond 147, 186–7
  Education and the Cult of Efficiency 144
Calvinism 3–4, 34, 41, 48, 65
capitalism
  American Protestantism 153–4, 157–8, 161–2
  Christological fiction 114, 118–21, 124, 126–8, 134–5
  economic novels 89–90, 91–103, 107, 109
  Gastonia novels 167–9, 171, 178, 183, 185, 187–8, 195, 197–9
  Harlem Renaissance 237
  labor fiction 29–32, 36–8, 42–5, 47–8, 56
  sanctification of 45
Christianity
  antebellum tradition 26
  and capitalism 3, 30–1, 42–3, 59–60
  Christian socialism 26, 90–3, 108–9
  denominationalism 34–9
  doctrines and denominations 34, 36–7, 38, 48, 51, 57
  domestic and religious values 63–4, 74
  dualistic metaphysics 66
  laws of God's creation 34
  promise of redemption 62–3
Christian socialism 26, 91, 98, 99, 104, 106, 109, 125, 127, 134
Christological fiction. *See also* Barton, Bruce; London, Jack; Sinclair, Upton
  conversions to socialism 124–35
  post-Civil War hagiography 111–20
  salvation politics 121–4
Christology 81, 111, 113, 118, 122, 174–5, 224
church system. *See also* American Protestantism; Christianity; congregational homogeneity
  Calvinist disestablishment 48
  class division 53–4
  clergy's role 48
  Congregational 49
  division of social classes 36
  elite ministers 42–5
  free-religious market 47–57
  institutional norms 37–8
  mass conversions 50–1
  Methodism, growth of 49
  power distribution 52–3
  voluntary 47–8
class conflict 7, 23, 26, 46, 111, 116, 124, 139, 145, 181, 183, 235. *See also* capitalism; class formation
class formation 3, 5
  American modernity and 23, 37
  antebellum 41
  apotheosis and 76–85
  Arminian soteriology 36
  during Awakening 25, 47
  Christianity and capitalism 59–60
  domesticity concept 60–4, 66
  middle-class use of religion 39
  social solidarity 18–22
class interest 11, 81, 111, 119
clerical economists
  cultural impact 42
  distinguished works 42–3
  popular names 42
collective representation 2, 15–16, 25, 135, 206, 209, 213, 214, 220, 226, 229, 235, 237
congregational homogeneity 54–5
  economic criteria for church membership 54
  economic elites' role 56–7
  examples of churches 53–4
  pew ownership 54–5
Connelly, Marc 226, 229–30
  The Green Pastures 228, 231–41
  Ol' King David and the Philistine Boys (1930) 234
  This Side of Jordan (1929) 234
conversion 25, 39, 48–50, 52, 63–4, 67–8, 72–5, 77, 81–3
  American Protestantism 143, 156
  Christological fiction 124–7, 130–5
  economic novels 89–95, 105–6, 108, 109
  Gastonian novels 184–6, 191–6
  Harlem Renaissance 207–9

Cullen, Countee 207, 211, 212, 218–19, 221, 224
   "The Black Christ" 206, 217
   "Christ Recrucified" 216
   "Heritage" 209, 218
   "Pagan Prayer" 205
Cummins, Maria Susanna, *Lamplighter, The* 70

Dargan, Olive Tilford 191–4, 199
   Call Home the Heart: A Novel of the Thirties 165, 174, 179, 184, 189, 193
   A Stone Came Rolling (1935) 194
Davis, Rebecca Harding 25, 60, 68, 76, 85–8. *See also* labor fictions
   Life in the Iron-Mills 59, 70, 78, 82
   Margret Howth 59, 69–72, 73, 82–4, 86, 92
domesticity 25, 59–71, 74, 76–7, 79, 81, 85, 87
   central convention 66
   cult of 68
Douglass, Frederick, *Narrative of the Life of Frederick Douglass, an American Slave* 224
Du Bois, W. E. B. 206, 208, 232
   collective call for redemption 204–5
   Darkwater 204, 211, 216
   "Jesus Christ in Texas" ("Jesus Christ in Georgia") 115, 214
   "Keep not Thou silent, O God!" 205
   "The Prayers of God" 205, 207, 209, 211, 217
   "The Second Coming" 212–13, 214
Durkheim, Émile 8, 11–21, 32–4, 77, 148, 171, 186–7, 190–1, 199, 206, 220
   on effervescence 31
   on material conditions of society 5

economic depression 1819 and 1837 29
economic novels. *See also* Howells, William Dean
   antebellum abolitionism 105–9
   apotheosis of capitalism 96–104
   Christian socialists' religious philosophy 89–96
   ontological difference of class 100–5
effervescence 31–3, 57, 186, 234, 241
Eliade, Mircea 22

Engels, Friedrich 4, 10, 12, 143, 182
   anthropotheism structure 11
Ethereum platform 1
Evangelicalism
   growth of churches 49
   labor radicals 39
   middle-class artisans 46–7
   revivalism 32–3, 47–9
   working class consciousness 46–7

Feuerbach, Ludwig 5, 9–14, 16
   on Christians' concept of God 57
   Essence of Christianity, The 9
First World War 143
Frederick, Christine, *The New Housekeeping: Efficiency Studies in Home Management* 143
free labor 35, 41
free-market capitalism 29–30, 32, 36–8, 43, 47, 56, 90
   Christianity and 30
free religious market 35, 47–57, 157, 209

Garland, Hamlin 91
Gastonia labor strikes
   antithetical economic systems 165
   apotheosis in the labor conflict 198–202
   death tolls 166–7
   Loray Mill conflict 26, 165–7, 173–4, 182–4, 186, 188–9, 191, 197–8, 200, 202
   National Textile Workers' Union 166
   Taylor System, implementation 166
Gastonia novels. *See also* Anderson, Sherwood; Dargan, Olive Tilford; Lumpkin, Grace; Page, Myra; Rollins, William, Jr.; Vorse, Mary Heaton
   Appalachian Christians 175–82
   on vital role of religion 165
Gilded Age America 89–93, 96, 99–100, 105
group interest 2, 22–3

Hale, Edward Everett 27, 91
Hallelujah (film) 240
Harlem Renaissance 27, 204–5, 209, 212, 214, 216, 220, 222–3, 226, 229, 241. *See also* Cullen, Countee;

Durkheim, Émile; Du Bois, W. E. B.; Hughes, Langston; Johnson, James Weldon; Hurston, Zora Neale; Toomer, Jean
Black Americans 205–6, 208–9, 212, 214–19, 221, 224–6, 229–33, 235, 238, 240
Black Christ 204, 206–7, 210, 212–23, 226, 228–9, 232, 236, 238–9
doctrine of salvation 214
Judeo-Christian subjects 209
plantation modernism on Broadway 226–41
Hemingway, *In Our Time* 119
Howells, William Dean
Annie Kilburn 89, 91, 101–2, 104–6, 130
conversion experience 89
A Hazard of New Fortunes 89, 93–5, 103, 105, 109, 130
indictment of capitalism 90–6
on liberal Protestant theology 89
process of fetishization or apotheosis 95–6
A Quality of Mercy 89, 93
A Traveler from Altruria 89, 95, 98, 101–2, 104
The World of Chance 89, 97, 105–6, 108–9
Hughes, Langston 204
"Christ in Alabama" 216
Hurston, Zora Neale 225, 228
"The First One" 224
Moses, Man of the Mountain 222

industrial revolution 3, 5, 7, 21, 23, 241

Johnson, James Weldon 222, 232
God's Trombones: Seven Negro Sermons in Verse 200, 221, 226, 228–9, 234

Kautsky, Karl 134
Der Ursprung der Christentumus 128

labor fiction. *See also* Davis, Rebecca Harding; Phelps, Elizabeth Stuart
concept of domesticity 60–8, 71
ethos of domesticity 85–8
mid-century maternalism 85–8
middle-class hegemony 60–8
salvation ethic 60, 62–7, 72, 74–6, 81–5, 88
sentimentalism 60–8
on working-class 60, 69–70, 72–3, 76–86
laissez-faire economy 41, 44–5, 47–8, 67, 95, 98, 124, 135
Lewis, Sinclair
Babbitt 26, 138, 151–3, 156–64
Elmer Gantry 26, 138, 152, 154–5, 161–2
literary prowess 137
Main Street 138, 150–1, 160–1, 163
taxonomy of apotheosis 146
Liston, Matt 1–2, 24–6, 165, 171
London, Jack 111–12, 119, 122
conversion narratives 124–5
devotion to socialism 125–9, 133–5
"How I Became a Socialist" 126
The Iron Heel 127–30
The People of the Abyss 126
"Revolution" 126, 128
The Star Rover 115, 127–8, 134
"Wanted: A New Law of Development" 126
"What Life Means to Me" 129
Lumpkin, Grace 180–2, 184, 189, 191
To Make My Bread 165, 170, 174, 177, 188, 196

Market Revolution 25, 29, 31–2, 34–5, 38–9, 46–8, 51, 53, 55–7, 64, 67
economic prosperity 53–4
Marx, Karl 122, 126, 134, 167
religious ideas 4–5, 10–13, 22
maternalism 25, 59, 69, 71, 76, 80, 85–8
Mathews, Shailer 154–7
Scientific Management in the Churches 154
McCowan, Archibald, *Christ, the Socialist* 115
McKay, Claude, "The Negro's Tragedy" 214
middle-class. *See also* maternalism
affective norms 64
domesticity 60–8, 74–6, 79, 81, 85, 87
hegemony 40–1
womanhood and motherhood 65

Norwood, Robert, *The Man Who Dared to Be God* 118

Page, Myra 176-7, 179-81, 188-9, 191, 196
  Gathering Storm 165, 170, 173-5, 178, 190, 192
  Southern Cotton Mills and Labor (1929) 176
Passos, Dos, *Manhattan Transfer* 119
patriarchs 41, 67, 224-5, 230
Pattison, Mary, *The Business of Home Management: The Principles of Domestic Engineering* 143
Phelps, Elizabeth Stuart 25, 60, 68, 75, 78, 85-8, 111. *See also* labor fictions
  The Gates Ajar 115
  Silent Partner, The 59, 70-1, 78, 80, 82, 121
  A Singular Life 115
  The Story of Jesus Christ: An Interpretation 115
political economy
  Biblical principles 44
  clerical economists and 42-5
  and laws of God 45
  Smithian 42, 45
Pope, Liston 26, 167, 172-4, 177, 179-80, 187
  Millhands and Preachers 165, 171
print culture 3, 21, 39, 48, 59, 61-3, 66-7, 81
Protestantism 3, 25. *See also* American Protestantism
  adoption of free-market political economy 35
  denominationalism 37-8
  institutional model 47-8
  during Market Revolution 56
  Second Great Awakening and 33
Pyle, Howard, *Rejected of Men* 115, 128

racial politics, apotheosis 221-5
religion. *See also* free-religious market; religion-0xΩ; sacralization; salvation ethic
  class struggle and 47
  cryptocurrency and 1-2
  radicalism 45-7
  sacred, concept 23

religion-0xΩ 1-2, 24
religious enthusiasm 3, 31, 63
revival 6-7, 21, 25, 30-2, 35, 36, 38-41, 45-6, 48-51, 63, 67
Rollins, William, Jr. 189, 191, 196
  The Shadow Before 165, 174, 188, 192, 199

sacralization
  abstract concept 11-13
  apotheosis structure 15-16, 22, 76, 135, 149
  of capitalism 3, 8, 26, 96
  dominant economic order 151
  elite class members 3, 8, 26
  industrial messiahs 146
  Taylor's specifications 137-8, 158
sacred objects 1
salvation ethic 4, 16-18, 20-1, 23, 33, 39, 60, 62-3, 57-8, 74, 81, 95, 116-17, 121, 124, 137-8, 145, 149, 153-4, 163-4, 170, 173, 191-2
  capitalist norms 60
Second Great Awakening 5, 25, 30-6, 38, 43, 45, 47-9, 51, 57, 64-5, 86
  class and soteriology 39-47
  clerical economists 42-5
  definition 57
  primary attributes 34, 38
  religious innovations during 45-7
  sentimentalism during 63-4
  social and theological innovations 64-5
Sellers, Charles 30, 32, 49, 53, 119
sentimentalism 69, 71-2, 74, 76, 87, 102
  middle-class 50-8
sentimental theology 25, 59, 63, 81
Sheeler, Charles 149-50
Sheldon, Charles M., *In His Steps: What Would Jesus Do?* 115, 118
Sinclair, Upton 26, 111
  Autobiography 122, 132-4
  The Cry of Justice 135
  Hell 118
  The Jungle 112, 115, 118, 131, 134
  Our Lady 118
  A Personal Jesus: Portrait and Interpretation 115, 118
  The Profits of Religion 118

Samuel the Seeker 112, 118
They Call Me Carpenter 115–16, 130
What God Means to Me 118
Singer, Avery 1
social control thesis 40–41, 45
social gospel 5, 109–9, 114, 116, 125–6
social groups 5, 12–13, 18–21, 23, 57, 77, 204, 209, 212, 219, 221
social redemption 106–7, 109
social salvation 26, 89, 92, 96, 109, 123
specular 2, 9–13, 15, 18, 22, 24, 33, 47, 52, 57, 93, 108, 151, 170, 214, 224, 226, 231, 241
Stead, W. T., *If Christ Came to Chicago* 115
Stella, Joseph
   Brooklyn Bridge 150
   New York Interpreted (The Voice of the City) 150
Stowe, Harriet Beecher 111
   Footsteps of the Master 115
   Minister's Wooing, The 86
   Uncle Tom's Cabin 61, 63–4, 73, 115

Taylor, Frederick Winslow
   Eastern Rate Case 138–9, 148
   "The Gospel of Efficiency: A New Science of Business Management" 146–7
   scientific management 137–49, 154–5, 157, 160, 166
   Taylorism 26, 137–8, 141–9, 151, 155–6, 158, 163–4
Toomer, Jean 209, 213–14
   "Box Seat" 213
   Cane 204, 207, 222

Vorse, Mary Heaton 187, 190, 192, 196–8, 200
   Strike! 165, 174, 183–5, 189, 191, 194–5, 201

Wallace, Lew, *Ben-Hur: A Tale of the Christ* 115, 118
Warner, Susan, *Wide, Wide World, The* 70
Weber, Max 22, 36, 37, 211–12
   on American mythos 4
   disenchantment theory 6–7
   Economy and Society 204
   Protestant Ethic 3
   sacramental theology 8, 14
   salvation based religion 206–7, 210–12, 221, 237–41
   theories of economy and religion 3–5, 16–19
White, Bouck, *The Call of the Carpenter* 115
Williams, Raymond 62, 64
Woods, Katherine Pearson, *Metzerott, Shoemaker* 118
working class
   American Protestantism 140–1, 146
   before Civil War 46
   in Christological fiction 113–14, 117, 121, 124, 128, 135
   earliest depictions 77
   in economic novels 91, 101, 102, 104–5, 107
   Gastonian novels 173, 178–80, 182, 186, 191, 195–6
   in Harlem Renaissance 206, 225, 237–8
   in labor fiction 53–5, 60, 69–72, 76–86
   Market Revolution 29, 33, 39, 41, 45–7
worship 1, 11, 16–17, 22, 24, 33–4, 36, 52, 56, 79, 129, 133, 149–51, 171, 184, 186, 189, 221, 223–4

www.ingramcontent.com/pod-product-compliance
Lightning Source LLC
Chambersburg PA
CBHW062129300426
44115CB00012BA/1867